TOKEN REFUGE

The Modern Jewish Experience

Paula Hyman and Deborah Dash Moore, Editors

TOKEN REFUGE

*The Story of the
Jewish Refugee Shelter
at Oswego, 1944–1946*

Sharon R. Lowenstein

Indiana University Press

BLOOMINGTON

Manufactured in the United States of America

Library of Congress Cataloging-in-Publication Data

Lowenstein, Sharon R.
  Token refuge.

  (The Modern Jewish experience)
  Bibliography: p.
  Includes index.
  1. Refugees, Jewish—New York (State)—Oswego.
2. Jews—New York (State)—Oswego. 3. World War,
1939–1945—Jews—Rescue. 4. United States—Emigration
and immigration. 5. Oswego (N.Y.)—Ethnic relations.
I. Title. II. Series: Modern Jewish experience
(Bloomington, Ind.)
HV640.5.J4L68 1986   362.8'7089924   85-42542
ISBN 0-253-36023-4
1 2 3 4 5 90 89 88 87 86

Contents

Acknowledgments

Theodore A. Wilson, mentor, friend, and colleague, introduced me to Oswego. I am indebted to him and to David A. Katzman for consistent encouragement and astute assessments. Leonard Dinnerstein suggested directions for research. Abram Sachar made the David K. Niles Papers available. Ruth Gruber introduced me to former refugees, shared her own work, and offered thoughtful comments. Henry L. Feingold and Carla L. Klausner helped with early drafts. Jonathan Sarna and Lawrence Baron added significantly to the completed manuscript. Remaining errors are my own.

I want to thank the following archivists and librarians: Joseph B. Howerton and Mary Livingston, Industrial, Social, and Fiscal Branch, National Archives, Washington, D.C.; Robert Parks, Franklin D. Roosevelt Library, Hyde Park; Dennis Bilger, Harry S. Truman Library, Independence; Nehemiah Ben Zev, American Jewish Historical Society, Waltham, Mass.; Myron Webb, YIVO Institute for Jewish Research, New York; Mrs. Rose Klepfisz, American Jewish Joint Distribution Committee, New York; Mrs. Helen Ritter and Mrs. Ruth Rauch, American Jewish Committee, New York; Abe Peck, American Jewish Archives, Cincinnati; and David J. Gilner, Public Services Librarian, Hebrew Union College, Cincinnati.

I am most appreciative of fellowships received from the Eleanor Roosevelt Institute of the Franklin D. Roosevelt Library, the National Foundation for Jewish Culture, and the Memorial Foundation for Jewish Culture.

Oswegans led me to former Oswego refugees, and they in turn helped give life to the vast collections of pertinent records. Michael Cahill of the Oswego County Historical Society introduced me to Ralph Faust, former Oswego High School principal, who in turn gave me the addresses of Steffi Steinberg Winters and Denise Battat, the daughter of Lea Hanf. They provided my first leads to former refugees. People who opened their homes to me for gatherings of former refugees included Fred and Jenny Baum, Hillsdale, New Jersey; Robert and Margaret Spitzer Fisse, San Francisco, and Ruth Gruber, New York. Initial responses ranged from enthusiastic to hostile. Gruber's book *Haven*, which grew out of my first interview with her, and the impact of the fortieth reunion, which she organized, made it possible for me to speak with far more people than would have been the case otherwise. The epilogue is a tribute to them.

Most important, this study would not have been possible without the love, support, patience, and encouragement of my husband, William Lowenstein, and our four sons, Lon, Glenn, John, and Reed.

TOKEN REFUGE

ONE

Introduction

ONE OF THE MOST DRAMATIC stories of World War II is the tale of one
thousand refugees selected from secured areas of Allied Italy and
brought to the United States in August 1944. The story of their
internment in upstate New York until eight months after Germany
surrendered places in perspective the hopes, frustrations, and impo-
tence of those who advocated the rescue of Europe's Jews; the motiva-
tions and personalities of policy-makers; and the ordeals and
tragedies of the refugee experience. A token group who experienced
eighteen months of American confinement before gaining permanent entry, they exemplify personal courage, stamina, and resilience.
Their story makes more immediate the loss of six million and offers a
tantalizing glimpse into what might have been.

Franklin D. Roosevelt had an exquisite flair for political gestures.
None was more poignant than his announcement on June 12, 1944,
that he was establishing the Fort Ontario Emergency Refugee Shelter.
The news, little noticed amidst the excitement stirred by the Normandy invasion, represented the failure of a bold, large-scale rescue
plan advocated by certain members of the administration throughout
the first half of 1944. The fate of that plan directly brought the token
one thousand to the United States.

Neither Western leaders nor their constituents lacked information about the fate of Europe's Jews. The details of the Final Solution
remained unclear, and the gruesome truth about Auschwitz still lay
hidden. But by the fall of 1942 officials had the names and locations of
many concentration camps, and newspapers carried stories of systematic mass murder.[1]

1

There is reason to believe that strong Allied pressure might have led some German officials and collaborating non-German politicians to become less efficient murderers. A minority among those responsible for the atrocities reacted nervously when, on December 17, 1942, the Allies accused the German authorities of "now carrying into effect Hitler's oft-repeated intention to exterminate the Jewish people of Europe" and condemned "in the strongest possible terms this bestial policy."[2] But the Allies did not again rebuke the Nazis until March 1944. At that time Washington and London simultaneously condemned "enemy crimes against humanity"—language considerably milder than that used fifteen months earlier.

Had the Allies wished to interfere with the killing, they could have done little more than issue condemnations and threats so long as German armies dominated Europe. In 1944, however, the situation was far different from what it had been two years earlier. German armies were retreating and the Nazi SS was struggling to complete its gruesome work before the Allies gained victory. Over four million Jews had already been killed. However, sizable populations still existed in France and Rumania, and Hungarian Jewry, swollen to one million, remained intact under a puppet regime with little enthusiasm for Nazi atrocities. Victory loomed and rescue appeared more feasible.

All rescue schemes depended on the availability of places of refuge. The United States was apparently becoming more receptive to the admission of refugees. Peacetime reconversion plans were in the making and the paranoia about national security had declined. Thousands of Japanese-Americans, interned illegally since early 1942, were being released to resume their broken lives. Overcoming anti-Semitic and restrictionist opposition would require great stamina and perseverance, but by 1944 this no longer seemed impossible.

Many Americans had long blamed foreigners for the nation's ills, particularly during times of economic crisis and war. The economic dislocations that accompanied rapid industrialization in the late nineteenth century produced populist outcries against unseen alien conspirators. Progressive reformers focused in the early twentieth century on the massive urban problems connected with industrialization, and they set about Americanizing as rapidly as possible the "new" immigrants pouring in from southern and eastern Europe. World War I cast a "pall of subversion" over the country and transformed progressive efforts into an insistence upon One Hundred Percent Americanism; a disregard for civil rights accompanied the demand for social conformity as proof of political loyalty.[3] The rise of Bolshevism, its call for international revolution, and growing radicalism in the United States further exacerbated fears.

Aliens and radicals came to be seen as indistinguishable. During the winter of 1919–20, the same year that a few Nazis gathered in Germany to form a small National Socialist Party, the attorney general of the United States, A. Mitchell Palmer, reacted to a series of bombings by staging illegal raids and mock trials, which resulted in the arrest of thousands of aliens and the deportation of hundreds. The Red Scare had taken hold of the country. Intense anti-alien feelings led to the infamous Sacco-Vanzetti case, which made headlines from 1920 to 1926 and resulted in the questionable conviction and execution of two Italian anarchists charged with murder.

Italians, Slovaks, Poles, and others experienced fierce hostility; nevertheless, "alien" and "radical" most often meant "Jew." Most Jewish immigrants had come from the area that gave rise to Bolshevism. Socialism, which to many Americans was indistinguishable from Bolshevism, asserted the dominant intellectual influence on the Lower East Side. And Jews comprised a disproportionate number of Russia's Bolshevik leaders. Strong anti-Semitic feelings permeated the anti-alien and anti-radical hatreds freely expressed by restrictionists.

Restrictionists waged a forty-year campaign before finally tasting victory during and after World War I. In 1917, despite a veto by Woodrow Wilson, they succeeded both in excluding Asians and in introducing a literacy test aimed at reducing immigration from Mediterranean and Slavic areas. Legislation in 1921 and 1924 established a National Origins Quota System and thereby institutionalized America's preference for citizens from northern and central rather than southern and eastern Europe.[4] Together, the three bills marked the end of an era that brought fifty-one million immigrants to this country, the single largest migration in recorded history.

For Jews in particular, the National Origins Quota System proved to be catastrophic in its failure to draw a distinction between immigrants and refugees, between people with the time and resources to proceed according to customary bureaucratic practice and persecuted people thrust into dire circumstances. An amendment in 1921 would have exempted from the quotas victims of religious persecution. But the motion received little support and was not reintroduced. Liberals were hesitant to make demands that would provoke restrictionists. The latter, still not satisfied with the National Origins Quota System, attempted in 1927 to reduce immigration an additional 10 percent during each of the next five years.

The Depression brought restrictionists growing support. The crash on October 24, 1929, occurred less than six months after the National Origins Quota System, plagued by administrative difficulties, became fully operational. In 1930 an effort to legislate the suspension of all immigration for two years died in committee, but in 1931 an attempt to cut quotas by 90 percent won Senate approval and came within one vote of coming to the floor in the House. It undoubtedly would have succeeded if restrictionists had waged an all-out campaign. However, Herbert Hoover made this effort unnecessary by using his administrative authority to achieve the same result.

During the Great Depression and World War II control over immigration policy, which became more restrictive, passed from Congress to the White House. On September 30, 1930, Hoover directed consular offices to interpret with utmost strictness the legal requirement that visa applicants provide evidence that they were not likely to become public charges for a period of five years. Immigration fell by 90 percent within five months.[5] Hoover expected both the Depression and his restrictive order to be short-lived but the Depression persisted and the order remained in effect.

American anti-Semitism, a strong component in restrictionist thinking, focused primarily on economic rather than religious or racial stereotypes. Nineteenth-century populists had thought that "international Jewish bankers" were their worst enemies. Twentieth-century nativists believed Jews and Bolsheviks to be synonymous. Both accused Jews of trying to subvert and dominate for economic ends. Such thinking became especially virulent during the Great Depression.

The idea of an insidious worldwide Jewish cabal found vicious expression in a spurious document that first appeared in Russia in the late nineteenth century and spread throughout the West during the 1920s. Translations of the *Protocols of the Elders of Zion* appeared in 1920 both in England and in Germany, where Adolph Hitler had recently become chief of the newly formed and small German National Socialist Party. A few months earlier the American Jewish Committee had refused to pay "a blackmailer" $50,000 for the *Protocols* to prevent their publication in the United States. Louis Marshall soon acquired a free copy. Henry Ford, who reprinted them in his *Dearborn Independent,* reported that they cost him $10,000. Harris A. Houghton distributed them in typescript form among Washington figures, and George Haven Putnam published them. Putnam and Ford, who was persuaded to print a retraction in 1928 after Jews boycotted his cars, gave American anti-Semitism credibility and respectability.[6]

The Depression years saw a fusion of anti-Semitic and anti–New Deal demagoguery. Decrying the New Deal as a "Jew Deal" that ignored the suffering of millions, Father Charles E. Coughlin, Charles E. Townsend, and Gerald K. Smith mounted an attack on Franklin Roosevelt that he never had to face from the Republicans, who remained in retreat following Hoover's ignominious defeat in 1932.

Townsend attracted over eight million members to seven thousand local political clubs and Coughlin drew far more to his radio ministry. In 1936 they joined with Smith, a rabidly anti-Semitic preacher, and organized a third-party challenge to FDR's presidential campaign.

The Coughlin-Townsend-Smith effort to unseat Roosevelt proved to be too little and too late, but it exposed feelings that evidently made a deep impact on the President. Always extraordinarily sensitive to public attitudes and political pressures, Roosevelt thought the challenge sufficiently serious to invite Coughlin, a one-time New Deal supporter, to Hyde Park for a discussion of their differences.[7] The president did not ignore the demagogues; it is unlikely that he dismissed the widespread appeal of their attacks on Jews. After the country went to war, overt anti-Semitism declined. However, a nationwide poll in December 1943 found that one-third of those questioned still believed that FDR had appointed too many Jews to jobs in Washington.[8]

Roosevelt's administration coincided with Hitler's chancellorship—he was elected president less than two years after the Nazis gained power and died less than one month before Hitler and the Third Reich ceased to exist—and he could not ignore the echoes of Nazi hatemongering that reverberated across this country. Most Americans had little interest in events within Germany. But polls, which Roosevelt followed avidly, indicate considerable sympathy for Nazi actions against Jews. Surveys in 1937 and 1938 found that one-third to one-half of the respondents believed charges that Jews had too much money, power, or influence in Germany or the United States. Ten percent blamed Jews totally for Nazi actions against them and nearly half thought Jews at least partly to blame. Between 32 and 45 percent agreed that anti-Jewish attitudes were intensifying.[9]

Franklin Roosevelt remained silent about Nazi persecutions and expulsions for five years. On March 24, 1938, when he broke his silence to call for an international conference in Évian, France, to address the growing refugee problem, he neither condemned the Nazis nor identified their victims as Jews. Preferring not to arouse restrictionists and anti-Semites, he used the euphemism "political refugees" and promised that no nation would be called upon to alter its immigration laws and regulations.

FDR issued his invitation in response to international and domestic developments. Several weeks earlier, after the League of Nations announced it would soon close both its Nansen Office and its High Commission for Refugees from Germany, the State Department reacted with dismay to a campaign for action mounted by columnist Dorothy Thompson and "certain congressmen with metropolitan constituencies."[10] Eleven days before FDR issued his invitation for the

Évian meeting, Germany annexed Austria and added 190,000 Austrian Jews to a German-Jewish community that had numbered 500,000 when the Nazis came to power. Both the refugee problem and demands that the administration act were growing. Congressional elections were only a few months away. Roosevelt's invitation, issued less than eight months before congressional elections, offered rescue advocates a glimmer of hope while assuring restrictionists that no fundamental changes would be made.

The Évian Conference, which brought together representatives from thirty-two governments on July 6–7, 1938, did more for the president's reputation as the humanitarian leader of the free world than it did for the salvation of Nazi victims. On the last day of the meeting, a German newspaper headlined: "JEWS FOR SALE: WHO WANTS THEM? NO ONE."[11] Unwilling to accept refugees within their own borders or to support American suggestions for huge refugee settlements in Africa, Asia, or Latin America, the delegates focused largely on the creation of an Intergovernmental Committee on Political Refugees (IGC). The IGC proved politically useful to sponsoring governments but produced only good intentions for refugees. A "bureaucratic monument to the spirit of futility," it enabled the State Department to discourage formation of an American agency that might have implemented actual rescue during the early part of the war.[12]

The refugee problem quickly exploded. Soon after Hitler claimed the concessions Britain and France granted him at Munich, the Germans forced the Sudentenland's German-speaking Jews into Czechoslovakia and its Jews with Polish passports into Poland. Czechoslovakia expelled its Jewish refugees to an island no-man's-land in the Danube. Within a few weeks the ranks of Jewish refugees had grown by hundreds of thousands. They fled Germany in the wake of *Kristallnacht,* the Nazi-orchestrated rampage on the night of November 9–10, 1938, which triggered mass arrests and intensified terror.

Desperate to escape, thousands bought worthless Latin American and Caribbean visas. Shiploads of Jewish refugees had to turn back after reaching Western ports. In May 1939 the *St. Louis,* carrying 930 Jewish passengers, received worldwide press coverage when, after being turned away from Cuba, it anchored off the American coast while American-Jewish organizations and relatives desperately sought help. Havana and Washington both refused to accept the refugees and they sailed back to Europe, where most were eventually killed by the Nazis.

The administration did, however, briefly encourage the full use of German and Austrian quotas, which were combined after the *Anschluss,* and the United States record on refugee admissions far surpassed that of any other country. Total quota utilization during the Nazi years ranged from 5.3 percent in 1933, when Jewish arrivals numbered 2300, to 40.6 percent in 1939, when Jewish immigration reached 43,000. The number of Jewish immigrants dropped sharply after America entered the war, and in 1944 again totaled only 2300. Except for those from Germany and Austria, most Jewish refugees came from countries assigned the smallest quotas—and even those quotas remained 60 percent unfilled. By 1943, when more than 4,500,000 Jews had been killed or transformed into refugees, approximately 811,000 had found refuge. However, many were in European states subsequently occupied by the Nazis. One hundred ninety thousand, 23.5 percent, obtained temporary or permanent admission to the United States.[13]

The outbreak of war brought new dangers to Jews in Europe and new threats to Jews in America. Most Americans had insisted on remaining aloof while the Spanish Civil War, the Japanese invasion of Manchuria, and the rape of Czechoslovakia drew the world inexorably closer to war. However, the Nazi-Soviet Pact in late August 1939, the invasion of Poland the following week, and the fall of France less than ten months later left England by mid-1940 to stand alone. Americans reacted with growing sympathy and increasing material support for the British, developments that alarmed isolationists, and angered anti-Semites, giving them common cause. The 1940 presidential campaign offered a new forum for hatemongers. Their insistent charge that Jews were pushing the nation into war led both FDR and GOP contender Wendell Willkie to warn repeatedly against Nazi efforts to divide America against itself.[14]

The refugee problem continued to grow and FDR turned to large-scale resettlement schemes that were unlikely to arouse restrictionists. He envisioned using hundreds of thousands of Jewish refugees and funds solicited from world Jewry to develop a barren area of the world. The project was expected to save lives and reclaim a desolate region without provoking serious opposition. A quasi-official President's Advisory Committee on Political Refugees (PACPR) was set up to review proposals and mobilize resources.

During the next three years, while Germany still appeared interested in large-scale emigration, the PACPR reviewed dozens of schemes. Interior Secretary Harold L. Ickes, Agricultural Secretary Henry A. Wallace, and leading figures in both the Army and the Navy favored an Alaskan proposal. They pointed to a 1939 study by Interior Undersecretary Harry Slattery that proposed that Alaska's population be increased to strengthen its security. However, although Roosevelt continued to urge the IGC to negotiate with the Germans on a "grander" scale, he refused to endorse the Alaskan scheme—the president much preferred untamed areas in Latin America or Africa, far from his own constituency.[15] He especially liked Angola. The British, who controlled Angola, favored Alaska. The Philippines, seeking to create a buffer in case the Japanese attacked, volunteered to accept refugees on the island of Mindanao. This offer might have been useful except that they also wished to protect Filipino farm exports and imposed restrictions that limited settlers to subsistence farming.

Resettlement remained a fantasy. By late 1941, when it was a dead issue, a mere 500 German Jews had been settled in Sosua, the Dominican Republic. Governments favored sites that were impractical or removed from their own constituencies. Alaska, Angola, Kenya, and Northern Rhodesia held the greatest promise, but not one proposal gained the necessary government approval. Jews would have shown little enthusiasm for such schemes even if the political, technological, and bureaucratic problems could have been overcome. Few refugees thought themselves suited for rigorous pioneering in undeveloped, difficult environments. And, most important, all proposals rested on the erroneous assumption, widespread not only among the Nazis but in the free world as well, that worldwide Jewry had the enormous capital that such development would require.

The fundamental issue remained not resettlement in some desolate corner of the world but entry into the United States, to which other countries looked to set an example. Soon after war broke out in Europe, FDR agreed to visa extensions for fifteen thousand aliens temporarily in the United States and to preferential treatment for several hundred artists and intellectuals seeking to immigrate. But he remained silent on the 1939 Wagner-Rogers Bill, which sought non-quota admission for 20,000 refugee children, and he did not support any of several efforts to liberalize restrictive legislation. The Roosevelt administration supported only one refugee bill. The 1940 Hennings Act granted temporary admission to 2000 children. However, the children in question were not Jewish and were not true refugees. They were "simply British children living in the war zone" of bombed London.[16] No other refugee legislation passed.

The president did not lend his support to ameliorative legislation, and, until the joint Allied statement in late 1942, he did not condemn Nazi behavior. He waited a week before remarking on *Kristallnacht* and he remained silent on the *St. Louis*. The "Final Solution" was tested with large-scale gassings of Jews on December 8, 1941, the day after Pearl Harbor, and approved nine days later. The Nazis adopted the "Final Solution" after German resettlement schemes failed and Germany extended its control over the areas that held Russian Jewry, the largest Jewish community in Europe. Mass killing methods used in Russia were labor intensive and inefficient. Further-more, the West's passivity and apathy permitted Nazi leaders to con-clude that in switching from forced emigration to mass murder they were doing the rest of the world a favor. Hitler aide Joseph Goebbels expressed typical Nazi thinking when, on December 13, 1942, he wrote in his diary: "The question of Jewish persecution in Europe is being given top news priority by the English and the Americans. . . . At bottom, however, I believe both . . . are happy that we are exter-minating the Jewish riff-raff."[17]

At the same time that the Nazis began putting into place the machinery for genocide, American Zionists and world Zionists moved to close ranks. After the outbreak of World War I the view that Jews in the Diaspora lived in *Galut,* in exile, found increasing favor. But most American Zionists, committed to life in the United States, rejected such thinking. Their support for Jewish settlements in Palestine focused on cultural and philanthropic rather than political activities, an approach that made possible the participation of non-Zionists. When, however, Nazi actions revealed the tragic precariousness of Jewish existence, American Zionists turned also to the search for a political solution, a shift made at the expense of relations with key non-Zionists.

The Biltmore Program expressed a new Zionist unity and deep-ened divisions within American Jewry. Launched May 9–11, 1942, at a meeting in New York that drew World Zionist Organization president Chaim Weizmann and Zionist executive David Ben-Gurion, it de-clared that American Jewry's first priority had to be the establishment of Palestine as a Jewish Commonwealth. The action repudiated agree-ments between American Zionist leaders and moderate non-Zionists within the American Jewish Committee and led to bitter disagree-ments within the Committee. In January 1943 the Committee issued an alternative statement that affirmed "deep sympathy" for Jews who wished to live in Palestine but insisted that Palestine could not provide the only solution for postwar Jewish rehabilitation. It rejected any "preconceived formula" for a "permanent political structure" in that land and disclaimed any "political identification" with any govern-ment established there.[18]

The first reports of mass shootings and gassings appeared in British and American newspapers one month after the Biltmore Con-ference, and American Jewry responded with mass protest rallies across the country. The first, on July 21, at New York's Madison Square Garden, drew an overflow crowd of twenty thousand. They heard a message sent by Franklin Roosevelt promising that America would "hold the perpetrators of these crimes to strict accountability on the day of reckoning which will surely come."[19] Four months later, on November 22, the State Department released far more detailed accounts of the killings. The story, buried on inside pages, triggered another round of much larger mass demonstrations. On December 2, half a million workers in New York City observed ten minutes of silence, local radio stations remained silent for two minutes, and NBC broadcast a memorial service.[20]

Organized American Jewry united in a spirit of cooperation. On December 9, 1942, the president received a representative delegation: leading Zionist Stephen S. Wise and the presidents of the American Jewish Committee, B'nai B'rith, the Jewish Labor Committee, and the Union of Orthodox Rabbis. They wanted Allied action to save European Jewry and asked that an American commission be created to study and report to the public on Nazi atrocities. FDR assured them that "the criminals would be held strictly accountable," that "every effort" would be made "to save those who could be saved," and that he would take under advisement the suggestion for a joint U.S./Allied commission.[21]

A few days later American Jewish leaders received a chilling cry for help from the Warsaw ghetto, where liquidation was underway. Called upon to "alarm the world," reminded that "only you can rescue us,"[22] representatives of thirty-two organizations met in Pittsburgh to lay plans for a major conference that would speak with one voice for American Jewry. They also formed a Joint Emergency Committee on European Jewish Affairs to conduct a campaign urging the government to assist Jews in immediate danger. However, announcement of a forthcoming Anglo-American meeting on the refugee problem diverted the latter's efforts. It turned instead to preparations for the Bermuda Conference.

The Joint Emergency Committee produced a twelve-point memorandum that asked the Allies to use neutral countries to negotiate the release of Jews and to promise such governments financial reimbursements for assistance to evacuated refugees. It called upon the Allies to increase immigration by revising administrative procedures, introduce a Nansen-type passport for unprotected "stateless" people, organize food programs for Jews unable to leave Nazi areas, form a new agency to implement rescue, and provide whatever funds such an overall program might need. Saving lives should take precedence over future political questions. Above all, temporary "havens of refuge" were needed in Allied neutral countries.[23]

While the major Jewish organizations (the American Jewish Committee and the Jewish Labor Committee did not attend the Pittsburgh meeting but joined the other groups soon after) laid plans for the Bermuda Conference and for a major Jewish gathering, a group of young Palestinian Jews introduced a new assertiveness into rescue demands. Beginning in early March 1943 with full-page ads in the *New York Times*, headlined "Jews Fight for the Right to Fight," and with performances at Madison Square Garden of Ben Hecht's "We Shall Never Die," which attracted overflow crowds, they drew supporters from across the country. Public agitation here and in Britain caused both Congress and the House of Commons to respond. The Senate, on March 9, and the House, on March 18, passed resolutions calling for the punishment of war criminals. And the House of Commons promised, insofar as military needs permitted, to give its "fullest . . . immediate . . . generous" help in providing "temporary asylum for refugees."[24] The Bermuda Conference promised an opportunity to coordinate efforts.

Washington and London each wished to be seen as the more humane, but both understood that neither wanted Jewish refugees. The State Department refugee officer saw his task as that of protecting national security, and his English counterpart in the Foreign Office saw his as protecting Britain's Palestine policy. The two men who bore direct responsibilities for refugee policy, Breckinridge Long in the State Department and Alec George Randall in the Refugee Department of the Foreign Office, thus worked in tandem not to aid refugees but to protect their respective countries from them. A lengthy memorandum from the British Embassy to the State Department on the eve of the Bermuda meeting expressed their common concerns: "There is a possibility that the Germans or their satellites may change over from the policy of extermination to one of extrusion and aim as they did before the war at embarrassing other countries by flooding them with alien immigrants."[25]

American and British representatives met in Bermuda to discuss the fate of European Jewry during the very days in which the Nazis completed the destruction of the Warsaw ghetto. The conference, held April 19–30, 1943, excluded Jewish organizational representatives. Sol Bloom, the token Jew in the American delegation, could be counted on not to make unpleasant demands. The elderly New York Democrat, chairman of the House Foreign Affairs Committee, had a reputation for being "easy to handle."[26]

Bermuda accomplished little more than Évian—the American and British delegations concluded with self-satisfying, platitudinous declarations and an agreement to revive the IGC. Twenty-two years later, Richard Law, the Parliamentary Undersecretary for Foreign Affairs who had headed the British delegation, characterized the meeting as "a façade for inaction."[27] Equally candid at the time of the meeting, Law had argued there that the Allies should not seek negotiations with Berlin because they might actually succeed and thereby relieve Hitler "of an obligation to take care of these useless people."[28]

Always more pragmatic than the Americans, the British admitted that such "useless" people aided the war effort by diverting German resources.

The Bermuda Conference embittered Jewish leaders but it also resulted in greater support for a public campaign. The memorandum that Jewish organizations could not present at the conference became the basis for resolutions and programs introduced at subsequent mass rallies. None felt more determined than the Bergson Boys, the young Palestinian Jews who responded with an all-out campaign to transfer refugee policy from the State Department to people committed to rescue. The *New York Times* carried a new series of full-page ads, an "Emergency Conference to Save the Jews of Europe" convened July 20–25 at New York's Hotel Commodore, and another mass rally took place at Madison Square Garden on July 26. The rally heralded the creation of the Emergency Committee to Save the Jews of Europe and focused specifically on the need for temporary sanctuaries.

Peter Bergson, the principal figure behind the new agitation, had worked in Warsaw and in London for the *Irgun*, a terrorist group in Palestine.[29] A man who had used several pseudonyms—he was born Hillel Kook, the grandnephew of the late chief rabbi of Palestine—he had arrived in the United States in 1940 and been stranded by Pearl Harbor. Skilled in the use of the media, he attracted support for the *Irgun* by creating such organizations as the Committee for a Jewish Army of Stateless and Palestinian Jews, the American League for a Free Palestine, and the Hebrew Committee of National Liberation. In 1943 he turned to the rescue issue and formed the Emergency Committee, the only Bergson organization that did not identify explicitly with Palestine and with Jewish nationalism. It functioned simply as one more American pressure group entitled to a hearing.

Indeed, Bergson's Emergency Committee was an American group. Secretary of the Interior Harold L. Ickes served as Honorary National Chairman and George Morris, president of the American Bar Association, accepted chairmanship of the Washington chapter. Other members included Assistant Secretary of the Interior Oscar Chapman, Interior Department general counsel Fowler Harper, Senator Guy Gillette, columnist Ernest K. Lindley, Representative Will Rogers, Jr., and ex-congressman William S. Bennett. Bergson's affiliation with the *Irgun* and revisionist Zionism made him anathema to Jewish communal leaders, but sympathetic non-Jews, unaware of the bitter cleavages within world Jewry, responded enthusiastically to his direct demands for action.

While Bergson gathered an impressive array of non-Jewish supporters, established organizations struggled to maintain fragile unity. On August 29, 1943, the American Jewish Conference drew more than five hundred delegates for a four-day meeting at New York's Commodore Hotel. Reports of the "Final Solution" had received official State Department confirmation two months earlier. Demoralized by Western inaction, the delegates could not agree on a proper response.

An American observer warned that a tragedy comparable to that which overtook the Jews in Warsaw should not be necessary "before you learn to cooperate, to compromise, to form a united front for the common good." A British observer reminded the delegates, "ideological squabbles between Zionists and anti-Zionists . . . seem strangely lacking in a sense of realism and responsibility."[30] Delegates bemoaned their lack of unity. However, at least one insisted that Jews were in essence "asking for the same thing." He thought the problem "a government question," for without government support, private groups remained powerless.[31]

Unity during the months that preceded the Bermuda Conference had depended on government cooperation, but that had proved futile. Resignation set in and produced alignments along ideological lines. Zionists now insisted that American Jewry devote its energy and resources to the long-range political goal of a Jewish State in Palestine. Little could be done for Jews presently endangered. And the "Jewish problem" would remain to endanger Jews in the future unless a Jewish state came into being.

The Zionists saw attention to rescue as a short-term digression that would be ineffective and would not only delay but subvert efforts to achieve the only possible solution. Others viewed the Zionist political campaign as activity in the service of a dream for which Jewish lives in Europe and Jewish acceptance in America would be sacrificed. They insisted that priority should be given to immediate rescue needs. The conference ended with a series of resolutions but no plan of action. The American Jewish Committee soon offered its resignation, as did the Jewish Labor Committee and the militant Orthodox Jews in Agudat Israel—the first because it refused to accept Zionism as the only solution and the latter two because they insisted on using every means to achieve rescue.

Bergson, who was not invited to participate in the American Jewish Conference and failed to gain its cosponsorship for an effort to get refugee policy out of the State Department, intensified his campaign to press rescue upon the government. The man whom many Jewish leaders suspected of being an opportunist seeking to embarrass and upstage traditional organizations orchestrated a campaign for a new agency with full power to implement concrete measures. On October 6, 1943, he marched with four hundred Orthodox rabbis in Washington, D.C., where, in FDR's absence, they presented a seven-point petition to Vice-President Henry A. Wallace. In addition to calling for a special intergovernmental agency that could act "on a large scale," it asked for the facilitation of immigration to both the United States and Palestine, the establishment of sanctuaries, and the shipment of food behind German lines.[32]

The campaign gathered support across America. Thousands signed similar petitions, including one that bore the names of more than thirty senators, one hundred representatives, and several Cabinet members.[33] On Sunday, October 10, six thousand American churches observed Yom Kippur as a Day of Intercession and called upon worshippers to pray for their Jewish "brethren" in Europe and to assist the Emergency Committee. And, on November 1, the Emergency Committee staged an "It Can Be Done" rally, during which the Swedish envoy to the United States accepted tribute accorded his country for its recent rescue of 6000 Danish Jews, and Leon Henderson, Roosevelt's economic advisor, severely rebuked FDR and Churchill for their inaction.[34]

The Emergency Committee next took its demands to Capitol Hill. Bergson supporters Senator Guy Gillette (D. Iowa) and Representatives Joseph C. Baldwin (R., N.Y.) and Will Rogers, Jr. (D. Calif.), introduced identical bills urging the executive to create a new refugee agency. On November 26 Sol Bloom's House Committee on Foreign Affairs tabled the measure. However, on December 20, just before Congress adjourned for three weeks, a similar bill, which had a dozen cosponsors in the Senate, won the unanimous approval of the Senate Committee on Foreign Relations. Both developments marked the beginning of the end for Breckinridge Long and for the State Department's refugee policy, the first because the House hearings gave Long an opportunity to discredit himself and the second because moving the issue to the Senate floor placed the administration on the defensive.

Bloom and Long each saw House hearings as an opportunity to refurbish reputations tarnished by the Bermuda Conference, whose deliberations five months earlier still had not been made public. Long testified for four hours in executive session on November 26. He persuaded committee members to reject the proposed new refugee agency; they tabled the measure to avoid appearing "entirely negative," a response that Germans might misconstrue.[35] Pleased with the reception Long received and unaware of the inaccuracies in his testimony, Bloom and the State Department gave his testimony wide distribution, thereby opening it to careful scrutiny.

Challenges quickly surfaced, including a "devastating point-by-point refutation" by the Rescue Commission of the American Jewish Conference.[36] Long ascribed wide powers to the IGC, when in fact it operated under highly restrictive limitations. The State Department official claimed that the United States had admitted 580,000 Jewish refugees during the previous ten years, but the actual number was less than one-third that figure. He attributed the underutilization of quotas to transportation problems, but troop transport ships regularly returned from Europe empty. Blaming his errors on a lack of preparation and an absence of notes and claiming that he was being victimized by Jewish agitators who needed to attack him in order to draw publicity, the determined restrictionist resigned five weeks later.

The House hearings discredited Long, but the victory was bittersweet, for they also publicly exposed sharp divisions among rescue advocates. Both House and Senate bills calling for a new rescue agency deliberately avoided mentioning Palestine, and that led Rabbi Stephen S. Wise to testify that such legislation would be relatively meaningless.[37] One month earlier the magazine *American Hebrew* had written about Bergson-sponsored demonstrations, "The spectacle is enough to make the angels weep." Sounding the charge that would echo through Zionist and non-Zionist, religious and secular circles alike, it suggested that "many people cannot but come to the conclusion" that some rescue advocates are exploiting the situation for reasons of their own."[38] Attacked by Jews who objected to his tactics and to his *Irgun* and revisionist connections, Bergson nonetheless continued to attract prominent non-Jewish support.

Political, labor, and religious leaders called for action. On September 9 the National Democratic Club and the National Republican Club issued a joint statement urging Congress to make available to fleeing Jews temporary visas valid until six months after hostilities in Europe ceased. In October, the annual convention of the AFL gave broad support to a resolution urging that America offer "temporary asylum." And in November, the annual convention of the CIO called upon Congress to grant Jewish refugees "full immigration opportunities."[39] A Christmas appeal for American sanctuaries included the signatures of Dr. Henry Sloane Coffin, President of the Union Theological Seminary; Bishop Angus Dun, Dean of the Protestant Episcopal Theological College; Archbishop Athenagoras of the Greek Orthodox Diocese of North and South America; and scattered local clergy.

Demands for action came from broad segments of American society, outcasts as well as prominent figures. On January 1, 1944, the inmates of Lewisburg Penitentiary urged FDR to use his full influence "to save the starving innocent children of Europe." A few days later Supreme Court Justice Frank Murphy, Vice-President Henry A. Wallace, and former presidential candidate Wendell Willkie appeared as the heads of a group of public figures who formed a National

Committee Against Nazi Persecution and Extermination of the Jews. They called upon Americans to heed their consciences and insist upon "sustained and vigorous" American and Allied action "to rescue those who may yet be saved."[40]

If Roosevelt needed additional evidence that the time for action had come, he received it from the Department of the Treasury. Treasury and State had clashed repeatedly during the previous months over the issuance of licenses needed to provide relief to refugees starving behind German lines. Treasury officials investigated State Department behavior and discovered interference in the transmission of information regarding the refugee situation. On January 13, 1944, Henry L. Morgenthau, Jr., received a stinging account titled "Acquiescence of This Government in the Murder of European Jews." Morgenthau softened its more inflammatory language, deleted a specific proposal for temporary American havens, and renamed it "Report to the President."[41] He presented it to Roosevelt on January 17, accompanied by Josiah DuBois, Jr., his general counsel and the report's principal author, and John Pehle, his director of foreign funds. The president responded five days later.

When FDR announced formation of the War Refugee Board, a new and independent agency with Cabinet status, it was clear that the State Department had outlived its usefulness in refugee matters. American Jewish organizations had grown more assertive, the Bergsonites had attracted broad and impressive support, and a resolution calling for a new federal rescue organization was on the Senate floor. A shift in the national mood was in the wind. No occupant of the White House ever had a keener sensitivity to such changes than did Franklin D. Roosevelt.

TWO

Rescue Proposal

PRESIDENT ROOSEVELT's announcement of the formation of a War Refugee Board appeared to signal that the United States intended at last to come to the aid of Europe's Jews. The new three-member board consisted of Secretary of State Cordell Hull, Secretary of War Henry L. Stimson, and Secretary of the Treasury Henry L. Morgenthau, Jr. But the WRB used Treasury offices and staff. Morgenthau had prevailed and a new day had dawned.

The War Refugee Board adopted two principal tasks, both of which appeared in the original report to Morgenthau. First, it released a barrage of messages to occupied Europe that threatened retribution for collaboration in Nazi crimes. The deportations could not be stopped, but perhaps they could be slowed if collaborators began to have second thoughts. Second, it worked to facilitate the flow of refugees to safe areas. Established escape routes existed from France and Rumania into Switzerland, from Poland and Slovakia into Hungary, from the Balkans into Turkey, from France into Spain, and from Yugoslavia into Allied-occupied southern Italy. Turkey, Spain, and Allied Italy appeared to be the crucial exit points. Their willingness to remain open to additional numbers of refugees, however, was conditioned upon assurances that they would not be overwhelmed. Rescue depended upon havens to which refugees could be moved.

Above all, the "Treasury Boys" wanted American havens, internment camps "similar to those used for the Japanese on the West Coast."[1] Morgenthau thought the proposal premature and deleted it. Temporary havens, discussed since the mid-thirties, had become the principal goal of the Bergsonites. Bergson supporters introduced the joint bills calling for such a body and they succeeded in moving the Senate version to the floor while similar efforts stalled in the House, action that Morgenthau credited with helping persuade Roosevelt to establish the WRB.[2] Less than two weeks after the board began operations, Bergson handed DuBois a memorandum similar to that which the Joint Emergency Committee had been unable to present to the Bermuda Conference.[3] The WRB's general program closely resembled its suggestions.

Peter Bergson did not meet Morgenthau, but he maintained a ubiquitous presence in the offices of the WRB and was known to many of its small staff of fewer than thirty. Former WRB director John W. Pehle, still loyal to FDR, no longer recalls having had much contact with Bergson. In early 1944, however, he aroused State Department anger because he used his government channels to relay communications between Bergson and Eri Jabotinsky, the son of Revisionist Zionist leader Vladimir Jabotinsky.[4]

Bergson had planned to travel to Turkey himself, but Pehle persuaded him to send Jabotinsky instead. The WRB director feared that Bergson's enemies would accuse him of leaving the United States to avoid being drafted, which would have damaged the credibility of the Emergency Committee. Pehle obtained State Department assurances that Jabotinsky would be permitted to reenter the United States, and, when the department reneged, he tried, unsuccessfully, to have him readmitted.[5] Pehle, who appeared at small Emergency Committee gatherings but did not associate with Bergson publicly, confessed unease to Morgenthau because he never knew what the skillful propagandist might do next.[6] Despite criticisms directed at the WRB and unease within it, Bergson, who remained closest to "firebrand" Josiah DuBois, Jr., retained free access to WRB offices.[7]

American Jewish leaders vigorously objected to the Bergson influence. And Morgenthau found it irksome.[8] His audacity and connections to the *Irgun* and Revisionist Zionists so aggravated Zionists and non-Zionists that efforts to have him drafted or deported began even before the creation of the WRB enlarged his influence. In mid-January 1944 Morris D. Waldman, executive secretary of the American Jewish Committee, visited the State Department to request an investigation directed toward "curtailing" Bergson's stay in the United States.[9] Four months later Nahum Goldman, World Jewish Congress president, asked the State Department why it still had not deported or drafted this perpetrator of "a gigantic hoax." Goldman threatened Pehle with a public denouncement of the WRB unless the director repudiated Bergson. Rabbi Stephen S. Wise, Goldman's WJC predecessor, described Bergson to Pehle as a man who would arouse so much anti-Semitism that he was "equally as great an enemy of the Jews as Hitler."[10]

Bergson's flamboyance and use of unconventional tactics both attracted and repelled the Treasury Boys, but his insistence that immediate rescue needs should have priority over postwar political matters aroused unequivocal support. Questions of immigration or a Jewish state could, to their minds, await the end of the war. First and foremost, temporary havens needed to be found; now the task would be to obtain sites within the United States.

Pehle and his staff would have to seek approval for such a plan within the administration, but before they could do this they would need to know that American Jewry would support the placing of Jewish refugees in camps within this country. The WRB director turned first to the National Refugee Service. The NRS functioned in a dual capacity. In New York, it operated the nation's largest and most comprehensive refugee-serving agency. On the national level, it acted as American Jewry's principal coordinator, spokesman, and ombudsman for refugees within the United States. Pehle and WRB Assistant Director Lawrence S. Lesser met on February 24 with NRS Board Chairman Joseph P. Chamberlain and NRS Honorary President William S. Rosenwald. They were to leave soon on a field trip to local affiliates in a dozen large communities and promised to test the idea of refugee camps during their travels.[11]

Chamberlain and Rosenwald found that the idea of interning Jewish refugees in the United States initially met resistance but, after careful explanation, won wide support. They returned able to promise full cooperation from both the NRS and its local affiliates.[12] Moses Leavitt, director of the American Jewish Joint Distribution Committee, the principal organization serving Jewish refugees in Europe, offered additional encouragement. He thought the proposal "the most important single step" the board could take.[13] FDR himself had already introduced the American public to the need for havens somewhere. His executive order establishing the War Refugee Board, which was prepared in the Treasury offices and given wide coverage, committed the administration to programs "consistent" with military needs that would hinder Nazi exterminations and facilitate rescue, including temporary havens.[14]

Pehle wanted another presidential declaration stating this commitment in stronger and more specific language. His staff prepared a draft in late February that condemned Nazi atrocities against Jews, promised retributive justice, and, after Jewish support was assured, included a promise to "furnish temporary asylum for all oppressed persons in imminent danger" from Hitler.[15] They would remain in the refugee centers until the war's end and then would return to their homelands.

The idea of temporary havens in America still had not been presented as a formal proposal, but the draft revealed that it had already undergone a significant revision. Initially, internment was to have been an interim measure, necessary only until security investigations could be completed, after which the refugees were to be released on some form of internment-at-large. However, in order to avoid arousing critics who would play on the nation's security fears, it was decided that refugees brought here would remain confined. Advocates wanted above all to gain support for unlimited asylum. The details appeared to be of secondary importance.

The draft presidential statement exposed significant differences between the WRB staff and the president. The Treasury Boys wanted to call specific attention to Nazi crimes against Jews, but FDR refused to single out Jews. He directed Special Counsel Samuel I. Rosenmann to transform the statement into a clarion call for freedom for all people. Morgenthau, Pehle, and DuBois had attempted to include the temporary havens proposal prematurely.

The Treasury secretary counseled tactical caution and did not fully commit himself. He thought the temporary havens idea "magnificent," but warned that it had only a 10 percent chance of gaining acceptance.[16] He encouraged Pehle to proceed but suggested that he obtain a congressional resolution that could be used to prod the president to act—the same tactic that had encouraged him to form the WRB. Pehle refused to accept a lengthy delay. They agreed to seek support on the board and among influential figures.

Board members never showed enthusiasm for the proposal. Morgenthau remained cautious. Undersecretary of State Edward Stettinius, Jr., who thought the White House would pose the "real hurdle," was characteristically noncommittal.[17] Henry L. Stimson responded that such a program would create postwar demands for changes in America's immigration law and should not be approved without congressional agreement. He noted in his diary that he gave Pehle "a long history of the Jewish problem in this country," including "the reasons for the growing opposition to unrestricted immigration of Jews" that had led after the last war to the National Origins Quota System.[18] Pehle recently recalled that the secretary considered Jews to be "unassimilable."[19]

Morgenthau did not commit himself unequivocally and Stimson raised a major stumbling block. The day after Pehle's meeting with Stimson, Drew Pearson reported in his syndicated "Washington Merry-Go-Round" column that the War Department had had "to carry the ball" the previous month in killing a Senate resolution reiterating American support for a Jewish homeland in Palestine because Hull "did not want to take a public stand against the resolution."[20] There was reason to suspect that, once again, Stimson was running interference for others.

Morgenthau undoubtedly suspected that Stimson's reaction expressed not only his own biases but the likelihood that the State Department did not intend to relinquish all influence on refugee policy. Henry A. Wallace noted in his diary that Morgenthau considered Hull "a marvelous underground maneuverer," who always sat silently, with his head down, but would later "pull underground strings to make things come his way at the White House."[21]

The temporary havens proposal had to be accepted as a rescue measure that would in no way circumvent American immigration laws. A report prepared by DuBois and WRB Assistant Director John B. Friedman offered several assurances. It promised that refugees brought to temporary camps would not be released, despite humanitarian opposition that might arise; in fact, they "would be treated in effect as prisoners-of-war" who would not be eligible for regular admission during their confinement and would have to leave the country at the war's end. Furthermore, America would not have to carry the burden alone. Nicaragua agreed to receive refugees "under the same conditions as the United States and in a number proportionate to the population of both countries."[22] Other nations could be expected to follow suit.

The fear that refugees might pose a threat to the nation's security also needed to be addressed. WRB counsels Matthew Marks and Milton Sargoy outlined a procedure that adhered to the old adage "the best defense is a good offense." All refugees in imminent danger or whose removal would facilitate the rescue of others, except those physically incapable of travel or suffering contagious disease, would be eligible. Selection would favor anyone suspected of being an enemy agent, everyone would be screened carefully at the port of debarkation, and suspected risks would be taken immediately into custody. Everyone else would proceed under armed guard to camps, where security would always be paramount. In other words, the program would reduce our security risks overseas without creating any additional threat at home.[23]

A third WRB memorandum offered four legal precedents for the creation of temporary havens within the United States. First, in the early days of World War I the officers and crews of several German ships turned to the then neutral United States to avoid British capture and were interned for the duration of the war. Second, the United States maintained interned POWs within its borders during both world wars. Third, during the summer and fall of 1943 more than fourteen hundred civilian Polish refugees experienced brief internment in California en route to Mexico, which offered them asylum. Fourth, in 1941 and 1942 more than thirty-five hundred enemy aliens were brought to the United States for internment after being rounded up in Central and Latin American countries in accordance with a series of unpublished wartime agreements made by the Roosevelt administration. Only thirteen hundred were repatriated before an exchange agreement with Germany broke down; the rest remained interned. In each case, Congress was not involved.

Wartime entrants did not require special legislation because "immigration into the United States is something freely allowable save to the extent that the Congress has seen fit to impose restrictions upon it." Only nonimmigrants with certain health problems faced congressional exclusion, and these would not be accepted for temporary havens. Furthermore, even if legislative authorization should be deemed necessary, the WRB memorandum argued, the president's war powers would be "sufficient."[24]

The WRB staff insisted that temporary havens had clear precedents, that they would not circumvent immigration laws, and that they would strengthen rather than weaken national security. The board, which had yet to be persuaded, officially received the proposal in late March and agreed to put it before Roosevelt. At Stimson's urging, however, they directed Pehle to include not one but four suggested responses. The original called for unilateral presidential action. Each of the three additions involved Congress: the president might consult appropriate legislative leaders before taking executive action, he might urge Congress to initiate action, or he might send a bill to Capitol Hill himself. Stimson also insisted on a cover sheet with a caveat that Congress definitely should be involved. And the board members signed only the cover letter, indicating their unanimous opposition to unilateral presidential action.[25]

The previous four years had seen increasing rancor between the White House and Capitol Hill. The victims were the agencies created by executive order and subsequently dependent upon congressional appropriations. Roosevelt chose to fund the WRB from a special Presidential Emergency Fund, in part because a 1943 battle over the Office of Price Administration turned into what has been described as "general guerilla warfare."[26] By 1944 suspicion that FDR might make unilateral "permanent position commitments" clouded all issues.[27]

Roosevelt's problems on Capitol Hill also extended to members of his own party. A mid-1943 presidential veto on a tax bill sparked a stunning revolt. Alben Barkley, a loyal New Dealer for twelve years, resigned as Senate majority leader and received a thunderous ovation and immediate reelection. Columnist Westbrook Pegler, a persistent thorn in the administration's side, hailed the incident as "the return of manhood and decency to Congress."[28]

Henry L. Morgenthau had become a lightning rod for Roosevelt critics during that tax revolt. Columnist David Lawrence politely described the rebellion as an uprising against "those non-elected advisors who exercise vast powers in the President's behalf."[29] Walter Lippmann was more direct. He declared that "the remedy is not resignations such as Barkley's but some new faces in the Treasury." Lippmann added that Congress heeded "men of proven knowledge" and "ability in action" in their fields.[30] He upheld Stimson as such a man but criticized Morgenthau for being neither a master nor even an apt pupil of war finance.

Presidential elections would soon take place, and the administration needed to mend its legislative fences rather than provoke additional ire. Cabinet members more concerned about politics than about rescue had good reason to oppose any unilateral action that would reopen congressional wounds. Furthermore, if the time was not auspicious for Roosevelt to provoke Congress, it was even less so for Morgenthau. The Treasury secretary had hoped that the growing stature of the WRB and his own quiet lobbying might be effective. But Stimson put him in a precarious position and Pehle found him increasingly wary.[31] DuBois wanted very much to "make the issue clear" on Capitol Hill[32] but Pehle was less confident.

House Majority Leader John W. McCormack, a reliable friend of rescue advocates, counseled that only a widespread and lengthy public relations campaign might overcome restrictionist opposition in both houses. Insisting that temporary havens could be established in the United States only through executive order, he recommended such action, if the president could gain support from leaders in both houses.[33] Prospects for this seemed bleak.

Meanwhile, Nazi deportations and murders proceeded and the administration faced growing criticism. FDR's vague March 24 condemnation of Nazi atrocities drew stinging attacks. *New York Times* columnist Anne O'Hare McCormick insisted two days later that the president could not continue to ignore demands for action. DuBois thought Roosevelt would soon feel compelled to deliver on his own promises.[34] New pressures for action developed.

A columnist for the liberal *New York Post* called for American "free ports." Samuel Grafton wrote on April 5 that goods commonly entered the United States to be stored in transit without being subjected to regular customs procedures. Why couldn't refugees be accorded similar treatment? He felt "ashamed" of having to pander to antirefugee prejudices by drawing such an analogy, but "the need is so sharp, the time is so short, our current example to the world is so bad, that it is necessary to settle for whatever can be done." And this meant that "it should not be impossible to do . . . for people" that which we do "in commercial free ports for cases of beans."

A nationwide Gallup Poll taken two weeks later suggested that 70 percent of Americans favored temporary havens, a figure that brought exhiliaration to WRB offices. The poll had been ordered by David Niles, presidential assistant for minority affairs. DuBois had given him a copy of the formal proposal only two days before the Grafton column appeared. Niles, an elusive figure with "a passion for anonymity," wielded considerable power and influence in the White House and developed a keen interest in the rescue proposal.[35]

Grafton and Niles brought opportune support. The Grafton columns—a second one followed April 15—ran in forty-one newspapers with a combined circulation of more than four million, and they were widely quoted by other writers. The first one appeared one day after Thomas E. Dewey won the Wisconsin GOP presidential primary and thus became the leading Republican contender. Rumors circulated that the former New York governor would soon announce his own plan for bringing 100,000 refugees temporarily to the United States.[36]

New York radio broadcaster Henry Pringle explained that "Free Ports" meant only "one immediate decision about the Jews of Europe—that they shall not be murdered by Hitler." His April 18 broadcast noted that non-Jews faced enslavement at the hands of the Nazis but two million Jews had already been murdered and another four million "are being killed." Why, therefore, did 130,000 Nazi POWs enjoy American hospitality while America's doors remained closed to Hitler's victims? "It does seem," he declared, "as though we could find an acre somewhere for the friends who never hurt us."[37]

"Free ports" quickly drew broad support. Newspapers publishing favorable editorials included the *Seattle Star, Charlotte* (N.C.) *News, New Orleans Times-Picayune,* and *Mitchell* (S.D.) *Daily Republic,* as well as the *Miami Herald, Chicago Sun,* and *Lynn* (Mass.) *Telegram News.* Additional endorsements came from the Federal Council of the Churches of Christ in America, the YWCA National Board, the American Friends Service Committee, and the Women's International League for Peace and Freedom. House Democratic Majority Leader John McCormack initially thought the idea might draw a presidential endorsement.[38]

The public momentum for "free ports" developed independently of the quiet campaign taking place within the administration. The first hint of the latter appeared at an impromptu press conference in WRB offices a few hours after Pringle's broadcast. Ira Hirschmann described for reporters the desperate situation of refugees and their reverence for the "god" Roosevelt.[39] When a reporter asked whether "free ports" were being given official consideration, Pehle responded that he could not comment on discussions in progress. The board had yet to give its approval but, much to the consternation of the WRB staff, several reporters assumed this had occurred.[40]

Three weeks later, after the board accepted a revised text that clearly discouraged unilateral presidential action, Pehle delivered it to FDR. The president, obviously familiar with the proposal, showed particular interest in a list of endorsements that Pehle had included, particularly in its significant omissions. Majority Leader John McCormack's inclusion on the list had little impact; he could already be counted on. The "other McCormack [*sic*]" (Robert) was not on the list and that was far more serious, for the *Chicago Tribune* publisher was an unrelenting administration critic.[41]

Roosevelt agreed to the proposal in principle. However, like Stimson, he introduced new obstructions and delays. On the one hand, he offered the use of naval transports that normally returned empty and indicated that the refugees should be located along the eastern seaboard because they would be returning to Europe at the war's end. On the other hand, he agreed only to consider establishing a single camp for one thousand refugees and even this depended upon the development of an appropriate "emergency" that could justify it.[42] Faced with such tokenism, Pehle expressed a preference for leaving the entire matter to Congress but he neither challenged nor criticized the president.

Five days later an appropriate "emergency" appeared on Pehle's desk. WRB Special Representative Leonard Ackermann wrote that removing even one thousand refugees from Allied Italy would ease a critical situation.[43] Pehle quickly developed a new proposal but it still did not win administrative support. Morgenthau raised the issue at a cabinet meeting on May 24. However, his announcement that Undersecretary of War John McCloy wanted refugees removed from Allied Italy struck Stimson, McCloy's superior, as an affront. The War secretary declared that the Army had no business with refugees and that he wished to wash his hands of the entire matter.[44] Attorney General Francis Biddle objected to even one camp, not on legal but on political grounds. Only Secretary of the Interior Harold L. Ickes, a Bergson supporter, expressed unequivocal support. Morgenthau left the meeting believing that the president remained "a little afraid" to act.[45] He and Pehle turned for support to presidential intimates such as columnist I. F. Stone, financier Bernard Baruch, and Justice Felix Frankfurter.

In another one of those timely public responses, Alfred E. Smith announced, the day after the cabinet meeting, that seventy-two prominent Americans had signed a petition calling upon the president to establish temporary havens in the United States. The former governor and Democratic presidential nominee had telegrammed requests for support to leading non-Jews throughout the country soon after Pehle's office prepared an official request for one camp to meet the need in Italy. Signers included a former vice-president of the United States, an associate justice of the Supreme Court, eighteen governors, four Nobel Prize winners, thirteen university and college presidents, key figures in business and labor, and a former law partner of Franklin D. Roosevelt.[46]

The president himself engaged in vigorous lobbying during the following two weeks. White House logs indicate that immediately after the cabinet meeting FDR held a conference with Senators Guy Gillette (D. Iowa) and Howard Burton (R. Ohio) and with Representatives Jennings Randolph (D., W. Va.), Harve Tibboth (R. Pa.) and William Stevenson (R. Wis.). Burton and Tibboth were key figures on the Senate and House Appropriation Committees, and Burton also sat on the Senate Immigration and Naturalization Committee. Randolph exercised considerable influence in the House Labor Committee. Roosevelt undoubtedly assured them that refugees brought to this country temporarily would not enter the American labor market but would instead be maintained at the expense of the United Nations Relief and Rehabilitation Administration (UNRRA), a view he expressed at subsequent news conferences.

Five days later Senator Gillette introduced a new resolution urging the president to aid "Jews and other special victims of Nazi hatred" who could escape. Gillette asked that they be received at Ellis Island "or other designated centers for temporary detention and care."[47] The Iowa Democrat reminded the Senate that his earlier bill calling for the creation of a rescue agency had prodded the president into creating the board, and he asked that the Senate once again push FDR into action. That same morning, May 29, the *Washington Post* carried a full-page Emergency Committee ad calling for temporary American havens. By continuing to demand the larger scheme, the Bergsonites may have helped blunt opposition to the token effort about to be announced.

Roosevelt made several public statements during the next few days that suggest that he was keenly aware of objections to a refugee camp expressed in the April Gallup Poll.[48] Newspapers first reported on May 30 that the president "applauded" the general idea of "free ports." Three days later FDR suggested that he might actually establish a shelter. Such a facility, open to gentiles as well as Jews, would directly benefit the United States Army by removing refugees from its path in Allied Italy. It would use an Army post and depend upon UNRRA maintenance. In actuality, Roosevelt had already approved establishment of a single refugee shelter and was considering two New York sites. Furthermore, UNRRA had refused to accept responsibility for the project because it operated only in neutral countries.[49]

During the first week in June seven members of Congress introduced separate bills urging presidential establishment of "free ports." Samuel Dickstein (D., N.Y.) chairman of the House Committee on

Immigration and Naturalization, then announced that he would open full committee hearings on the resolutions if the president did not act by June 21.[50] During that same week, the White House also recorded an unusual number of congressional visitors. Their identities suggest that the principal topic was the Bretton Woods Conference on postwar economic cooperation, scheduled to open July 1, but the visits gave FDR numerous opportunities to test reactions to the establishment of a refugee haven.

At the same time that activity on behalf of refugees intensified, the Allies launched their long-awaited second front. That event, on June 6, both obscured the refugee issue and strengthened the argument that any refugees brought to the United States would remain only a short time.

During the first week in June the War Refugee Board also received notice of Adolph Eichmann's infamous offer of "blood for trucks."[51] The legitimacy of the Nazi suggestion that as many as one million Jews might be released in return for ten thousand vehicles was never tested because the British immediately imprisoned Joel Brand, the Zionist rescue operative who had brought the message from Budapest. Brand didn't regain his freedom until October 7, 1944, and by that time three-fourths of the Jews in Hungary had been deported to Auschwitz. However, in early June the Brand offer stirred considerable hope in the WRB offices.

Roosevelt officially approved the Oswego Emergency Refugee Shelter—a name he chose to emphasize the temporary nature of the project and to indicate that the government would accept responsibility for little more than shelter—at a meeting with Morgenthau and Pehle on June 8.[52] They were shocked the following day when the president reacted to Dickstein's stated intent to open congressional hearings by "jump(ing) the gun" and publicly announcing the Oswego Emergency Refugee Shelter before officially informing Congress.[53] His communication to Congress three days later was anticlimactic.

In stark contrast to the high hopes of refugees selected for the project, Oswego got off to an inauspicious start. The president did not issue an executive order but merely signed instructions to the departments responsible for the camp, an action that lacked the status of an official presidential order. Recognized as a token gesture, the president's act was buried on the back pages of newspapers filled with stories from Normandy. It evoked no immediate opposition.

Morgenthau's "Boys" had had the temerity to dream that they would bring hope and salvation to thousands, perhaps hundreds of thousands. That dream included far more than American camps. The temporary havens proposal was in fact part of a larger rescue plan to which Palestine was central. In this, they had FDR's cooperation.

THREE

Diplomatic Gamesmanship

THE WAR REFUGEE BOARD altered the Anglo-American rapprochement on refugee issues, but the nature of the change was not immediately apparent. Alec George Randall, chief of the refugee department within the Foreign Office, initially dismissed the new American agency as another of Roosevelt's politically expedient gestures that would require a similar British demonstration of humanitarian concern. Since the president included in his WRB announcement a notice that American overseas missions would soon ask the governments to which they were accredited for a full accounting regarding their efforts to provide refugee assistance, the Foreign Office issued parallel instructions to its consulates. Randall assured the War Office, however, that "this is all rather of the order of 'eyewash,'" intended only "to enable the State Department to deny reports that His Majesty's Government are backward in their solicitude for refugees."[1]

The Foreign Office thought the board a nuisance rather than a menace, but the War Office saw it as a threat. The first area of Anglo-American disagreement, noted by the WO less than two weeks after the formation of the WRB was announced, centered on the question of currency transfers. The WO expected the WRB to demand a revision of blockade policy in order to aid Jews behind enemy lines, a change it firmly opposed.[2] The Treasury Department, which had been in conflict with the State Department over the issue for several months, did act without British consent and licensed the International Red Cross to convert $100,000 for aid to Jews in occupied Hungary and Rumania. That action and word that Roosevelt was about to

28

publicly condemn Nazi atrocities without conferring with London led Foreign Minister Anthony Eden to call a special meeting of the War Cabinet on March 10.[3] The British could not prevent additional licensing, but they persuaded FDR to delay and revise his anti-Nazi declaration.

Morgenthau and the WRB staff expected Roosevelt to issue the declaration on March 14 and remained totally in the dark when he did not do so. They did not know that the State Department had passed a copy to Ambassador Lord Halifax on March 10. Neither did they know that on the evening of March 13 War Secretary Stimson, Navy Secretary Frank Knox, and General George Marshall had informally conveyed Anthony Eden's anger to the president and that Roosevelt had agreed to a postponement.

The British wanted a jointly released declaration similar to "the many solemn warnings already given," but one that criticized only German satellites and not Germany herself.[4] The president had already softened the draft given to him one month after the WRB began to operate. He refused to remove Germany as a target of his condemnation but he agreed to a second delay so that the British could prepare a statement for simultaneous release.

Morgenthau and Pehle puzzled over the declaration's fate and turned to Bernard Baruch for help. That venerable presidential advisor, whose estate Roosevelt used as a secret retreat, acknowledged his own bafflement. Baruch knew "something [was] wrong," and he doubted that the problem stemmed from subordinates down the line, but he could not identify the source of the difficulty.[5] When FDR did at last issue a statement (*New York Times*, March 25, 1944), he declared:

> In most of Europe and in parts of Asia, the systematic torture and murder of civilians—men, women and children—by the Nazis and the Japanese continue unabated. In areas subjugated by the aggressors innocent Poles, Czechs, Norwegians, Dutch, Danes, French, Greeks, Russians, Chinese Filipinos—and many others—are being starved or frozen to death or murdered in cold blood in a campaign of savagery. . . . In one of the blackest crimes of all history . . . the wholesale systematic murder of the Jews of Europe goes on unabated every hour. . . .All who share the guilt shall share the punishment.

Rather than the condemnation of genocide intended by the WRB, Roosevelt's statement became a criticism of "crimes against humanity committed in the name of the German people." And Morgenthau attributed its timing to the Nazi completion of their Hungarian occupation four days earlier.[6]

The British continued to be divided as to the seriousness of America's increased interest in refugees and rescue. Two indiscretions, the first by a WRB representative and the second by a State Department diplomat, suggested that little had really changed. During his March trip to Washington, WRB Special Representative to Turkey Ira Hirschmann gave reporters an exaggerated account of his achievements and prematurely announced that Germany had granted safe passage from Rumania to Haifa for 1500 Jews abroad the SS *Tari*. The disclosure, which caused the Germans to renege, made it appear that the WRB valued publicity more than results. British diplomats in Turkey offered confirmation of that impression when they reported that American Ambassador to Turkey Laurence Steinhardt considered the announcement "the essential thing" and showed no interest in other recently arrived refugees in Ankara.[7]

Pehle recognized that the Foreign Office preferred to view the WRB as "a political move in an election year."[8] However, complaints from the War Office about "great and increasing" WRB pressure for Jewish camps indicated that the latter took the WRB more seriously.[9] Using the Middle East Relief and Refugee Administration (MERRA), a department within the Repatriation Office of the British Embassy in Cairo, the British had been operating camps for Greeks, Yugoslavs, and Dodecanesians since 1940 in Egypt, Syria, and Palestine. At the Bermuda Conference British and American representatives had agreed to jointly sponsor two camps for the stateless and non-repatriables, that is, for Jews. However, when the WRB appeared nine months later, there still were no camps for Jews and no plans to establish them.

The first camp promised for Jews, at Fedhela, French North Africa, had been proposed by the British and restricted to refugees who reached Spain. England wanted that camp so that it could be used to persuade Spain to keep its border open. The refugee traffic across the Pyrenees Mountains included downed British fliers and escaping prisoners-of-war useful to British intelligence. However, conference delegates did not establish procedures for implementation. Furthermore, the Free French and American military authorities feared arousing Arab opposition. The delay led Churchill personally to prod Roosevelt into action. The French acquiesced but imposed restrictions that reduced would-be occupants to prisoner-like status.[10]

Fedhela, which was to have housed ten thousand refugees, never held more than a few hundred. Jewish refugees in Spain objected to exchanging relative freedom for French internment, In March 1944 Washington and London agreed to impose "involuntary removal."[11] However, by that time refugee traffic to Spain had declined sharply and no longer included British fliers. Britain lost interest and did not supply ships to Spanish ports as promised. Nevertheless, the camp continued to be reserved for refugees from Spain.

The second camp, consisting of four sites with a total capacity of forty thousand, was to be in Tripolitania, Libya. The British agreed to it in exchange for Roosevelt's help in obtaining the Fedhela camp.[12] But the plan evoked only perfunctory interest until the WRB appeared, at which point the Foreign Office found itself caught between WRB demands and War Office opposition. When the latter persisted despite assurances from the Egyptian Department that a facility known to be temporary and created "without ostentation" would not arouse local Arab anger,[13] the Foreign Office assured the War Office that, even if it should negotiate an agreement "in principle" with the WRB, it would "stall" actual work.[14]

Three months passed before the Foreign Office acceded to WRB demands for the Tripolitania camp, and then it agreed only to one site for no more than fifteen hundred refugees who had Yugoslav nationality and had made their way to Allied Italy.[15] Despite the restrictions, another five months passed and construction did not begin. In November 1944 the Foreign Office concluded that "times change" and that the Libyan camp no longer had the "same importance." In addition, it thought that the WRB, which was reducing its European operations as the Allies advanced, was "a dying body."[16] State Department lethargy, WRB failure to propose a North African camp maintained exclusively by the United States, and British obstructionism worked against Fedhela or Tripolitania becoming Jewish havens.

Trying desperately to fight a war and prevent their empire from collapsing in a flood of rising nationalisms, the British wanted above all to placate Arabs in the Middle Eastern lands that stood as a gateway to India. The Allies could take Jewish loyalty for granted, but Nazism and Fascism found influential supporters throughout the Arab world.

The British were most vulnerable in Palestine, where Zionist development, encouraged by the 1917 Balfour Declaration favoring a Jewish national home, had dramatically increased that land's capacity for population and had attracted increasing numbers of Jews and Arabs. Beginning in 1929, Arab fears of becoming a minority produced periodic riots that grew more violent as it became apparent that only such actions led the British to impose limitations on Jewish immigration. Nazism and the reluctance of the Western world to accept Jewish refugees transformed Zionism into a desperate effort to bring Jews into Palestine despite Arab hostility and British restrictions. The approach of war hardened British determination to protect its increasingly tenuous position.

Four months before war erupted, the MacDonald White Paper had decreed that Jewish immigration would be limited to a total of 75,000 during the next five years. As the expiration date of May 17, 1944, neared, approximately 26,000 Palestine certificates remained undistributed, and Zionist criticism mounted. The certificates had been withheld to extend the White Paper and thus postpone having to address the question again. Having established the WRB as Zionist demands increased and wanting to use the board to deflect criticism of his own inaction, Roosevelt indicated to Morgenthau that he wished to force Palestine open.[17]

By 1944 significant refugee movement could come only from the Balkans, and most who fled headed for Turkey. That produced additional pressure on Britain's Palestine policy because Turkey did not admit refugees without assurances they would continue to Palestine. Several tragic sinkings occurred in 1942 because Turkey refused refugees on crowded, unseaworthy vessels. In September of that year the Foreign Office asked Turkish authorities to check with the British ambassador before refusing aid to any ship in trouble in Turkish waters, an action that the Colonial Office protested because of its "embarrassing implications."[18]

Few Jews reached Turkey the following year and Britain felt comfortable acceding to Turkish demands that it guarantee that all Jewish refugees in Turkey would receive Palestine certificates. That promise, given secretly in July 1943, remained unknown to fleeing Jews. The British subsequently revealed it to the Jewish Agency in order to "draw off . . . the ire" of rescue advocates but insisted that it not be publicized to stimulate refugee traffic.[19] Fewer than two hundred Jews arrived in Turkey during 1942, and no more than twelve hundred reached Palestine, legally and illegally, via that country during 1943. Nevertheless, when Pehle sought Palestine certificates for refugees in Allied Italy and when flights from the Balkans increased as Russian troops advanced in 1944, London insisted that Palestine certificates were already reserved.

The War Refugee Board demanded that Britain help facilitate movement from the Balkans, and the British responded by revising their promises to Turkey. The Foreign Office now limited Turkey to 10,300 certificates, at the rate of no more than 1500 each month, and promised that it would seek havens elsewhere if more refugees arrived. At the same time, it resisted WRB efforts to obtain such havens.

Undersecretary of State Edward Stettinius, Jr., led a mission to London at a time when the British were particularly sensitive to the issue of refugee traffic into Turkey. The Stettinius mission, in April 1944, gave the WRB its first opportunity for face-to-face Anglo-American discussions on the refugee issue. Ambassador to London John Winant set the tone for the talks by presenting the Foreign Office with a demand for an "immediate" rescue proposal suitable for presentation to the Joint Chiefs of Staff.[20] Unfortunately, Stettinius and Wallace Murray, the State Department officer selected to represent the

WRB and a man whom John W. Pehle viewed as "the worst possible person" for the assignment,[21] did not convey a similar sense of urgency or commitment. Stettinius and Murray returned home "proud" that they had British assurances that an adequate number of Palestine certificates remained available and that additional havens would be found if necessary.[22]

WRB instructions, prepared by Josiah DuBois, Jr., had urged insistence on temporary havens in Palestine, which were to be presented as a useful alternative to growing Zionist pressure for termination of the White Paper. DuBois argued that temporary havens in the United States would also reduce Zionist pressure on Roosevelt. Sympathetic to the Zionist cause but aloof from it, the WRB staff wished to challenge neither the White Paper nor American immigration laws. They wanted only to use the Zionist conflict to strengthen their case for temporary havens.[23]

Palestine held the key to any significant rescue operation. The United States, North Africa, Cyprus, and Portugal were all considered potential locations for temporary havens. However, Palestine's geographic proximity, international status, low population density, and accessibility to food supplies made it the single most attractive site. Could Jewish rescue and temporary havens be separated from questions of ultimate settlement? FDR was postponing questions about postwar governments and boundaries in order to focus exclusively on winning the war. Could the same be done in order to save Jews? The Bergsonites and the WRB staff insisted that it had to be done. Stimson had argued in the case of American havens that the issues could not be separated. However, Palestine was Britain's problem and he did not discourage the WRB staff from pressing the British to make such a separation.[24]

The British responded to increased American pressure by becoming even less cooperative. In July 1944 Sir Clifford Heathcote-Smith, the Intergovernmental Committee representative in Italy, forwarded to London and Washington captured German orders for the deportation of non-Italian Jews in northern Italy. Knowing that deportation meant certain death, he asked the Allies to seek papal intervention. At the WRB's urging, American IGC representative Myron Taylor met with Pope Pius XII. The Pope later reported that he asked the Germans to halt the deportations but that they responded that he had no *locus standi* for such a request.[25]

A British representative did not accompany Taylor to the Vatican because the Foreign Office indicated such intervention was improper. Communications within the Foreign Office, however, reveal that propriety was not the issue. A draft reply not sent to the WRB said that "any suggestion of an approach to Hitler to release Jews would be directly contrary to the settled policies of the two governments concerned."[26] And Edward Walker, an assistant to Alec George Randall, noted on an interoffice memorandum that Heathcote-Smith "betrays a certain lack of sense of proportion" or at least "knowledge of the British problem."[27]

Despite their ability to resist American pressure, the British repeatedly overrated WRB influence in Washington. Winant's demands and the talks with Murray convinced Alec George Randall that the Foreign Office should make some concessions. He concluded that "President Roosevelt himself is behind this refugee policy," and "it will not do for us to go with a blank negative to the Americans." He saw joint sponsorship of a camp in Tripolitania as "a far less objectionable alternative."[28]

British Embassy reports from Washington strengthened Randall's growing belief that London should show some flexibility. Political officer Michael Wright reported in late May that the WRB was Roosevelt's "own ewe lamb." Too intimidated to do anything "that might look remotely like taking our side," the State Department was now "friendly but futile." In sharp contrast, the WRB was "offensive but effective." He expected temporary havens to be approved. Since few Jews would be left to benefit, he concluded that Pehle really wanted "to beat us for our refusal to allow unrestricted Jewish immigration into Palestine." Wright hoped that Pehle and the WRB would soon "be cut down to something more nearly approaching life size."[29]

The WRB's challenge to Britain's Palestine policy was unmistakable. However, FDR's orchestration of the challenge was less obvious. Morgenthau, Winant, and Taylor each pressed WRB demands upon the British more vigorously after conferring privately with the president. In late May FDR ordered Ambassador Robert Murphy, the senior American diplomat in the Mediterranean area, to see that "as many [Jews] as possible" were sent to Palestine.[30] Because the British had not yet acted on the camp promised in Tripolitania, he also ordered Murphy to investigate possible sites in Sicily and on the Italian mainland. At the same time, Winant began to press both for new refugee facilities in the Mediterranean and for the issuance of Palestine certificates in Allied Italy. The Foreign Office felt itself under "direct attack."[31]

FDR stepped up pressure against the British in late spring 1944 after learning that Allied Forces Headquarters (AFHQ) had acted to reduce the flow of refugees into Allied Italy. Since invading in September 1943, Allied troops had been struggling up the Italian boot heel against fire from much larger enemy forces. Intended not only to liberate the country but to draw German fire while preparations for the Second Front continued, the operation lacked sufficient men and supplies and encountered much heavier resistance than expected. In addition, the troops were burdened by civilian needs. The Allied Control Commission (ACC) formed a Displaced Persons Subcommission, but it too lacked adequate supplies. By spring 1944 food shortages had become so severe that the American Fifth Army had to feed 200,000 civilians.[32] Refugees meant an additional burden.

The refugee burden evoked resentment but also sympathy. Most of the 15,000 refugees who crossed the Adriatic Sea from partisan-controlled Yugoslavia during late 1943 and early 1944, the peak period, did so on small schooners directed by American Army Intelligence men. And, in early December, when some line officers asked that this activity be restricted, AFHQ refused.[33] But in January 1944 the high command of the Mediterranean theater of operations experienced a turnover. General Dwight D. Eisenhower, the American commander, transferred to the European theater of operations, along with his principal staff, to prepare for the invasion of Normandy. Less than a month after the Mediterranean command passed to Field Marshal Sir Harold Alexander and a predominantly British officer corps, Yugoslav partisans complained about receiving fewer supplies and less cooperation for refugee evacuations.[34]

Four months later AFHQ canceled military assistance to stateless and non-repatriable refugees crossing the Adriatic but not to wounded partisans and their families. The order was issued May 4, the same day that Marshal Tito (Josip Broz), the partisan leader, sent word to AFHQ that he would accept the Combined Chiefs' request to increase assistance to escaping Jews in exchange for reimbursement in supplies or the currency of his choice. The request, initiated by Morgenthau, recognized that the partisans included a significant number of Jews and had extensive contacts in neighboring Hungary. However, the restrictive order rendered Tito's acceptance useless.[35]

The restriction had American diplomatic support. WRB Special Representative Leonard Ackermann and WRB worker John Saxon both had immunity from the United States Trading with the Enemy Act so that they could negotiate with enemy aliens in order to rescue Jews. On learning of the restriction, Ackermann turned to Ambassador Robert Murphy for help. But Murphy wanted the military not only to withhold assistance but to take direct action to prevent non-Yugoslav refugees from reaching Allied Italy.[36]

The president ordered the restriction rescinded as soon as he learned about it at his May 24 cabinet meeting. However, it remained in effect until June 14, and, when it was rescinded, the British commander threatened to reinstate it.[37] The WRB thanked the Foreign Office for its "wholehearted agreement" and blamed the three-week delay on "other branches" of His Majesty's Government.[38] However, the British did not disagree among themselves. A Foreign Office memorandum complained that, in view of the "steam" behind American efforts, refugee evacuations were becoming "difficult to oppose successfully."[39]

British opposition became more overt when Pehle sought to enlarge Ackermann's operational authority by naming him special representative to Italy as well as to the Mediterranean area. The WRB director assumed the change would require only perfunctory approval from the Combined Joint Chiefs of Staff. However, a War Office note to the IGC described Ackermann's new appointment as "a pretty tall order," which "amounts to full powers to take any action he thinks fit . . . to rescue Jews."[40] And Pehle did not obtain approval until he agreed that, out of respect for established organizations and procedures and not because of any desire to discourage refugee traffic, Ackermann could engage only in "investigation" of the refugee situation.[41]

Whereas AFHQ argued that they did not have accommodations for greater numbers of non-repatriable refugees, Ackermann thought the problem one of attitude rather than numbers. He reported that the military believed that the refugees were coming from areas of Yugoslavia in which they were in no real danger, so that accommodating them in Italy meant giving them "a free ride."[42] The situation in both Yugoslavia and Hungary was far more precarious than AFHQ recognized. Nazi deportations continued in Yugoslavia and refugee movement depended on the shifting fortunes of the partisans. In late March, when the Nazis completed their conquest of Hungary, roundups of Jews began first in the region adjacent to Yugoslavia.

Ackermann reported that the military not only underestimated the precariousness of the refugee situation but miscalculated spaces available for refugees. At the time of the restrictive order, AFHQ claimed that 1850 refugees arrived weekly and only 8000 camp spaces for non-Italian refugees remained.[43] But Ackermann subtracted the number of partisans brought to the area for medical care or training and concluded that actual weekly refugee arrivals numbered only one thousand. Furthermore, he noted the presence of 14,000 non-Italian repatriables, most but not all in Italian camps, who qualified for removal to Britain's MERRA facilities. The situation was far from critical. In his view, authorities had time and "breathing space" so that they could encourage new arrivals while making arrangements for an eventual overflow.[44]

Before it issued the restrictive order AFHQ had attempted to evacuate the 14,000 non-Italian repatriables under its control. MERRA initially agreed to accept the entire group in its mideast camps. But it soon reneged on the grounds that a shortage of medical personnel would not permit it to accept more than 4000. The WRB resolved this problem by locating refugee physicians in the United States willing to work in MERRA camps. MERRA ignored the offer. The WRB did not know that MERRA's increasingly uncooperative behavior was due to Foreign Office pressure.

The Foreign Office did not learn until November 1944 that it had been "misled" into interfering unnecessarily. At that time it discovered that the War Office had tampered with reports from Allied Italy in order to stiffen Foreign Office resistance to WRB pressures. The refugee movement across the Adriatic included far fewer Jews than actually reported. Most refugees from Yugoslavia "were in fact families of Marshal Tito's Partisans removed to safety so that the morale of their menfolk might be kept up," and "not Jewish fugitives maintained to placate our political pressure groups contrary to military interests."[45]

Roosevelt's Oswego announcement brought promises of additional camps. FDR had insisted that he would not approve even one shelter unless he could assure Congress that other facilities would be established in the Mediterranean area so that Oswego would not become a precedent for a much larger American program.[46] The MERRA camps, now under UNRRA's administration, quickly agreed to accept an additional 15,000 repatriable refugees. The French authorities in North Africa bowed to American pressure and opened camp Jeanne d'Arc in Philippeville, Algeria. And AFHQ agreed to accept responsibility for an additional 18,000 non-Italian refugees.[47] However, although the fate of Jews in Hungary was still unclear, the concessions had more political than actual value.

When it became clear to the British that Roosevelt would soon act, they too made a gesture, approving Heathcote-Smith's request for Palestine certificates for 300 non-repatriable, that is, Jewish, families in Allied Italy. Optimistically expecting Allied troops to encounter an "inevitable influx" of refugees as they advanced northward toward and beyond Rome, Heathcote-Smith made a second request for certificates for an additional 800 families, which the British refused.[48] Within the Foreign Office he continued to be seen as "a most obstinate man," who needed to be taught "forcefully and tactfully" that Palestine quotas had to "last as long as possible."[49]

Following FDR's Oswego announcement, the WRB wrested from the British an agreement to accept joint responsibility for any "special category Jews" freed in accordance with an offer made by Hungarian Prime Minister Miklós Horthy. Probably no more than 20,000 qualified for the "special category," but the International Red Cross estimated the figure at 40,000 and the British feared being overwhelmed with as many as 800,000 to one million. They agreed to accept joint responsibility only after Morgenthau and DuBois traveled to London with written assurances that their country would accept its "fair share" and privately promised Anthony Eden that the United States would not seek a similar arrangement for other groups of Jews.[50]

With an Allied victory only a question of time, the Allies received several offers to ransom or release Hungarian Jews. At the same time that the Nazis deliberately encouraged the hope that large numbers of Jews might still be rescued, they systematically proceeded to annhiliate this last major community. The first deportations occurred on April 28. On June 9, when FDR announced the Emergency Refugee Shelter, 290,000 had been deported. When deportations stopped in early June, another 520,000 were gone.[51]

Oswego remained the only temporary haven for Jews. The MERRA camps accepted an additional 15,000 repatriables, mostly Yugoslavs, who probably included a few Jews, but it was too late to make a difference for would-be refugee arrivals into Allied Italy. The French camp in Philippeville, like the one at Fedhela, established prisoner-like restrictions and accepted Jews only from Spain. Said to be capable of holding 10,000 but never occupied by more than 2500, it served primarily as an excuse for closing Fedhela. In October 1944 the American Jewish Committee announced that it expected havens similar to Oswego to be opened in Ecuador, Venezuela, Paraguay, and Mexico.[52] Mexico provided sanctuary for several thousand (non-Jewish) Polish refugees. But Oswego did not become a model for additional havens in the United States or elsewhere.

FOUR

Disparate Expectations

FORT ONTARIO COMPRISED eighty lush acres overlooking the Great Lake for which it was named. Stately shade trees protected rows of white barracks that provided a backdrop for red brick homes surrounded by a broad green parade ground. The scene was one of idyllic beauty.[1]

The fort, once a British fur trading post and the oldest garrison in the United States, lay within the city limits of Oswego, a Great Lakes seaport of 22,000 inhabitants. Settled by successive waves of German, Irish, French Canadian, Polish, and Italian immigrants, Oswego had such a varied religious and ethnic mix that no one group could gain dominance. Old World languages and national customs continued to prevail in four of its seven Catholic and one of its thirteen Protestant churches. Jewish settlement had been constant since the 1840s and the town's twenty-six Jewish families, predominantly merchants and professionals, included leaders of the Chamber of Commerce and the Elks Club. They prided themselves on being "part and parcel of the mechanics and workings of the town."[2]

Oswego is located at the point where Lake Ontario spills into a river that carries its waters to the Hudson. After completion of the Erie Canal in 1825 the town hoped to become the principal transfer point between steamships on the Great Lakes and connecting river barges and railroads. But that did not materialize and Oswego continued to depend economically on the small garrison stationed at the fort. The town became a milling center during the mid-nineteenth century and subsequently moved into production of matches, boilers, paper bags, boxes, and light machinery. Its shopkeepers continued, however, to rely heavily on the troops at the fort. Military men made good customers and frequently married Oswego daughters. Such couples frequently returned to Oswego to live out their retirement years amidst conservative, middle-class tranquility.

World War II brought unsettling changes throughout the United States, but Oswego faced special challenges. The first occurred in 1939 when the fort became a Negro post. Ruth Gruber, an Interior Department representative, later reported that many townsfolk were "convinced that President Roosevelt was mad at them for being Republicans."[3] But black troops were also profitable, and no unpleasant incidents occurred. The following year, Roosevelt carried Oswego by more than eleven hundred votes. When the black troops were transferred two years later, the community felt it had received a terrible blow. This time the Army turned the fort into an educational camp for illiterates, most of whom were southern. Again, "consternation set in."[4] But again business remained good, no incidents occurred, and Oswego accepted the change. The ultimate blow occurred on March 15, 1944. The government closed the fort. A Chamber of Commerce delegation immediately traveled to Washington to plead that it reopen.

The president granted Oswegans their wish, but turning the fort into a refugee camp was "the farthest thing" from their minds.[5] Gruber later described local citizens who felt they had been "afflicted."[6] Economic disaster appeared imminent. The town had learned that troops, of any color or background, meant revenue. But refugees would not have funds. In addition, although Oswego's Jewish families felt well integrated, there were townsfolk who used "Jew" and "refugee" interchangeably and said "damn refugee" as "casually and contemptuously" as southerners said "damn Yankee." [7] Speculation soared as Oswego uneasily awaited this new development.

FDR's Oswego announcement also created consternation in the Washington agency that was to have direct responsibility for the project. Created almost as an afterthought in March 1942 to manage the 110,000 Japanese and Japanese-Americans evacuated to ten camps in the wake of Pearl Harbor, the War Relocation Authority existed as an anomaly, far removed from the citadels of power. Milton Eisenhower, who had moved from the Department of Agriculture with several key aides, resigned as WRA director after three months to protest the administration's insistence that Japanese-Americans remain interned.

Dillon S. Myer, Eisenhower's principal aide and successor, also believed internment "dreadfully wrong."[8] He saw the struggle for greater freedom as a "battle on behalf of racial tolerance in the United States" and refused an opportunity to become director of the Bureau of the Budget in order to continue the fight.[9] Viewing camp life as "an unnatural existence which should be avoided if any alternative was possible" and having no knowledge of refugees, the WRA did not welcome its Oswego assignment.[10]

At least in the Japanese Relocation Centers, the WRA both formulated and implemented policy; at Oswego it would enact policies determined by the War Refugee Board. The WRB brought the camp into being, selected its occupants, and, until June 6, 1945, retained responsibility for overall policy. It based all policy decisions on the project's possible influence on larger refugee questions. The War Relocation Authority had no interest in larger refugee questions and operated instead from the perspective of an agency having to respond to the daily problems of camp life.

Initial planning efforts quickly exposed sharp differences between the two agencies. Experience in the Japanese Relocation Centers had taught the WRA that camps established before policies were clearly formulated encountered the most rebellion, while those opened after policies were stable operated more smoothly. But the WRB wished camp policies to evolve gradually so that public opinion might continually be tested and public support encouraged. In its actual camp administration the WRA remained at least as fearful of public reaction as was the WRB. Public protests had forced repeated revisions in plans for the Japanese relocation centers. Public and political pressure had in fact "determined the form of that entire program."[11]

Comprehensive planning preceded the shelter's opening only in the matter of security. Insisting that immigration laws would not be circumvented, Roosevelt wanted it understood that the refugees would be *in* but not *of* the United States. They would be maintained temporarily but would have no visa status. And he assured Congress that the Army would assume full responsibility, meaning that the Army would not permit any refugee escapes. Initial plans called for the Army to install spotlights at 100-foot intervals along an existing 6-foot chain-link fence topped by barbed wire. And it expected to assign 150 men to guard the camp perimeter.

Neither the spotlights nor the armed guard were put into place. The WRA persuaded Pehle that a small "token" civilian force within the fort would be sufficient.[12] The WRB director concluded that, in the event of any unauthorized leaves, he could justify the change by insisting that he had relied on Army Intelligence screening conducted in Italy. The War Department had more interest in removing refugees as quickly as possible from Italy than in directing security at Oswego.[13]

Pehle wished both to satisfy the War Department and to act before opposition surfaced, and he thus insisted upon haste. WRB

Special Representative Leonard Ackermann was to conduct the selection and move everyone to the port at Naples within a two-week period, while "the tears are flowing in Washington and there is much popular feeling throughout the country on the subject of 'free ports.'"[14] "Elaborate" health checks and "unnecessary" security screenings were to be avoided.[15] Obvious security problems and "loathsome" diseases had to be excluded, but other conditions could be addressed in Oswego.

The WRB established specific criteria, but these too were to be overlooked if their observance meant delay. The president wanted refugees for whom no other havens were available, which meant Jews, and he also wanted a "good mix," which meant a "reasonable proportion" of other groups.[16] He had promised Congress that the group would include mostly women and children, so able-bodied men of military age were to be excluded. Ackermann was asked to select two or three rabbis, no more than half a dozen doctors, and a sufficient number of skilled workers to maintain the camp. Furthermore, the selection should not split families.

Wartime communications are often unreliable, and Pehle's instructions did not reach Ackermann until the selection had nearly concluded. The WRB special representative proceeded on the basis of a ten-minute chat with Ira Hirschmann at the Algiers airport. The group Ackermann selected had keener interests in immigration than Pehle foresaw but otherwise closely resembled the community he had in mind.

One-fourth of the group came from Rome and three-fourths from camps and towns throughout the rest of Allied Italy. Ackermann assigned the Rome selection to Heathcote-Smith. Aided by Captain Lew Korn, a former WRA program officer now the American representative on the Displaced Persons Subcommission, he managed the rest. Besieged by more than three thousand applicants, Ackermann and Korn relied heavily on assistance from Allied officers and from Delasem, a local Jewish organization. When a viral infection forced Ackermann to seek hospitalization for several days, most of the traveling fell to Korn, who worked sixteen-hour days. Having to make choices proved heartrending, but arranging the logistics presented an equal challenge.

An abandoned mental asylum in Aversa served as the central collection point. The *Henry Gibbins,* a troop transport ship scheduled to join a convoy, waited in the Naples Harbor and could not be delayed. With the Eighth Army on the move, Ackermann had "to beg, cajole, plead, and threaten" to obtain food and trucks.[17] The refugees, who remained unaware of the difficulties, recalled their first impressions in a skit performed at the fort fourteen months later:

It took us three days from Ferramonti!
It was a dreadful journey!
We're sitting now in a mad-house where madmen fooled each other!
That is the first step of our rise to happiness—oh brother!
The sun shines without pity. I'm hungry as a hound!
They do not care, they're busy. They disinfect the crowd![18]

Having suffered years of fear and trauma, the refugees had a great psychological need for precise information, and that is exactly what the WRB could not provide. The first and greatest source of difficulty arose from a statement that each family head signed before being accepted. It read:

I declare that I have fully understood the following conditions of the offer of the United States Government and that I have accepted them:

A.1. I shall be brought to a reception center in Fort Ontario in the State of New York, where I shall remain as a guest of the United States until the end of the war. Then I must return to my homeland.

A.2. There I shall live under the restrictions imposed by the American security officials.

A.3. No promise of any kind was given to me, either in regard to a possibility of working or permission to work outside the reception center, or in regard to the possibility of remaining in the United States after the war.

B.1. I declare further, since I cannot take along any valuta under existing laws, that I shall accept in exchange for my valuta the same amount in dollars, which the authorities of the United States will eventually pay me after my arrival in America.[19]

The WRB considered the agreement, offered in French, Italian, and German as well as English, to be clear and indisputable, but that was not the case. The English phrase "I shall remain" became *Je pourrai rester, Posso rimanere,* and *Ich bleiben kann.* The translations conveyed the impression that one could remain in the fort if he wished, not that he had to do so. Other differences in meaning pertained to security restrictions, limitations on work, and return. But, seeing that they were "guests" of the United States, most of the refugees preferred to view the agreement as a precautionary rather than a contractural measure. Certainly, few expected to be confined against their wishes.[20]

False suppositions were most prevalent among the Rome group. Eager to encourage candidates, Heathcote-Smith assumed the best and painted glorious pictures of the life that awaited refugees aboard ship and in America. In sharp contrast, Ackermann and Korn insisted that they had no answers to refugees' specific questions. They promised "only safety, security, and shelter for the duration," and reported that applicants appeared "willing to take their chances."[21] However, when the entire group assembled, people eager to flee years of terror and trauma, people needing to believe in dreams, ignored Ackermann's and Korn's caution and clutched at Heathcote-Smith's promises.

Expectations quickly clashed with reality. The *Henry Gibbins* turned out to be far different from the ocean liners that several had enjoyed in earlier years and others now fantasized about. The president's "guests" who looked forward to "fun" at last while leaving the "cruel, guilty world"[22] of the Nazi inferno found endless rows of triple-tiered canvas hammocks rather than private cabins with sheeted beds. Refugees had to eat their meals quickly while standing at tall tables rather than dining leisurely on white linen. And those who had scrounged fabric to sew bathing suits had no pool in which to swim. Thirty-one-year-old Abraham Ruchvarger (Avram Ruchwarger), a Yugoslav physician, and his bride of three months, blond nineteen-year-old nurse Zdenka Baum Ruchvarger (Ruchwarger), enjoyed a private cabin and took their meals with the ship's officers because they volunteered to join the medical team aboard ship.[23] All other refugees shared accommodations usually occupied by troops.

After rushing to board ship and waiting in the Naples Harbor for five sweltering days while the convoy formed, the group spent seventeen days crossing the Atlantic, days marked by fear as well as illness. Soon after entering the Atlantic the convoy came under enemy fire. Standard procedure called for the ship to release billowing clouds of thick black smoke to camouflage itself, but someone neglected to open the exterior vents. The smoke filled the lower decks, compounding the terror induced by the attack. Furthermore, after years of inadequate nutrition and even acute hunger, sea travel and a normal diet proved to be an unfortunate combination. Many remained ill the entire voyage and most suffered at least part of the time.

Some plunged into despair and even asked to be returned to Italy while others joined Interior Department representative Ruth Gruber's English classes, presented musical entertainments, and focused on the promise of better times ahead. Optimists noted that it had been "nonsense" to expect Roosevelt to transport them in a luxury ship during war. What was important was that America awaited them with "Freedom, brotherhood, and justice."[24]

Ruth Gruber, a thirty-two-year-old, multilingual Ph.D., social worker, and journalist, quickly established rapport with dozens of refugees. A special assistant to Interior Secretary Harold L. Ickes, she joined the refugees while the ship remained at anchor in the Naples

Harbor, remained with them during their first few weeks at the fort, and frequently returned to the camp thereafter. Her personal warmth and fluency in Yiddish and German caused many to turn to her for counsel, cementing relationships that continue to the present. Aboard ship and throughout internment, she helped diffuse dissension.

Nevertheless, an undercurrent of unrest swelled and persisted throughout the voyage. WRA workers who attempted to organize volunteer work parties encountered demands for pay and better treatment. In addition to requests for removal from the ship, hastily arranged protest meetings produced demonstrations of passive resistance and even suggestions that the group refuse to disembark in America. WRA representative Ralph Stauber reported that such threats were just talk, but they indicated the "mental climate" aboard ship.[25] Because policy remained uncertain, Stauber, Korn, and Gruber had instructions not to discuss the nature of the group's internment. The situation made internment "a burning question," exacerbated all irritations, and led Stauber to report an "imperative" need for immediate, precise policies.[26]

Unlike most adults, adolescents loved the voyage. Suffering less illness, they formed a volunteer work "gang," developed a camaraderie with crew members, and made a game of the experience. The crew had not been allowed leave in Italy and traded clothing for Italian coins and other souvenirs. Sixteen-year-old David Hendel accepted clothing from sailors whom he thought preferred to give soiled garments away rather than take them home. That seemed consistent with other evidence of American wastefulness that he also did not understand, such as the nightly dumping of great quantities of food not consumed each day by ill passengers. Whatever the reason for the sailors' generosity, Hendel and a few friends arrived in the United States with newly acquired shoes and complete outfits of clothing, eager for the adventure that lay ahead.[27]

A hurricane was reported to the south, but rain stopped in midafternoon as the Statue of Liberty emerged under an overcast sky and refugees gathered on deck to chant the *Shehehiyanu*, the ancient Hebrew prayer of thanksgiving. It was Thursday, August 3, 1944, and the group remained aboard ship one last night while returning wounded servicemen were removed to various hospitals.

When the refugees disembarked the Army subjected them, without explanation, to the same routine performed on all returning servicemen. The refugees neither expected nor understood the procedures. Twenty-six-year-old Fredi Baum considered a leather belt he had saved throughout his refugee experience to be a "prized possession" and saw it shrink when he was sprayed for delousing. Having to resort to string to hold his pants up just as he arrived in America seemed "to add insult to injury."[28] Hendel recalls that "after we got our clothes back we looked like real refugees."[29] Jenny Baruch, now Mrs. Fred Baum, still hears the screams that she heard when she was eighteen and delousing evoked dreadful fear.

Native-born Americans did not know of and did not seek to alleviate the terror that accompanied Hitler's refugees, and the latter, while understanding intellectually that they had indeed reached a different world, could not immediately adjust emotionally to new realities. The presence of dozens of armed guards added to their unease. Two hundred MPs who lined a roped-off corridor from the pier to three nearby trains supervised the processing and joined the refugees aboard the trains. Only military personnel, WRA representatives, and authorized members of the press were permitted in the area.

Military stiffness crumbled when one MP suddenly broke rank and screamed with excitement. Army Private Herbert Altman, who had immigrated with his wife six years earlier, unexpectedly saw his in-laws, a Polish couple in their sixties, on the gangplank. The older man, now "bent and hollow-cheeked," at first did not recognize the husband of one of his three daughters, all of whom now lived in the United States.[30] While Altman swept Eisig and Golde Diamant into his arms, other Americans who had gathered at the pier hoping to find relatives had to remain behind temporary barriers. Only the young MP's spontaneous outburst temporarily disturbed the tight control in evidence everywhere.

Ruth Gruber had selected fifteen people for brief interviews with photographers, translators, and journalists. They included:

Thirty-seven-year-old Seratina Poljakan: She lived with her husband and small son in Zagreb, before the *Ustaci,* a terrorist organization sympathetic to the Nazis, invaded her home and killed her husband before her eyes. She fled with her son to the home of her parents and brother, only to see them killed by the *Ustaci.* When the Nazis invaded Yugoslavia, she was remarried. The family fled to a small island in the Adriatic, where partisans mistakenly killed her second husband. Seratina and the boy hid in the mountains, often without food, until the partisans helped them cross to Italy.

Fifty-year-old Matilda Nitsch: A Roman Catholic Czech whose husband was deported by the Germans, she "drifted" into Yugoslavia and opened a boarding house that eventually became a way station for the underground. She estimated that she had helped at least one hundred Jews escape the Nazis before she was imprisoned by the Italians.

An Austrian family, Leon and Olga Maurer, eighteen-year-old Walter, and baby Harry: Dubbed "International Harry," the baby was born in an

American ambulance on the way to the *Henry Gibbins* in the port of Naples.[31]

Arrival in the United States often brought bittersweet tears. One young couple brought with them a six-month-old child for burial. The baby, born in a concentration camp, weakened by malnutrition, and ill with pneumonia, died only one day before the parents walked down the gangplank at Hoboken.

The Atlantic crossing, debarkation procedures, and the presence of armed guards during the two-day train ride to Oswego created uneasy feelings, and arrival itself produced waves of conflicting emotions. However, nothing made as much of an impact on the entire group as did the six-foot chain-link and barbed-wire fence that awaited them at the fort. It contradicted everything that America represented. All felt shock and anger but none more so than the nearly 60 percent who had eluded internment entirely in Italy or had lived there under "free internment" restrictions, having only to report daily to local police. They now faced imprisonment that had not even been imposed upon them "by an enemy."[32]

Calling the refugees "guests" did not make them feel less like prisoners. As they expressed their feelings months later:

> I feel myself a monkey in a zoological garden!
> Are we to be on display? There's missing [*sic*] but the warden!
> What are we—a sensation for tedious people's pleasure?
> I can see only prison, not Roosevelt's guests in leisure!
>
> What world are we to live in? What have we then committed?
> Are we the foe—the driven? A murderer—outwitted?
> We were the cast out people in Hitler's Nazireichen:
> Are we the outcasts in highest freedom's nation?[33]

The fence kept them from loved ones and exposed them to strangers. Relatives who traveled to Oswego could only communicate through the chain links, in full view of curious townsfolk. Throngs of well-wishers and curious Oswegans gathered during the first two weeks. Several passed sweets and gifts to the newcomers. Three women tried to give silver coins to Olga Maurer. Embarrassed, the young mother refused until the women persuaded her that they meant only to give good luck pieces to her baby. All three subsequently became her friends.[34] Exuberant Geraldine Rossiter impulsively organized a human pyramid and passed her bicycle over the fence to refugee youngsters. The irrepressible teenager returned after dark and slipped into the camp repeatedly without being detected.[35]

Unlike the government, which kept them quarantined while it

tested public reactions and considered various policies, the 982 refugees had definite ideas about what they wanted. Most important, they had surprisingly close connections to the United States. Three hundred of the 496 "units" (families or unaccompanied individuals) had already registered for immigration. At least 14 units had visas that the war had prevented them from using, and 4 had advisory approval for visas. One-third of those registered for immigration already had affidavits of support from American citizens. Fifty-one individuals qualified for nonquota or preference visas because they had American spouses or adult children, and 34 families had immediate relatives serving in the American Armed Forces. More than one-third had immediate family living in America. Most hoped to remain in this country.[36]

Several applied for Oswego while waiting to obtain a quota number that would enable them to join spouses and children who had already entered the United States. They viewed Oswego as a means of expediting family reunions. This group, for whom internment and continued separation seemed especially harsh, included:

Dr. Hugo Graner: A forty-nine-year-old physician born in Hungary, he had a wife and two children who had immigrated in 1938 on the Austrian quota. Arrested and sent to a Nazi camp in northern Italy, from which he escaped, he obtained work as an ambulance doctor for the British in the Allied Transit camp at Bari, Italy. In the meantime, his wife had become a seamstress and an American citizen in New Jersey. She learned of his whereabouts from a newspaper list published three days after he arrived in Hoboken.[37]

Regina Loewit: She and her husband both received visas in August 1938 but the Nazis arrested him before they left Vienna. Walter spent a year in Dachau and Buchenwald. Upon his release, the couple fled to Italy with Lea Wadler, Regina's sixty-five-year-old mother. When Italy entered the war, Walter fled to France but Regina remained behind to care for her mother. He was interned in France, they were interned in Italy, and contact was broken. One month before they sailed for Oswego, he immigrated and found work in a New York armaments factory. His employer and the Society for Ethical Culture pressed unsuccessfully for Regina's release. He arranged to visit her biweekly but eleven months passed before they were allowed to remain together overnight, and their separation lasted an additional seven months.[38]

Berthold Gunsberger: A forty-three-year-old Austrian dairyman born in Czechoslovakia, he remained behind while his wife and son immigrated on the Italian quota. He experienced several years of internment. Brief hospitalizations did not reverse the serious mental and physical deterioration that ensued during his additional internment in Oswego.[39]

TABLE 1
U.S. Relatives of Oswego Refugees

Wives	7	Mother-in-law	1
Husband	1	Grandmother (of an orphan)	1
Sons	39	Uncles (of an orphan)	2
Daughters	26	Siblings	179
Stepsons	3	Brothers-in-law	68
Sons-in-law	18	Sisters-in-law	46
Daughters-in-law	9	Stepbrother	1
Mothers	6	Stepsisters	5
Fathers	4	Uncles, Aunts, Cousins, Nephews, Nieces	307

Total 713

Nonrelated Sponsors 192

Applicants for Oswego shared one or more of five specific motives. They wished to rejoin family members already in the United States (see table 1), they needed to restore their health and wanted American medical care, they had children whose education had been interrupted and wished to enroll them in American schools, or they had specific professional and vocational goals. Some thought that by coming to the United States they might more easily rejoin family members in another country far from either Europe or America. The latter included:

Joseph Schlamm: A seventy-five-year-old widower who had been in the importing business, he fled Vienna in 1940 to join a daughter in Benares, India. Italy entered the war and interned him before he could sail from Trieste. Fluent in English but without any relatives or associates in the United States, he remained alone and ill at the shelter and died there in April 1945.[40]

Chaim Feffer: A thirty-five-year-old whose sweetheart had emigrated to Canada several years earlier with her family, he spent several years in various camps throughout Hungary, Yugoslavia, and Italy following his own flight from Poland. Unable to mail letters from warring Italy to Canada, he addressed an envelope with only her name and the designation, "Montreal, Portugal." Alert mail sorters in that neutral country forwarded the missive to Canada. By the time she received it, he had arrived in Oswego. They married in the shelter and she returned to Montreal to wait for him. They eventually moved to New York, where he obtained work as a watchmaker.[41]

Mordecai and Dora Zylberstajn: A Polish couple in their sixties, they had two sons, both physicians, working for the British. One worked in civil defense and the other was a major in the British Army. Britain granted the couple visas in 1940 but war prevented their use. After their arrival in Oswego, one of their sons obtained British applications for priority passage and the WRA made shipboard arrangements for them, but Britain, without explanation, refused to supply the necessary final papers. Unable to join their only remaining family, the couple eventually settled in Carmel, California, a "major tragedy," according to one WRA official.[42]

Florentine Simon: An unmarried fifty-year-old woman from Germany, she had only two brothers, both of whom lived in Palestine. One was a physician in Jerusalem and the other, an attorney in Tel-Aviv. Ten days after she sailed for Oswego, a notice arrived in Italy approving her application for a Palestine certificate. While in Oswego she continued to seek emigration to Palestine. Unsuccessful, she moved to Minneapolis when the shelter closed.[43]

The group also included two dozen survivors of an ill-fated ship that had tried to run the British blockade against illegal immigration into Palestine. In 1940 *Betar*, the Revisionist Zionist youth organization, gathered more than four hundred Czech, Slovak, German, and Austrian Jews at a Czechoslovakian port on the Danube and put them aboard the *Pentcho*, a paddle steamer built for fifty. While docked at a Yugoslavian river town they were joined by one hundred elderly Jews whom the Nazis had released and threatened to rearrest. A vermin-infested voyage that should have taken eight days lasted a seemingly interminable five months and ended with the ship being wrecked on a reef in the Aegean Sea. Picked up by an Italian warship, the youthful settlers and elderly evacuees were interned first on Rhodes and then in Italy.[44]

Whether the Oswego refugees hoped to remain in the United States or settle elsewhere, whether this country represented a long-term or short-term goal, all needed to rest and recuperate far from Europe's horrors. Many had been refugees for as long as seven or eight years and had seen family members and friends wantonly slaughtered and slowly wasted. Nearly one hundred had been imprisoned in Dachau or Buchenwald. Dislocation and trauma had taken their toll. Italian camps did not include torture and willful cruelty, but Italy suffered severe food shortages, and few refugees, interned or free, escaped the deprivations of hunger and disease. *Pentcho* survivor Hanus Goldberger, forty-eight, lost eighty pounds and turned gray during his ordeal. Like many others, he appeared at least ten years older than he was. All who came to Oswego needed first to regain their health.

The government conducted two initial health checks, which provided very different pictures. The first, a cursory screening in Italy, suggested that the group consisted primarily of older people in "fair to good" condition, who were worn "by difficult traveling and living conditions and the heat."[45] No serious illnesses were reported among the dozen stretcher cases. A more thorough examination at the fort revealed that half a dozen had incurable or serious illnesses, such as inoperable cancer, active tuberculosis, unexplained paralysis, and Malta Fever, and that eleven stretcher cases required immediate hospitalization. Several suffered from malaria, asthma, and hypertension; arthritic and rheumatoid problems were common; and nearly everyone needed dental care, much of it quite extensive. Hundreds required eyeglasses, hearing aids, and orthopedic devices. And two young men needed prostheses. Nearly all were "physically and emotionally broken" and undernourished.[46] Many wanted rehabilitative surgery. Those who came specifically for American health care included:

> Arthur Lehman: A sixty-two-year-old former architect and essayist in Germany, he had been widowed in 1942 and was living in Italy with his radio engineer son. Only "for health reasons" would he have chosen to leave his son, even temporarily, and travel to America.

> Abraham Drahline: A forty-two-year-old stateless Russian whose wife and son had been deported to Poland from France while he was away on business, he planned to return to Paris to resume his business and, if possible, to find his family. But first he wanted to regain his health.[47]

Families with children thought educational opportunities as important as health care. Most students had already lost several years. Remaining in Italy meant prolonging the interruption. Those specifically seeking American schooling included:

> Dr. and Mrs. Rafailo Margulis and their sons, Rajko and Aca: "One of the most dapper of the fugitives," fifty-nine-year-old Dr. Margulis, erstwhile chief medical officer of a large Belgrade hospital and lieutenant colonel in the Yogoslav Army's medical corps, disembarked at Hoboken in suit and tie. The family was living freely in Rome, where the two boys could have completed their medical studies at Rome University, when glorified stories about the Oswego project persuaded them to opt instead for America. After settling at the fort, the boys gained admission to Harvard Medical School and received promises of scholarship assistance from Jewish organizations. Despite personal lobbying by Eleanor Roosevelt and Mrs. Henry Morgenthau, Jr., they could not obtain permission to leave the shelter to resume their studies. When Dr. Margulis developed terminal cancer and wished to return to Yugoslavia, the family joined sixty-two other Yugoslavs in accepting repatriation during the spring and summer of 1945. The boys subsequently returned to the United States on student visas, completed their medical studies at Harvard, and married their Oswego sweethearts.[48]

Mr. and Mrs. Erich W. and their two sons, ages twelve and eleven: Having one child with special needs but concerned about the welfare of all the children, the former Czech coal company manager compiled a card index giving the educational status of every elementary and secondary student aboard ship in order to facilitate American school enrollments for the fall term. While in the shelter, the older boy, retarded and epileptic, developed more frequent and intense seizures. Institutionalized in January 1945, he was later transferred to a facility in California to be near his family's new home.[49]

A few of the refugees expected Oswego to serve as a means to specific job and economic opportunities in America:

Ernst Wolff: The sixty-three-year-old Austrian screenwriter, who had worked for MGM in Paris for several years, expected to disembark and leave immediately to join friends and colleagues awaiting him in Hollywood. He had joined the group because, while doing translation work for the Allies in Rome, an American officer had expressed a desire to be helpful and Ernst had replied, "Get me to Hollywood." He eventually made it, but not until he spent eighteen months as an internee in upstate New York.[50]

Ernest Braun: A thirty-one-year-old Austrian of independent means and a student of ancient languages and medicine, he had discovered a formula for a surgical compound that avoided skin irritations often caused by similar products. He hoped the trip to Oswego would enable him to bring his work to the attention of American medical authorities. While he was in Oswego, the product was successfully tested at Syracuse University. In July 1945 he received word in the shelter that the United States Army and Navy wished to begin production.[51]

Leonard Ackermann's irritation with Heathcote-Smith's selection procedures would have been far greater had he known that the Rome group included not only more than a dozen able-bodied men of military age but also eleven White Russians who were not in fact World War II refugees. Because Ackermann miscalculated the number of expected applicants in Rome and reserved one-fourth of the available spaces for them, Heathcote-Smith could accept nearly all who applied and still recruit others in order to obtain the "proper mix." No one was more surprised than those "others" when they found themselves under military escort to internment in an American camp. They included:

Luba Chernitza: A fifty-one-year-old White Russian widowed during the Bolshevik "Reign of Terror," she had fled with her infant son and younger brother to Siberia and to Manchuria, where the child died. In Shanghai, she taught music and earned her brother's passage to the United States. By the time she earned her own passage, she could obtain only a temporary visa and had to content herself with a visit to California, where her brother became a successful ship builder and achieved fame for his ship models, several of which became part of FDR's collection. She settled in Rome. Graduating from an art institute as the oldest member of her class, only two years before war broke out in Europe, she was still trying to establish herself as a sculptress when invited to apply for Oswego.

"Prince Peter" Ouroussoff: The descendant of Russian nobility, he worked as a bank clerk in England and in France. After the Nazis occupied France, he fled to Italy with his Italian-born wife. They viewed Oswego as a door to better American economic opportunities.

Michele and Olga Mikhailoff and their twenty-four-year-old son, Vadim: Olga moved to Italy in 1912 for her health and settled in Capri, where she later met and married Michele. She worked as a set designer and director for theatrical shows, which he produced. Both also acted and painted murals, some of which graced fine homes and hotels in Naples, Rome, and Capri. A British and an American officer visited their home in Capri, from which most of the White Russians in Oswego came, and invited them to join the group.[52]

The camp that awaited the refugees was neither aware of nor concerned with their expectations. The War Refugee Board had assumed, as had the president, that the government should be responsible only for "maintenance," which meant the minimal care necessary for the well-being of the group and the treatment of health problems, such as tuberculosis, which threatened individual or group safety. There were no plans to provide elective and rehabilitative health care and no plans for American schooling. The government offered basic food, clothing, and shelter. Refugee residents were to cook their food, maintain their camp, and create the activities they wished to have, including all classes for children and adults. Most arrangements, however, were considered tentative. On matters other than security, policies would be formulated as specific needs arose. The difficult task of confronting the contradictions between government and refugee expectations lay ahead.

FIVE

Tenuous Beginnings

"You symbolize the tiny vessel of oil rescued by the Hasmonean from the iniquitous power of the Greeks in the time of the second temple which signifies 'Chanuka.' Let's hope to God that this time the miracle will be greater and many jars of oil like you will be spared from the wicked Nazis. Amen."[1] Leading the *Kaddish,* the Jewish mourner's prayer, Rabbi Sidney Bialik, the spiritual leader of Oswego's tiny Jewish community, concluded official welcoming ceremonies. The ancient prayer extolling God brought bitter tears, for nearly every refugee family had suffered tragic losses. But the mood quickly changed as the crowd moved toward long rows of shaded refreshment tables to one side of the sunny parade ground. It was Sunday, August 6, 1944, and the War Relocation Authority had invited government officials, leading Oswego citizens, Jewish leaders, and the press to join in welcoming the shelter's new "residents," the euphemism used to soften the reality of internment.

Refugees who listened carefully heard, in English and in German, the government's general intentions. Speaking on behalf of Interior Secretary Harold L. Ickes, WRA Director Dillon S. Myer declared the fort a "haven" that would be their new home "for the duration of the war" or until they could "be safely returned" to their homelands.[2] The refugees listened quietly as he expressed the hope that here they would dispel tragic memories. But Myer's words made less impression than did the fact that the camp was to be administered by an agency of the Department of the Interior, which for Europeans commonly meant the police. The misunderstanding persisted for months.[3]

54

TABLE 2
Religions of the Oswego Refugees

NATIONALITY	Jewish	Roman Catholic	Greek and Russian Orthodox	Protestant
Yugoslav	326	32	11	
Austrian	210	20	5	2
Polish	140	6		
German	85	6		5
Rumanian	17			
French	15			
Turkish	10			
Russian	9		8	
Czech	34	7		
Danziger	7	1		
Spanish	5			
Libyan	4			
Bulgarian	4			
Belgian	3			
Hungarian	3			
Italian	1	1		
Dutch	1			
Greek			4	
Total	874	73	28	7

Seventeen families were religiously mixed: 9 Jewish and Roman Catholic (4 Yugoslav, 3 Austrian, 1 German, 1 Polish); 3 Jewish and Protestant (2 German, 1 German/ Danziger); 3 Jewish and Greek Orthodox (2 Yugoslav, 1 Austrian); 2 Greek Orthodox and Roman Catholic (2 Russian, 1 Russian/Italian).

Others who spoke included Joseph Hebrew Smart, a devout Mormon who would be shelter director; Joseph T. McCaffrey, Oswego's mayor; Anne Laughlin, WRB representative; Rev. A. S. Lowrie, of the Oswego Council of Churches; and Leon Levy, a Yugoslav attorney selected to represent the refugees. Most heralded a new beginning for a new community. However, "community" would remain an elusive goal. Mere chance had thrown together a population for whom tragic memories provided the strongest commonality.

Government officials expected Judaism to provide cohesiveness, but religious variations divided Jews, and national differences proved enormously influential. Those who identified themselves as Jews numbered 89 percent (see table 2), and several who listed themselves differently had been born Jewish or were married to Jews. However, even among those who were Orthodox, that is, observant of religious commandments, national differences often overshadowed religious similarities. Among the largest national group, the Yugoslavs, those

TABLE 3

Citizenship of the Oswego Refugees

Country of Origin	Number of Individuals	Stateless among Them
Yugoslavia	369	0
Austria	237	221
Poland	146	76
Germany	96	89
Czechoslovakia	41	2
Russia	17	16
Rumania	17	13
France	15	5
Turkey	10	8
Danzig	8	3
Spain	5	0
Greece	4	0
Libya	4	0
Bulgaria	4	0
Belgium	3	0
Hungary	3	3
Italy	2	0
Holland	1	0
	982	436

who were Orthodox tended to identify more closely with other Yugoslavs than with other Orthodox.

The refugee population was approximately one-third Yugoslav, one-fourth Austrian, 15 percent Polish, and 10 percent German. Among the fourteen minority national groups, the Czech was the largest. Nearly half of all the refugees, however, were now stateless, their citizenship having been nullified by the Nazis as part of their effort to maintain racial purity by making Jews outcasts (see table 3).

The national groups readily revealed distinctive behaviors. Yugoslavs seemed "more like evacuees" only temporarily displaced rather than refugees. WRA representatives aboard the *Henry Gibbins* described them as the "most articulate, antagonistic, and difficult to deal with."[4] Yugoslav Jews did not face significant anti-Semitism until April 1941, when Axis armies invaded their country. Most Oswego Yugoslavs had lived in the eastern Adriatic Sea provinces of Dalmatia and Montenegro or had fled there because the Germans left those areas to the Italians until September 1943. The Italians, who insisted on confining Jews themselves rather than turning them over to the Nazis, promulgated anti-Semitic policies to placate their Nazi allies but subverted those same policies through sloppy enforcement. Many of the Yugoslavs still possessed a little property and currency. They had suffered great losses but during a relatively brief period, and, with Tito's partisans, many had engaged in acts of defiance.

In sharp contrast, Austrians seemed much meeker, more cooperative, and far less distinctive as a group. The intellectuals among them formed alliances with Yugoslavs or Germans, and the Orthodox did the same with Poles. The Austrian Jewish ordeal had lasted three years longer than the Yugoslav and had been the most vicious. Beginning with the *Anschluss* in March 1938, when Austria bowed to overwhelming pressure and voted to accept Nazi rule, the Nazis used Austria to test tactics meant to induce mass Jewish flight. Subjected to a more brutal and intensive campaign of terror than that conducted previously against Jews in Germany, they had fewer financial resources and less ability to resist. Hermann Goering expected to rid Austria of its 200,000 Jews, of whom 190,000 lived in Vienna, within four months. Most fled much sooner.[5] And many who came to Oswego were still in a state of shock.

Only the Poles, most of whom were Orthodox, identified primarily as Jews rather than as a national group. And, more than any other group, they fit American stereotypes about refugees. The WRA staff found them to be less antagonistic and more appreciative than the Yugoslavs or Germans and more easily identifiable than the Austrians. Unlike the other principal national groups, they were more likely to be blue-collar workers rather than businessmen or professionals. Another unusual feature of the group was that it was not primarily an indigenous one. Only eleven of the sixty-three family heads who listed Poland as their country of origin had come from Poland itself. The others had fled or been expelled from Germany, Austria, Rumania, Holland, France, Switzerland, or northern Italy. They felt no cultural affinity with Poland and never developed a strong national organization in the shelter.

Like the Yugoslavs and in strong contrast to the Poles, the German Jews had a deep sense of heritage. However, even more so than the Austrians, they suffered an acute identity crisis. When the Nazis gained power in 1933 Germany's 500,000 Jews enjoyed a high standard of living and viewed themselves not only as true Germans but as people of achievement and influence in the intellectual center of Europe. Emigration was relatively simple in the early Nazi years, but few chose to leave until *Kristallnacht* and the terrors that followed, by which time they had been made stateless, pauperized pariahs. Now possessing little more than their lives, knowing they could never go back, and feeling completely disoriented, they clung to German culture as a source of stability and status in a world gone mad.

Variations in the length of time and degree to which national groups had been subjected to Nazi barbarities merely exacerbated differences that had long distinguished European Jews. The Balkanization of Oswego stemmed from age-old rivalries, the most bitter of which was that between Germans and Yugoslavs. Like the former, the latter consisted largely of religious liberals of middle- or upper-middle-class status who enjoyed broad social acceptance among non-Jews. Seventy thousand Jews inhabited prewar Yugoslavia, of whom 40 percent prided themselves on having inherited the Sephardic tradition, which stemmed from Jewish history's golden Iberian years, and 60 percent viewed themselves as pacesetters within the highly Germanized Ashkenazic tradition. Neither group had any inclination to accord German Jews the higher status they claimed.

While German Jews struggled to maintain their sense of superiority and belittled Yugoslav Jews for not having endured comparable suffering, the Yugoslavs scorned them for being Germans at heart and for not having taken up arms against the Nazis. Abe Furmanski, a thirty-five-year-old Polish Jew, spoke for many when he complained that German and Austrian Jews interned with him earlier had demonstrated greater regard for German officials than for other Jews, behavior which "[made] our position worse."[6]

Language served as a lightning rod for seething national rivalries. Unbeknown to Joseph Smart, the issue smoldered aboard ship and during welcoming ceremonies at the fort. Twenty-five-year-old Fredi Baum, who spoke five languages, appeared the natural choice to serve as translator. He had performed similar work for the Allied Forces in Italy and had assisted with the selection of refugees in Rome. However, it galled the German Jews to have a Yugoslav interpret for them and to hear German spoken less than perfectly.

The issue flared into the open two weeks after the refugees arrived at the shelter, during the first non-Orthodox Sabbath evening service. When Rabbi Hajim Hazan, a forty-six-year-old Yugoslav who spoke almost no German, delivered the sermon in Serbo-Croatian, German Jews walked out. Thinking the service to be over, Joseph Smart left and walked into an angry confrontation outside. The director quickly apologized for his own premature departure and did so again in a posted memorandum. Genuinely interested in Judaism and respectful of differences, he obtained apologies from both groups and an uneasy compromise whereby German became an alternate language for sermons.

Yugoslavs constituted the largest national group but the German language had the greatest number of adherents, and this circumstance aggravated historic tensions. The refugees listed twenty-one mother tongues. However, 40 percent were fluent in German and all but twenty-five or thirty of the adults understood at least a little of the

TABLE 4
Languages of the Oswego Refugees

Mother tongue	Number speaking	Bilingual or tringual among them	Languages spoken with equal fluency
German	392	26	Italian, Yiddish, Polish, Czech, Hungarian, Dutch, Croatian, Rumanian, Slovak
Yiddish*	85	17	German, Polish, Ukrainian, Ruthenian
Serbo-Croatian	93	3	Ladino, German
Croatian	73	4	Serbian, German, Italian, Hungarian
Serbian	27	1	Ladino
Yugoslav	58		
Ladino*	53	22	Croatian, Serbian, French, Greek, Italian, Turkish, Yiddish, Yugoslav
French	26	2	German, Yiddish
Polish	55	16	Yiddish, German, Croatian, Serbian
Czech	18	2	German
Hungarian	31	1	German
Russian	18	2	Ukrainian
Italian	14	2	Yiddish, Serbo-Croatian
Rumanian	5		
Slovak	4		
Hebrew	1		
Greek	4		
Bulgarian	2	2	German, Ladino
Flemish	1	1	French
Arabic	1	1	Italian
Turkish	1	1	Greek
Unknown	20		
	982		

*Yiddish (Judeo-German) includes elements of Hebrew, Slavic, Old French, and Old Italian. Ladino (Judeo-Spanish) derives from medieval Castilian and includes Hebrew, Greek, Turkish, Portuguese, and other Mediterranean components.

language (see table 4). In sharp contrast, few non-Yugoslavs understood Serbo-Croatian.

The group's linguistic profile reflected both European proclivities and the fact that the ability to acquire additional languages became a crucial survival tool. A total of 713 refugees spoke languages

TABLE 5

Citizenship or Last Citizenship of Family Heads in Oswego

	Female	Male	Total
Yugoslav	43	108	151
Austrian	12	147	159
Polish	17	60	77
German	12	44	56
Czech	6	13	19
Russian	3	10	13
Rumanian	0	3	3
French	1	0	1
Turkish	0	4	4
Danziger	1	4	5
Spanish	0	2	2
Greek	1	0	1
Libyan	0	1	1
Bulgarian	1	1	2
Hungarian	0	2	2
	97	399	496

in addition to their mother tongues, with the number of additional languages distributed as follows: one—157, two—257, three—176, four—86, five—30, six—4, seven—1, nine—2. German had the greatest number of adherents, but English had become the language of greatest study. With the help of newspapers and an English dictionary, her "prized possession," Regina Gal, a thirty-five-year-old Polish widow with two small children, used her nine-month Italian internment to study the language.[7] Many did the same. Ruth Gruber's classes aboard ship drew dozens, and classes offered in the fort attracted hundreds.

Linguistic jealousies nurtured old conflicts but the Yugoslavs faced challenges on the question of their numerical dominance as well. They constituted 38 percent of the total refugee population but only 30 percent of family heads (see table 5). In sharp contrast, the Austrians numbered only 24 percent of the total and the Germans only 9.7 percent, but they included 32 percent and 11 percent, respectively, of family heads. Austrian and German family heads together outnumbered Yugoslav family heads 215 to 151.

The Yugoslav families included considerably more children. More than 24 percent of the Yugoslavs but fewer than 6 percent of the Austrians were seventeen years old or younger. The Yugoslavs made up 38 percent of the total population but 50 percent of the school-age children (those six to eighteen years old). In sharp contrast, total population and school-age population figures for the other three dominant groups were: Austrians, 24 and 9 percent; Germans, 9.7 and 5 percent; and Poles, 14.7 and 16 percent (table 6).

The greater number of children among the Yugoslavs reflected both prewar demographics and wartime experiences. Yugoslav families were younger and more intact. Forty percent of the Austrians, 29 percent of the Poles, and 26 percent of the Germans had suffered involuntary marital separations but only 17 percent of the Yugoslavs had done so. The married Yugoslavs in Oswego without their spouses also included eight men and two women who left non-Jewish mates behind to look after property and several women whose husbands continued to fight with the partisans. In other words, unlike the other refugees, a number of the separated Yugoslavs knew something of their mates' whereabouts, a "definite (psychological) asset."[8]

The entire group also presented an abnormal age and sex profile (table 7). Ages ranged from newborn "International Harry" to eighty-

TABLE 6

Students in the Shelter: Religion and Citizenship by Age

	Ages 6–13	Ages 14–17	Ages 18–24	Total
RELIGION				
Jewish	105	43	34	182
Catholic	6	3	2	11
Greek Orthodox	3	1	2	6
Protestant	1	0	1	2
CITIZENSHIP				
Yugoslav	66	16	23	105
Austrian	10	4	5	19
Polish	12	15	3	30
German	5	4	1	10
Czech	6	1	2	9
Russian	3	2	1	6
Rumanian	0	0	1	1
French	4	1	0	5
Turkish	0	0	1	1
Danziger	0	0	1	1
Spanish	1	0	0	1
Greek	1	0	0	1
Bulgarian	0	4	0	4
Belgian	6	0	0	6
Hungarian	0	0	1	1
Stateless	1	0	0	1
	115	47	39	201

TABLE 7

Oswego Refugees: Distribution by Age and Sex

Age	Female	Male	Total
Under 16 years old	89	98	187
16–20	25	20	45
21–30	35	8	43
31–40	119	49	168
41–50	78	142	220
51–60	70	133	203
Over 60	40	76	116
	456	526	982

year-old Isaac Cohen, but there was a disproportionate number of older people. Nearly one-third were over fifty. Fewer than one-fifth were sixteen and younger and fewer than 5 percent were in their twenties; four-fifths of the latter were women. Those over sixty were nearly three times as numerous as those in their twenties. And most over forty had aged prematurely.

Generational conflicts intensified national group rivalries. Only 6 percent of the Yugoslavs were over sixty years old but 19 percent of the Austrians were. The Poles were also younger than the Austrians and Germans. Most Poles were in their thirties and forties, most Germans in their forties and fifties, and most Austrians in their fifties. And, among those sixteen to forty-one, the group on whom most work depended, there were 60 percent more women than men. A critical shortage of males for manual labor meant not only that the burden fell on older residents but that it fell disproportionately on specific national groups.

Historical differences, as well as war ravages and WRB selection criteria, accounted for the group's unusual age and sex profile. As early as 1936, American Jewish philanthropic leaders worried that Germany's Jewish community was becoming "a gigantic old age home whose inmates would have to be maintained by Jews abroad."[9] Younger people were the first to flee, but even before the Nazis came to power, assimilation and low birth rates had created old Jewish communities in both Germany and Austria. When Nazi terrors began older Jews remained longer and fewer of them found havens.

Religious differences, as well as national and generational ones, created frictions. Few non-Jews lacked ties to Jews, and their presence caused no problems. The significant division appeared between Orthodox and non-Orthodox Jews. The former had tried and failed to obtain representation on the refugee Advisory Council that was organized the first week. However, Smart thought that giving Orthodox

Jews representation on a body that granted others only national representation "violated" democratic principles.[10] Unable to obtain two seats on the council, most Orthodox Jews chose not to vote for any representatives.

The Orthodox Jews were the first to organize themselves and they remained the most cohesive group. Ackermann reported that they included a core group of 35 to 40 people, those who had survived without violating their consciences by breaking dietary laws. The number requesting kosher food rose to 70 aboard ship and to 180 during the first week in the shelter. The mess chief called for 10 more in order to achieve a better balance between the one kosher and four nonkosher kitchens, and the number quickly increased to 225. The kosher kitchen opened only nine days after the shelter did. By then, an Orthodox synagogue and religious school also existed.

The Orthodox Jews immediately affiliated with the American branch of Agudat Israel, headquartered in New York. Insisting on the primacy of religious law and rabbinical authority in all Jewish life and society, Agudat Israel organized in the early twentieth century throughout central and eastern Europe in direct opposition to assimilationist-inspired changes it perceived in Conservative and Reform Judaism and in secular Zionism. It did not establish itself in the United States until 1939 but quickly became an aggressive lobbyist for Jewish refugees at a time when established organizations hesitated to do so. Most American Jews rejected Agudat Israel's militant religiosity and separatism.

The War Refugee Board and the War Relocation Authority expected to accommodate religious desires as the need arose. Agudat Israel immediately made those needs known. Contacting the government the day after FDR announced Oswego and repeatedly thereafter, it offered extensive assistance as soon as the refugees arrived and encouraged Rabbi Mosco Tzechoval and Israel Rothschild, the refugees' leading Orthodox figures, to petition for proper facilities.[11] Agudat Israel equipped the kosher kitchen and supplied meat the first week. The government then assumed responsibility and the religious group took care of special and holiday needs.

Despite "constant" problems,[12] the shelter administration strove to comply with Orthodox requirements. Meat acceptable at the time of purchase sometimes became unacceptable en route because transportation difficulties cause delays and thus violated the religious requirement that meat be washed every three days. Orthodox refugees couldn't understand such delays in a land so far from battle, and staff members found their requirements incomprehensible.

The Chief of Mess Operations concluded that the observant Jews in the shelter were "more Orthodox than [American] Orthodox," which she attributed to their having "swung to the far end of the pendulum" because for "so long [they] had been denied."[13] In actuality, American Jews who call themselves "Orthodox" vary considerably in their interpretations of religious observance.

A "group apart," the Orthodox Jews celebrated regained religious freedom with what one member of the staff described as "ecstasy."[14] On the first Sabbath after the group arrived, thirteen-year-old Joseph Langnas became the first boy to celebrate his Bar Mitzvah in the camp. Five days later, during Rosh Hashanah services conducted by Rabbi Mosco Tzechoval, the Orthodox marked the beginning of the Jewish New Year by consecrating a Holy Ark and four Torah scrolls provided by Agudat Israel. The sanctuary, in a brick building remodeled by the Army, included seating for 230 men and 130 women as well as classrooms for 75 children. A *heder*, in which children studied traditional texts, opened within a few weeks.

Much to its surprise, the government soon learned that all Jews would not use one synagogue. Smart offered to share the Army chapel and, after the cross was covered, initial unease disappeared. Other problems proved more persistent. Whereas all the Orthodox Jews found common bonds in the Yiddish language and Ashkenazic culture, equivalent ties did not unite those who formed the liberal congregation. The latter, predominantly Yugoslav but including nearly every nationality, represented an uneasy association of Yiddish-speaking Ashkenazim and Ladino-speaking Sephardim. Since German evoked disagreement and few non-Yugoslavs understood Serbo-Croatian, Italian served as the vernacular used with the Hebrew of the prayer book.

More akin to America's Conservative than to its Reform Jews, the congregation's nearly four hundred worshipers—the High Holidays drew such crowds but weekly attendance rarely numbered more than three or four dozen—evolved their own patterns of observance. The more traditional among them prevailed in establishing *mechitza* (separate seating for men and women), but most did not choose to observe *kashrut* (dietary laws), a European pattern that contrasted sharply with the American practice of giving more significance to observance of the latter. B'nai B'rith in Syracuse provided a Torah, and other items came both from Syracuse and from the Synagogue Council of America.

All religious activities, non-Jewish as well as Jewish, including supervision of an Agudat Israel teacher provided to instruct children in both congregations, were to be supervised by Rabbi Tzechoval and an Advisory Council subcommittee. Traditional tensions seethed beneath apparent Jewish harmony. The Agudat Israel representative initially sent to the camp reported that "half" a scholar would suffice because the refugees included no one with extensive talmudic learning; he recommended that the teacher selected should work with liberal as well as Orthodox children to avoid the former going to a "trefa [nonkosher] organization" and in the hope that he might bring them into the fold.[15] The teacher proved to be too aggressive in his efforts to proselytize and had to be dismissed. Most children in the liberal congregation preferred to pursue religious studies and prepare for Bar Mitzvah with volunteers among the refugees.

As with religious needs, the government expected to provide basic living facilities and leave their use and maintenance to camp residents. The policy provided accommodations considerably more complete than those of evacuees in the Japanese Relocation Centers, which had to be built by volunteers from among the evacuees before the entire Japanese-American population could be moved from makeshift facilities. Nevertheless, shelter arrangements failed to meet standards the National Refugee Service thought essential.

NRS recommendations addressed psychological needs common to refugee populations. They warned that traumatically dislodged people who tasted freedom and indulged in hopes for the future would "bitterly" resent "any restraint or control."[16] Above all, after years of uncertainty and brutality, Oswego's new residents needed an orderly environment, fully furnished before their arrival, which did not smack of prison. It was important to avoid overcrowding if at all possible and to offer places to which individuals could retreat from the pressures of group living for periods of quiet and privacy. Like the NRS, the WRA understood the importance of having facilities complete and policies clearly formulated before camp residents arrived, but it had no control over such matters. The only NRS recommendation implemented by the War Refugee Board was that families should be kept together.

Housing arrangements created a strained environment. The fort included a number of wooden barracks built in 1939 as temporary structures and the Army converted these into refugee apartments. Each remodeled barracks contained four apartments on each of two floors and communal toilet and shower facilities for men and women. Family size determined who would receive one, two, or three rooms and the buildings to which they would be assigned. Unaccompanied women received one-room apartments but bachelor men occupied dormitories in permanent brick buildings. The apartments included only beds. Dressers, tables, and chairs had yet to be built in camp workshops. Three months later, two dozen families still lacked such furnishings. By that time, however, eighty families had been moved to newly opened barracks to relieve overcrowding. Most important, apartments were separated by fiberboard partitions through which even the softest conversations could be heard.

Housing difficulties exacerbated other tensions throughout the life of the shelter, but food presented the greatest initial adjustment problems. The WRA had planned according to evacuee appetites, but the refugees, suffering widespread malnutrition, required portions equal to those "fed [to] combat troops."[17] Menus also proved unsatisfactory, a situation that acquired enormous importance for many who had long been deprived. Most Japanese evacuees were American-born and shared the preferences of other Americans, but the refugees had different tastes—many looked with disdain upon white bread and dry cereals, thought milk suitable only for children, and would not accept vegetables. Most important, European diets relied far more on fats and sugars. The refugees never understood why foodstuffs had to be rationed and were often in short supply in America, a wealthy nation far from the battlefields.

Most serious, the camp did not address special dietary problems. Shelter residents who needed fat-free, low-sodium, ulcer, or diabetic diets could not fend for themselves as had Japanese evacuees with similar problems. And they lacked the cohesiveness to organize as had those who observed *kashrut*. Only the parents of newborns managed to do so. Others had to rely on the regular kitchens, which did not have staff for special needs. More than ten months passed before a kitchen opened in the hospital building for the more than eighty residents who needed special diets. Problems of quantity and taste resolved themselves far sooner. Within three months, Ruth Gruber found herself "besieged" for advice on weight reduction.[18] And eating only white bread soon became a common practice, an unfortunate sign of Americanization.

For people who had lost everything, clothing, like housing and food, acquired "exaggerated emotional significance."[19] Ten-year-old Charlotte Gal and Albert, her eight-year-old brother, arrived dressed in shirts and shorts fashioned by Regina, their seamstress mother, from a shirt donated by an American sailor. Many appeared "in rags, shirtless, and almost naked." A former Yugoslav attorney wore only English Army shorts. And a significant number entered the shelter barefoot or walked in "shoes" fashioned of sackcloth and rope. Because of "appalling" confusion several remained in this condition for weeks.[20]

Clothing distribution difficulties inflamed national resentments. Initially, the WRA established a storeroom for donated used and overstocked items and divided these among the national groups for distribution to their members. Filip Baum, Fredi's father and a man who worked diligently to achieve cooperation, assisted in the distribution and had to endure angry charges that he "favored" the Yugoslavs. Private organizations, such as the American Association for Yugoslav Jews, complicated the problem by contributing clothing earmarked for its own constituents. Such actions prompted the Jewish Labor Committee to complain that the Yugoslavs and Austrians received considerable help from compatriots, but the Poles, in whom it was most interested, were neglected. However, Elise Neuman (Liesl Newman), a Viennese who was then thirty-four years old, still believes the Poles "got more help and money than anyone else."[21]

Selection problems also plagued the clothing program. Contributed articles tended to be out-of-season and were frequently of poor quality. The assortment almost never included all sizes. By the third month, the shelter stopped accepting donations and began purchasing essential items for distribution as grants. Because it used local welfare practices for guidance, it provided coats but not hats or gloves and, except for workers and schoolchildren, neither shoes nor stockings. Local welfare practices defined such items as supplemental aid provided by private organizations.

Delivery delays and Oswego merchant activity added to the confusion and concern. Local merchants were permitted to bring merchandise into the camp for sale during the first month when the refugees remained quarantined. However, only people who had independent resources had funds to spend, and those who accepted money from friends or relatives reduced their eligibility for WRA allowances. The WRA's perference for doing business with local merchants despite wartime shortages, which made it necessary to wait for depleted Oswego stocks to be replenished, meant that most refugees, dependent upon WRA cash grants, faced long delays. Furthermore, the refugees were atypical welfare recipients who found application and interviewing procedures particularly demeaning. Most of them failed to anticipate cold weather needs. The staff also did not foresee the problem of winter clothing and the second-quarter budget did not allow for additional clothing. The foresighted and most aggressive fared best, a painful lesson.

Housing, food, and clothing difficulties caused consternation, but prisonlike procedures produced shock. Shelter "residents" could neither leave the fort nor receive private visitors. Visitors were to be welcome after September 1, but when the refugees would be able to leave the fort remained unclear. Furthermore, residents had limited access to radios and newspapers, a cruel oversight for people so hungry for news of the war.

Customs confiscations exacerbated feelings of repression. In accordance with strict wartime regulations, all "enemy aliens," that is, former Austrians and Germans, had to relinquish their German-language notebooks, manuscripts, and personal letters, as well as photographs, stamp collections, books, cameras, and gold pieces. Many had to give up treasured mementoes, but journalists, professional photographers, and film directors lost material needed for projects documenting Nazism. Customs retained most items until mid-October and held some for several additional months. Smart repeatedly objected to a lack of information on held items and complained of the "widespread discontent" that resulted, but to no avail.[22]

Mail censorship was equally irrational. Newspapers across the country carried rosters of the new arrivals, and mail poured into the camp—more than 28,000 letters and 10,500 parcels during the first three months. An August 19 letter in the Washington, D.C., *Times Herald* asked, "Aren't there enough Fifth Columnists in the United States already? Who is going to determine if these refugees are all the goody-good kind?" Soon after, the War Department, objecting to cursory screening procedures, insisted that the Office of the Postmaster invoke complete postal censorship.

Maneuvering to soften the blow, Smart stalled for eight days to give shelter residents time to distribute an address to which mail could be sent directly without first arriving at the camp. The delay made censorship "utterly meaningless," for on September 1, the day before it became effective, the shelter began issuing six-hour passes to Oswego. Smart argued that the new modified-leave policy made censorship "unwarranted . . . unworkable . . . and unenforceable," and that it would remain "a source of irritation and resentment [that would] grow to ugly proportions."[23] The War Department, which wanted the order enforced for at least three months, agreed to lift the restriction on incoming mail after two weeks but did not do so on outgoing mail for another six weeks.

Press accounts published during the month-long "quarantine" stressed that the refugees felt deep gratitude and required minimal expenditure. On August 6 the *New York Herald Tribune* reported "Refugees Awed by Luxuries of New Life Here." Writer M. Jan Racusin noted that daily diets cost a scant 43½ cents and caused "endless wondrous chatter" among people who considered them "feasts." Two days later *PM* described a child clinging to a pillow while his mother explained its use. Such scenes were not uncommon. Like many others, Kathe Kaufman, her photographer husband, and their eight-year-old daughter had survived in a cave. Clean beds and a door with a key brought real joy.[24]

Only *The Day* reported any dissatisfaction. World Jewish Congress president Nahum Goldman had asked Samuel Margoshes, a congress board member and editor of the popular Yiddish daily, to visit the shelter and report his observations. Margoshes's stories, appearing August 13, 14, and 15 in his "News and Views" column, sharply criticized the government's restrictions and lack of preparation. But he spoke for residents whose feelings remained unknown to the general public.

The camp had a well-meaning administration hampered by insufficient authority and inadequate knowledge of the people for whom it was responsible. It had a deprived and tormented population sharply divided on everything except what it wanted from the United States government and Jewish organizations. No precedents existed for resolving the differences.

SIX

Emotional Conflict

What sin have I committed? Am I a prisoner? I
was free in Italy, before we left! Are we enemies? Is this the country of freedom and justice? The German prisoners have more
freedom than we![1]

BEING *IN* AMERICA but not *of* America put the refugees on an emotional roller coaster. The barbed wire–topped fence stunned them,
customs confiscations angered them, mail censorship irritated them,
and the loss of freedom hurt them. At the same time, some parents
tucked young children into clean sheets on individual beds for the
very first time. And when voices joined exuberantly to chant the *Sh'ma*
on Friday nights and Saturday mornings, the sounds of war began to
recede.

For many, the first steps toward a resumption of normalcy involved resuming contact with separated loved ones. Naftali and Rywa
Flink, a Polish-born couple in their sixties, received the first incoming
call. Their son, United States Army Sergeant Joseph Flink, had immigrated with his wife six years earlier on the Austrian quota. A second
son had been lost in Austria, and the whereabouts of a daughter last
seen in Switzerland remained unknown. Joseph read his parents'
names in a New York newspaper and turned to the NRS for help in
contacting them, action that his parents saw as proof that "Miracles are
still happening."[2]

More "miraculous," just a few weeks after arriving in Oswego, the
six unaccompanied Weinstein children, three boys and three girls
between the ages of ten and twenty, read in *Aufbau,* a German-
language newspaper, that their mother and three younger siblings
were safe in Switzerland. Originally from Czechoslovakia, the family
split into two groups and lost contact with one another while fleeing
from Belgium to France and to Italy. The six older children reached
Rome with their father, only to see him arrested and deported shortly

70

before the city's liberation. Thrilled to learn that their mother and younger siblings were safe, they would remain separated more than eighteen additional months.[3]

The first month brought, in addition to news of loved ones and the group's first Bar Mitzvah, a *Brit Milah* (covenant of circumcision) and two weddings. Olga and Leon Maurer refused to have "International Harry," born in a truck on the way to the Naples pier, circumcised on the prescribed eighth day by a ship's doctor. They waited until a *mohel* (performer of the rite) could travel to Oswego from New York.[4]

News of the shelter's first bridal couple captured American hearts and drew a shower of gifts.[5] Blond and pretty Marianna Hartmeyer (Manya Hartmayer), a twenty-one-year-old from Berlin, met handsome Ernst Breuer, a twenty-six-year-old Viennese photographer-artist, and his sister, Alice (Liesl) in a Vichy concentration camp at Gurs. Separated from her Belgium-bound family at fifteen by a Gestapo agent, Manya soothed her own pain by singing for fellow prisoners. She and Liesl drew the attention of a rescue group and found themselves walking across the Alps to Italy. Ernst managed to join them in Rome, where the girls found work as cabaret singers and where they met Margarete Frank and Paul Aufricht. The latter couple, a thirty-six-year-old Berlin-born Parisian beautician and a forty-seven-year-old Viennese merchant, had been inseparable since their meeting in a Rome apartment that was used for the preparation of false identity papers.

The two couples married in traditional ceremonies less than three weeks after arriving at the fort, the Breuers first because they first completed legal requirements. Not authorized to perform an American ceremony, Rabbi Tzechoval assisted Oswego's Rabbi Bialik. Honeymooning in barren one-room apartments—Manya decorated hers with crepe-paper streamers and milk bottles filled with wild flowers—they shared both their happiness and their most intimate moments, the latter an unfortunate reality because barracks apartments provided visual but not soundproof privacy.

All spirits rose in September, for that month opened with the lifting of the quarantine. Residents received six-hour passes for Oswego, where they strolled on sidewalks lined with carefully tended colonial homes and explored shops that, despite wartime shortages, still appeared to be "stuffed" with goods that for years they had known only in fantasy. They met "kindness . . . hospitality and willingness to help" and considered this their "greatest and happiest experience" since arriving in the United States.[6]

Beginning with labor Day weekend, when the quarantine was lifted, visitors poured into the camp. More than ten thousand friends, relatives, organizational representatives, government officials, and area citizens visited. Sixty-year-old Chaim Fuchs hugged Gustave Fox, the son he had not seen for six years, so fiercely that the younger man's glasses broke. Neither seemed to notice. The father, alone in the shelter, had suffered torture in Dachau and found it hard to believe that he now embraced the one family member he knew to be safe. Now a buyer for a hardware company in New York, Fox had immigrated six years earlier on the Austrian quota while his father and other family members waited for Polish visa numbers.[7]

One visitor, Eleanor Roosevelt, created waves of excitement throughout the camp. The "First Lady of the World," accompanied by Mrs. Henry Morgenthau, Jr., arrived on September 20 without escort cars or guards for an "entirely unofficial" visit. Hundreds shook her hand throughout the day as crowds waving American flags accompanied her to a service in the Orthodox synagogue, to ceremonies in all five kitchens, and to tours of the barracks. Mrs. Roosevelt and selected guests also enjoyed a special luncheon prepared by fifty-two-year-old Jacob Grunberg, a former Viennese pastry chef. Additional September visitors included Zionist leader Stephen S. Wise, entertainer Molly Picon, and the Reverend Dom Odo, Duke of Wittenberg. The latter called on Felix Blumenfeldt, a fifty-seven-year-old Austrian Roman Catholic who had served many years as the duke's palace chauffeur.[8]

The attention and activity generated by the refugee shelter caught Oswego unprepared, and it reacted with mixed feelings. On the one hand, despite initial concerns, the refugees appeared to be an economic bonanza. When the rush of visitors overwhelmed the town's two small hotels, a number of Oswegans opened their homes to paying guests. Rumors claimed that the visitors included wealthy New York relatives who would make Oswego prosperous.[9] On the other hand, rumors also accused the government of outrageous generosity at a time of severe wartime shortages. Every refugee family was said to have been given new electric stoves and refrigerators. At the same time, the hiring of dozens of locals was said to enable the foreigners, who were described as including many men of military age who were "huskier" than drafted Oswego men, to live "the life of Riley."[10] Mothers of fighting sons and farmers short of farmhands sometimes looked with bitterness on foreign men "living off the fat of the land."[11]

The WRA wished to avoid all criticism and looked to local business and civic leaders for approval and support. With help from Edwin Waterbury, publisher of the *Oswego Palladium Times* and president of the local Chamber of Commerce, Joseph Smart called a meeting on August 18 that led to the formation of an Oswego Citizens

Advisory Committee. That group, which made possible the enrollment of shelter children in Oswego schools and the introduction of
six-hour passes, played a vital role in maintaining good community
relations. Chaired by attorney Ralph Mizen, it organized committees
to resolve any difficulties with visitor accommodations and with refugee business and recreation in town. Most important, it created a
"rumor clinic," which used the *Oswego Palladium Times* to quickly
repudiate wild tales. The system so impressed Eleanor Roosevelt that
she wrote in "My Day," her syndicated column, "something of this
kind in every U.S. community might be wonderfully useful."[12]

The War Refugee Board had not asked Oswego schools to enroll
shelter youngsters because it feared that to do so might bring into
question its commitment to return the group to Europe. Instead, the
NRS agreed to provide teachers within the camp. But refugee pleas
and demands persuaded Smart to pursue opportunities in Oswego.
The community's schools were underenrolled because the draft and
the lure of defense jobs had produced an out-migration of younger
families. Parochial schools readily offered to admit youngsters of their
faith and, after Smart assured the public schools that Jewish organizations would pay for materials and textbooks, they did the same. The
school year opened on Tuesday, September 5, with 189 shelter residents between five and twenty-one years old sitting in Oswego classrooms.

The school issue proved much easier than the matter of free
access to shopping and recreational facilities. A vocal minority
thought it wiser to maintain control by arranging for the refugees to
visit in town only on conducted bus tours. However, at the conclusion
of the meeting, Smart reported that the new Oswego Citizens Advisory Committee wished to open its schools and its community to
shelter residents.[13]

The WRA wanted to ease internment restrictions and the WRB
wanted to use Oswego to strengthen its case for additional shelters.
Both wished to avoid irritating the president, who had been sensitive
to public criticism of government "largesse" in Japanese Relocation
Centers. Dillon Myer persuaded John Pehle to present school enrollments and Oswego passes to FDR as changes already made at the
urging of Oswego leaders.[14] To avoid local irritation and reduce the
possibility of an unfavorable incident, they initially limited passes to
150 daily.

Publisher Edwin Waterbury estimated that 90 percent of Oswegans immediately accepted the shelter and thought the remaining
10 percent lacked any real influence. But Oswego did not escape the
anti-Semitism that permeated America in the thirties and early forties. "Refugee" meant "Jew," and early tales of rich New York kin and

of able-bodied men avoiding both manual work within the camp and combat overseas rested on common anti-Semitic stereotypes. Geraldine Rossiter remembers being called a "Jew lover." And more than one Oswego housewife undoubtedly sympathized with a local matron who lamented, "If they're so intellectual and such a high type, I guess there won't be a chance of getting a servant among them." However, most refugees never heard derogatory remarks and most Oswegans prefer to forget them. Furthermore, Waterbury represented the great majority when he proudly exclaimed, "I don't think any of us expected there would be so many outstanding people at the Fort."[15]

To shelter residents, then and now, Oswego meant warm acceptance and hospitality. A number of refugees, particularly performing artists, frequently visited in leading homes. On the other hand, one reporter found that Oswegans who did not themselves feel secure socially hesitated to mix shelter and town guests. A middle-aged couple who occasionally entertained a young Polish husband and wife on Saturday afternoons explained that they would not invite town guests at the same time because, although they thought the attitude of some "damnable," they would not challenge it.[16] Only the Catholic and Greek Orthodox children enrolled in Oswego's parochial schools generally enjoyed informal social exchanges. Even the Jewish youngsters who were elected class officers found themselves unwitting members of opposing "gangs" when "townies" gathered to taunt refugee children on their way to and from school.[17]

Prejudice existed but the community's civic leaders, educators, and merchants discouraged its expression. A dozen letters critical of the refugees were published in the summer of 1945 in the *Oswego Palladium Times*. Edwin Waterbury ordered an investigation and discovered they bore fictitious names.[18] Nevertheless, they expressed views that the rumor clinic found difficult to dispel, views that exaggerated the government's beneficence, portrayed the refugees as lazy evaders of military service, and accused them of self-aggrandizement. Such feelings tended to be greatest among people who felt excluded from the local power structure or who felt they had sacrificed the most for the war.

Critics who resented the refugees' apparent inactivity assumed that they preferred dependency. Those who feared for their sons at war did not know that nearly two dozen refugee families had sons in the American Armed Forces, or that forty refugee men and women tried to enlist and were refused on the ground that they did not live officially in the United States. In addition, refugee men of military age who appeared able-bodied frequently suffered debilitating conditions or injuries. Most yearned to be productive and to support the

American war effort. Their "idleness" irritated some Oswegans but devastated many in the fort.

WRA officials recognized the need to offer productive work opportunities. Dillon S. Myer wanted light industry in the camp but government regulations forbade the manufacture of goods that would compete on the open market against American products. He wanted to develop shoe repair and clothing renovation for overseas relief, but a Japanese Relocation Center did this, could not find a market, and tried to sell its goods to the shelter.

Outside work possibilities seemed more promising. Requests for refugee workers poured into WRB and WRA offices. An aircraft parts manufacturer only forty miles from Oswego desperately needed one hundred laborers for "high priority" work that was neither confidential nor restricted and could be performed by handicapped and disabled people. The company offered either to build living quarters at the work site or to provide daily transportation.[19] Most area employers needed agricultural and food-processing work. Wartime manpower shortages, serious in 1943, when fort soldiers worked nearly one thousand man-days in nearby orchards, became critical in 1944.

Requests to utilize refugee labor outside the camp evoked very different responses from the WRA and the WRB. The WRA viewed them as a useful step toward release on internment-at-large. Thus far, it had used such opportunities to free 35,000 from Japanese Relocation Centers and resettle them throughout the nation's interior. The WRB feared that permitting outside work would undermine its efforts to obtain additional camps. It agreed to permit fifty refugees to work briefly in nearby orchards and in a local Birds Eye storage plant during the fall of 1944 only because it also feared that refusing to do so would arouse local hostility. When local employers did not unite to increase the pressure for refugee workers, the WRB refused to approve subsequent requests. Employers did not press the issue because POWs increasingly filled their needs.

It is a tragic irony that those who favored bringing large numbers of POWs to this country succeeded, whereas those who wished to do the same for refugees did not. The United States took in 425,000 enemy POWs, of whom 372,000 were German. Three hundred fifty-five thousand were already here when the Oswego refugees arrived. The War Department did not plan to bring more, but congressional pressure "tipped the scales" and persuaded it to bring an additional 70,000.[20] Before the war's end every state except Nevada, North Dakota, and Vermont had a POW camp. They helped greatly in easing the nation's critical manpower shortage.

Two base camps and eleven satellite facilities housed 4500 German POWs near Oswego. Arriving throughout the summer of 1944—

Oswego refugees saw German POWs on the decks of two ships in their convoy—they performed road maintenance, camp beautification, and agricultural and canning work. Shelter teenagers soon encountered them in the fort and, a few weeks later, refugee workers worked alongside them in a nearby Birds Eye cannery.

German POWs helped ready the fort for the refugees and had not yet completed groundwork when they arrived. A poignant confrontation ensued after a group of refugee youngsters set out to explore the far reaches of the shelter. Finding "evil incarnate, the Nazi himself, right in our camp," Walter Arnstein and his friends yelled, in German, "We are Jews. . . . You understand, you pigs? Jews! You didn't get us all! We are Jews! Jews!" One of the Germans stepped forward and made a wide, sweeping, exaggerated bow. The others broke into "wild laughter." Before the teenagers could react, the POWs' supervisor, a bored policeman, ordered both groups to mind their own business.[21]

The refugees thought the Germans' presence incomprehensible, "truly beyond belief," particularly when they learned that the United States paid Germans to work in American orchards while American farmboys fought them in Europe.[22] The issue aroused angry bewilderment and remains a chilling memory of government "insensitivity."[23] However, it did not lead to protests. It may be that the issue so threatened the refugees' views of FDR that they could not face it. At any rate, few experienced direct contact, and this occurred only during the first few weeks. Shelter residents did not know, of course, that WRB proponents had promised to treat them similarly to POWs, nor that, had this been done, they would have had a number of advantages.

American Alien Registration laws clearly defined the POWs' legal status and the Geneva Convention stipulated the government's obligation to them. The refugees were not registered under the former because that would have meant recognizing their entry into the United States, and there were no international laws granting protections to refugees.

American employers, the War Department, and the Roosevelt administration all saw the POWs' presence as advantageous. Employers wished to hire them, the War Department wanted to woo them, and the Roosevelt administration found them profitable. POWs, Japanese-American evacuees, and Oswego refugees all performed outside contract labor. Oswego refugees eagerly sought outside work—September registration for orchard and canning work drew 246 applicants, more than fives times the number needed. Smart suggested that, as in the case of the POWs, the government could offset its maintenance costs by utilizing refugee labor in labor-short industries.

But racial, religious, and economic stereotypes produced a greater demand for German workers.

POWs proved to be good business. Employers paid prevailing rates for American labor, POWs received minimum wages comparable to those paid Oswego refugees, and Uncle Sam pocketed the difference. That amounted to one hundred million dollars, one-fourth more than the POWs cost to maintain.[24] War Department enthusiasm stemmed from the hope that POW letters home would encourage additional surrenders and that POWs would take democracy home with them after the war. The department conducted a crash program in democratization and claimed, after the war, that its efforts had transformed "the Nazi sniper [into] the American farmer."[25]

Nazis in American camps fared better than Americans in German camps. The Geneva Convention required diets equal "in quality and quantity" to the diets of the captor nation's troops at base camp.[26] Because standards for American and German troops differed greatly, a typical POW wrote home, "Here we eat more in a single day than during a whole week at home."[27] However, because the War Department held that content prisoners would make better workers, would bring victory sooner, and would help create a better postwar world, POWs fared better in the United States than international agreements required.

At Fort Niagara, the base camp in upstate New York, POWs enjoyed weekly films, a 1200-volume library, and soccer, boxing, volleyball, and badminton. They had their own school with a twelve-member faculty, their own newspaper, and their own orchestra. Their presence aroused "little concern," and German-speaking residents in the area donated books and other materials.[28]

POWs fared better than refugees and evacuees on several counts. The government gave them complete, coordinated summer and winter wardrobes. It provided POW officers private bungalows and the services of individually assigned orderlies. It also exempted them from work and gave them monthly allowances of twenty to forty dollars. Private organizations brought a wide variety of recreational activities to all three types of camps, but only the POWs had opportunities to earn credits toward university degrees—they could enroll in correspondence courses, in English, from the University of Chicago—and to take qualifying professional exams.

The WRA lacked authority and planning comparable to that of the War Department's Prisoner of War Special Projects Division. It saw internment not as an opportunity but as an unfortunate circumstance. Recognizing the deleterious effects of extended camp life and frustrated by its custodial role, it focused not on long-range goals but on proposals to close its camps. Having already freed 35,000 Japanese-Americans from relocation centers, it expected to do the same for the newly arrived refugees.

The refugees also did not expect to remain confined. During the first few weeks, relief over having reached America and seeing their children enrolled in American schools offset for many the shock of internment. Rumors of imminent release accompanied Eleanor Roosevelt's September 20 visit. When Advisory Council Chairman Leon Levy noted all her efforts on behalf of "those who have suffered," there was an implied assumption that she could deliver freedom.[29] Mrs. Roosevelt did not wish to raise false hopes but her mere presence did just that, and dozens pressed personal petitions into her hands. When the promise she symbolized did not find fulfillment, depression set in. Hopes again rose as the November presidential election neared. Surely, their benefactor would set them free after the election. On November 7 FDR secured his fourth term, but again, freedom did not come.

Winter came instead. And it brought the realization that the refugees might be facing an indeterminate sentence. Harsh winters are normal in that Great Lakes region, but the winter of 1944–45 arrived with unusual haste and ferocity. A mid-November squall, continuous storms, and freezing temperatures broke all records. Oswego received more than forty-three inches of snow by late December and nearly twice that much during the next three months.

The refugees had come from a Mediterranean climate, their average age was considerably above that of surrounding populations, and they had neither the experience nor the stamina for such weather. Four suffered fractures during the first storm and fractures increased thereafter. Smart reported that "a large number" had to rely on others to bring meals to them.[30] Even the able-bodied had difficulty moving from building to building. And when high winds whipped through the wooden barracks and froze water pipes, keeping warm and fed became everyone's obsession. Only the children easily adapted.

Winter proved a far harsher jailer than did the government. Many found escape in flights of fanciful return to warm and sunny Italy. The Fiermonti camp had been cursed with malaria. In 1943–44 the Bari camp had experienced a clothing shortage that led to underclothes being made from mosquito netting and to boots and shoes being fashioned from pieces of salvage. Bari memories also included disinfestation, which had produced hysterical fears that the facility might be a "German camp in disguise."[31] But such experiences faded from memory and Italy loomed as far more attractive than Oswego. Now shelter staff appeared to be the enemy and those who cooperated came to be seen as collaborators. Ruth Gruber noted that a social worker who had fled Hitler in the thirties and now worked in the camp on loan from a private Jewish agency "bore the brunt" of such animosity. Shelter residents demanded to know how she could work for "such people."[32]

All authority was resented and the resentments forced the resignation in early December of the Advisory Council. That meant that the camp no longer had a refugee forum. Nationality groups became more insular. Frustrations formerly vented toward members of other groups now festered between members of the same group. Real and imagined slights acquired exaggerated significance and resistance to authority took on increasingly paranoiac overtones. Work became "forced labor," internal security became "the Gestapo," and "protection" and "favoritism" were seen as influencing all.

The relentless winter intensified feelings and responses characteristic of the refugee experience. The Welfare Department chief thought that many had survived because of "thoroughly asocial" attitudes that made it possible "to think and act only in terms of self-preservation."[33] A former member of the Advisory Council specifically attributed to previous camp experiences the "vehement aversion" to all authority and rules.[34] A postwar psychological study concluded, "The refugee starts his life in an atmosphere of defeat and disorder," and thus "approaches every task in a spirit of anxiety, uncertainty, dread," and, therefore, cannot trust.[35]

Continued internment also nurtured paranoiac tendencies. The inmate or internee frequently suffers feelings of "mortification," and these may be sharpened if the mixing of age, ethnic, and racial groups produces feelings of "being contaminated" by contact with undesirables. Such feelings are further exaggerated because the institution weakens or supplants such traditional sources of support as families and economic structures, violates individual needs for privacy, and discourages tendencies toward fraternalization and clique formation. Adaptation is left to individual devices, which frequently include contrariness, withdrawal, or "conversion," that is, acting out the role of "perfect" internee.[36] Conditions at the shelter proved to be no exception. Valiant people did not succumb, but they remained a minority.

Despair deepened and the camp suffered a tragic suicide. Searchers braved fifty-mile-an-hour winds and ten-foot snow drifts to find pretty and frail thirty-two-year-old Karoline Bleier. The previous day, December 28, she had left her husband and two infants in their barracks apartment, walked to an isolated and unprotected spot, and sat down in the blowing snow and bitter cold. An autopsy indicated that "she had swallowed one hundred tablets of aspirin.[37] Fear for two children left behind with her first husband, intensified by increasing news of Nazi death camps, had produced survivor's guilt too great to bear. Hers was the single suicide, but it symbolized the growing disintegration throughout the winter of 1944–45.

The situation prompted the WRA to seek expert counsel. Curt Bondy, Chairman of the Department of Psychology at Richmond Professional Institute of William and Mary College, had been an assistant director of the Kitchener Refugee Camp in England and a consultant on refugees for the Dutch Government. Author of several articles on the behavior of interned populations, a linguist who did not need translators, he arrived the day after Bleier's frozen body was discovered. He remained four days and interviewed individuals and groups, staff and residents, leaders and followers.

Bondy concluded that the shelter suffered problems common to all internment camps, but that it also faced difficulties arising from specific circumstances. Loss of freedom and status reversal—in all camps some lose traditional sources of recognition and others are elevated to positions not available to them in ordinary life—produce a sense of isolation and give many a feeling of degradation. But the uncertainties associated with the shelter exacerbated such destructive psychological responses. Bondy warned that the refugees could be expected to become "more unbalanced, more nervous, more dissatisfied and more resentful"[38]

Changes needed to be made in internment, work, refugee representation, and discipline. The camp should be closed, but if this could not be done, Bondy wanted to introduce month-long visits to family, friends, or volunteer hosts and to reduce daily tensions. Filling jobs that required difficult and even dangerous manual labor posed the single greatest administrative problem. He asked that uniform wages be replaced by a system that offered greater rewards for the least desirable work. Furthermore, calls for workers should be based on the actual number needed, not the number expected to show. Both the administration-sponsored Advisory Council, which consisted of two representatives elected by each of the four major nationality groups and two elected by the minorities, and a Labor Committee formed by workers themselves had spoken for refugee workers, but by March neither existed. He recommended formation of a new refugee organization with greater status and authority than had been given the Advisory Council.

He expected work problems to persist even if the WRA granted brief leaves, differentiated wages, and gave refugees a voice in policy. Therefore, strict discipline would be necessary. A former inmate of Buchenwald himself, Bondy noted that he had originally opposed the use of coercion but that, reluctantly, he had come to believe that camp life produced negative behaviors that sometimes required strong responses. He recommended the withholding of daily passes and, in extreme cases, detention on Ellis Island. But such measures would have to be explained in advance, applied consistently, and enforced without hesitation.

The Bondy report found a mixed reception in Washington. Interior Secretary Ickes thought it notable only for calling attention to the fact that "we are not doing the job at Oswego as well as it might be done."[39] A feisty long-time advocate of rescue and resettlement, known to his subordinates as "Old Curmudgeon,"[40] he felt frustrated both by his lack of overall authority for the project and by the seemingly endless problems associated with it. In exasperation, he wondered if those who were dissatisfied should return to Europe or go wherever "they would be more likely to merge into the social environment."[41]

Bondy's recommendations stirred interest only in the WRA and did not become policy, but they did draw attention to the question of repatriation. Specifically, the WRA began to see repatriation or the threat of it as an alternative to coercive measures. Community analyst Edward Spicer argued that the Yugoslavs had been the single most dissatisfied group "from the day they boarded the ship at Naples," and, now that Tito's victories made repatriation an increasingly likely option, they should be permitted to remain in Oswego if they could be made to understand "the score from here on out."[42] During the coming months, sixty-six Yugoslavs did accept repatriation.

The camp would not be closed, the Yugoslavs remained the only group for whom repatriation was possible, and psychological deterioration continued. Ruth Gruber reported several examples.[43] One of two professional chefs in the shelter had been living freely in Rome and had an American visa that the war had prevented him from using. He insisted that he applied for Oswego only because of assurances that he would be free within a few weeks. Wanting only "to make something of myself" and reading ads daily in the *New York Times* that offered as much as $500 monthly for people with his culinary skill, he felt helpless and grew increasingly bitter. Others began to feel less able to resume ordinary life. A young woman told Gruber that initially she wanted to leave the camp, but "Now I don't know." No longer having "to worry about such things" as providing for herself gave her a growing sense of security.

The lack of privacy and quiet proved even more devastating than frustrated ambitions and institutional dependency. One of many residents who pleaded for Gruber's help in getting out of the camp cried that she lived alone but could find no escape from people who reminded her of "nothing but my unhappy past and my uncertain future."

Stress often expressed itself in emotional outbursts. A middle-aged professional man created a terrible scene in the mess hall because his meat portion appeared smaller than his neighbor's. But those who maintained control and dignity sometimes suffered most. Welfare worker Ruth Ehrlich observed that the effort might require "such an extreme withdrawal" that even contact with those closest became "intolerable." Thus, even the most dignified not infrequently dissolved into tears upon hearing "only a few words" from a sympathetic friend.[44]

Periodic tremors shook the entire camp and added enormously to the stress. Leaks in February 1945 about discussions in Washington pertaining to the closing of the War Refugee Board and efforts to close the camp produced wild rumors of imminent freedom. Refugees bought every trunk and suitcase available in Oswego. And when days turned into weeks and nothing happened, the flight of fancy turned into a still deeper descent into gloom. Each new swing of the pendulum between euphoria and disillusionment cut deeper paths of pain.

Before winter released its icy grip, the vast majority of adult residents showed signs of one or more camp neuroses such as explosive irritability, irrational suspiciousness, bitter resentment, or resigned withdrawal. Six suffered severe psychiatric disorders.[45]

B.F.: Sixty-two years old, a former Austrian textile merchant originally from Poland, he had a wife whose whereabouts were unknown and was alone in the shelter. Hospitalized in a psychiatric facility on Long Island in early January after several severe outbursts, he returned more than three months later and continued to need an alternative to camp living. When the shelter closed, immigration officers ruled him inadmissible; he returned to the Amityville Convalescent Hospital on Long Island.

G.G.: Thirty-nine years old, a bookkeeper originally from Poland, she too lived alone in the shelter. Placed in the Amityville Hospital in January, she remained unable to care for herself and did not return to the camp.

E.P.: A sixty-two-year-old Austrian housewife, she lived with her sixty-five-year-old husband, a former bookkeeper. Childless and without American relatives, they had suffered numerous separations and internments. Both were "extremely nervous" but "tried hard" to adjust. In early March she fell into a catatonic stupor and was "completely incommunicative" until receiving electric shock treatments at Amityville. Returning to the shelter before the end of the month, she remained in a precarious condition but did not qualify for immigration with her husband when the camp closed.

J.R.: A forty-seven-year-old Austrian barber, he was single and had no American relatives. Admitted to the Philadelphia Psychiatric Hospital in early February for hysterical deafness and erratic behavior, he returned six weeks later little improved. Judged inadmissible for immigration, he returned to Philadelphia for care.

R.O.: A twenty-four-year-old living in the shelter with her parents and sister, she married in the shelter. Diagnosed manic depressive and hospitalized in Syracuse, she returned to the shelter showing little improvement but did qualify for immigration when the camp closed.

F.K.: A sixty-two-year-old Austrian merchant, he was the saddest case. He was partially paralyzed, deaf, and suffering from a chronic case of typhoid fever because of torture in Dachau and subsequent deprivation in other camps. His wife and two daughters, both of whom had husbands serving in the Armed Forces, lived in California. They desperately sought his release so that they could care for him. They succeeded in November 1945 and he died less than three months later.

The WRA called Rudolph Dreikurs, a Chicago psychiatrist, to the camp less than three months after Curt Bondy visited. He had fled Vienna several years earlier and had gained recognition as an Adlerian committed to the use of group activities to treat individual problems. From March 29 to April 9, 1945, he conducted individual evaluations. The fact that the current camp population included only a few borderline and only one or two unquestionably psychotic cases struck him as "remarkable." Not only were there surprisingly few truly distrubed people, but the "severity" of individual cases bore no relation to the degree of terror previously experienced.[46]

Dreikurs noted that shelter residents presented a psychiatric profile no different from that of the general population. However, the camp had far more cases of neurotic personality disorder than the 110 reported by refugee physicians. Personality disintegration, apparent in a deterioration of reasoning skills and a high incidence of psychosomatic illnesses, was widespread, but the condition resulted from existing circumstances and would respond to environmental improvements.

Originally asked for advice regarding individual cases, Dreikurs provided an analysis of the group's dynamics and suggestions for developing a more supportive community. He identified three categories of shelter residents.[47] The first and most difficult, people neither deranged nor abnormal, showed impaired emotional and intellectual functioning, which resulted in numerous conflicts in social situations and in great personal suffering. Some had been troubled all their lives and others had first become aware of difficulties during the refugee experience. Many in this first category found it impossible, both "morally" and "emotionally," to accept shelter regulations and restrictions. They had survived through defiance and deceit, they had refused to submit under far more difficult circumstances, and he thought that they might become openly defiant at "any moment."

The second group also exhibited anticonformist behaviors, generally for the first time because such tendencies had previously been latent or channeled into constructive endeavors. This group included a number of attorneys frustrated because they had the least chance of resuming their careers. Trained to rely on their own interpretative skills, they had practice in using argumentation to overcome opponents. Dreikurs described one such man who had enjoyed considerable power and influence in Europe and had "felt his own strength and power" and "maintained his equilibrium" while bringing his family safely through a series of incredibly dangerous and traumatic experiences. Now, in the camp, he felt condemned to idleness. And not having accepted defeat before, he responded by privately engaging in acts of masochism and publicly assuming the role of agitator against the camp staff.

The third and largest group displayed various forms of neuroses. A widow whose dream of being reunited with her scattered children had previously enabled her to maintain her courage now developed numerous organic-neurotic symptoms because she could no longer stand to be separated from a daughter living in America. Another who had protected and supported her children during years of flight now succumbed to depression because she could not accept regulations that prevented her from supporting her family. Such individuals often created disturbances that encouraged feelings of distrust and persecution among others who might not have developed paranoiac traits. At the same time, they did not develop schizophrenia or "true paranoia." In each case, they held "persecutory ideas" that were "still close to reality and based on actual events" that needed only slight misinterpretation.

Barracks living produced continuous justifications for aggressive, hostile behavior. Dreikurs described "three characteristic conflicts" that derived from "the sexual conditions in close living." A young married woman "suffered extremely from the fact that the neighbors commented freely on her nightly pleasures," a young girl frequently interrupted her parents because she felt they had made love "enough," and a six-year-old boy suffered screaming attacks "whenever his parents got together." It was "impossible to get reliable information," but "growing promiscuity" was also a serious problem that disrupted families and put great stress on the "humiliated" partner, a problem exacerbated by the peculiar status of the refugees as nonimmigrants and nonvisitors—they could marry but not divorce because the latter required that they come under a judicial jurisdiction.[48]

Dreikurs also noted a process of social realignments in response to generational antagonisms arising from differences in attitudes toward continued internment and toward work requirements. Younger people more often found camp life intolerable, wanted out as soon as possible, and resented being pressured to perform undesirable work and to conform. Older people more often found security within the camp, feared having to leave, and resented those whom they saw as shirking necessary work. Generational differences now superseded national group frictions but did not offer alternative identities or substitute means of achieving cooperation. The situation appeared to be explosive and would continue to worsen unless changes were made.

The psychiatrist concluded that the refugees most needed to recognize the extent to which they formed "a real community." He suggested four changes that would help to create a more supportive society, one involving everyone and three for specific population segments. He called for a staff addition, a trained group worker who could conduct activities such as group sings to foster a spirit of unity. Pressing for cooperation merely intensified antagonisms and increased the incidence of psychosomatic illnesses. Because staff members lived within the camp and mirrored refugee tensions, he recommended that they should be required to leave the fort for a specific period of time every week. Regularly scheduled interdepartmental meetings were also needed. And he insisted that refugees urgently needing a respite from camp life had to be given temporary leaves.

Dreikurs also focused on the problems of shelter children. In several cases, parents could not, for physical or psychological reasons, care adequately for their children. In others, the children had problems that made them unmanageable for parents. In either situation, the children needed to be placed as soon as possible in a separate, supervised children's home within the shelter. Communal living placed unusual burdens on all shelter children, involving them to an unusual degree in adult life at the same time that it weakened parental authority and increased peer influence. Dreikurs wanted a well-organized children's recreational program and insisted that it could not wait until summer.

The WRA forwarded individual evaluations to the WRB as evidence of the need for sponsored leaves but thought Dreikurs's overall recommendations "impractical."[49] Nevertheless, most eventually became policy.

The camp never had a resident psychologist or psychiatrist, and, although Smart and the Welfare Department sought such an addition to the staff, neither Bondy nor Dreikurs made such a recommendation. The welfare chief concluded that "there was a great awareness of problems," but "this did not mean action."[50] A few who exhibited severe antisocial behavior or became dysfunctional were hospitalized on Long Island or in Philadelphia, and a few others received brief outpatient treatment in Syracuse, generally in the form of electric shock treatments. The camp's social workers carried a caseload of 150 refugees. But they worked extensively with only 50, most of whom were children. The refugees looked to them not for therapeutic counsel but for help with practical problems such as housing, clothing, and disagreements with the medical staff. For the many who suffered various neuroses because of the environmental situation, treatment either was unavailable or consisted only of small environmental improvements.

Medical problems closely paralleled emotional stresses. The group's general physical condition quickly improved. After three months many had gained thirty to sixty pounds, and worries about overweight replaced fears of malnutrition. But depression, anxiety, and hysteria became more evident, and physical complaints increased both in volume and in severity. People who suppressed fear and anger most often developed illnesses for which an organic explanation could not be found. Repeated medical visits only increased their frustration. Winter weather limited trips to the camp clinic but increased the demand for house calls. The line of clinic patients lengthened as the weather improved. It was not unusual for four or five physicians to see fifty to sixty patients. Dreikurs explained:

> It was probably significant and not incidental that a number of patients suffered from a heart neurosis with similar symptoms consisting of severe attacks of fear, with pain around the heart and other heart symptoms, but without organic findings. . . . A short analysis of the psychological problems of these patients revealed the real meaning of the symptoms. They were all directed against the life situation. . . . All these people were extremely kind and nice people, most of them rather successful, who suddenly found themselves in a situation where they could not do any significant work and lost hope. At this moment, an incidental excitement started an ailment which became their only interest; from then on they lived only for their neurosis.[51]

Under the circumstances, acrimonious patient-doctor relationships could not be avoided. Many had come to the United States to obtain medical treatment from "American specialists" and they did not want refugee physicians. The doctors, burdened by the same stresses as their patients, had neither the patience, stamina, nor specializations to meet their needs. Furthermore, because camp life erased all separations between work, family, and social activities, group antagonisms and individual conflicts necessarily colored patient-doctor relationships. In addition, the WRA assigned the physicians the task of determining suitability for work, and this responsibility trapped them between refugees and staff on the single most explosive issue in the camp. The situation spread distrust and resentment throughout the camp and created friction between the medical and welfare departments. The refugee doctors were "despised, rejected by the residents and the staff alike."[52]

Visitors to the shelter, at least those content with surface impressions, noticed few problems. They saw that the refugees slept in clean beds, appeared suitably clothed, and no longer suffered malnutrition. Shelter residents married, gave birth, saw their children off daily to American schools, and moved about freely in Oswego. They had full religious freedom and conducted religious classes for their children. Certainly, no group of World War II refugee internees enjoyed comparable comforts or freedoms.

But internment, however benevolent, took its toll. Lives hung suspended between past horrors and future uncertainties, in a present beset with sexual, familial, occupational, and social difficulties. Before winter spent itself, a pattern of psychological and physical deterioration had become well established. Tensions built to explosive levels. And the labor problem drew the fire.

Refugee mother and child experience a family reunion through the fence. (Photo copyright by Leni Sonnenfeld.)

Scene from the gate looking up the road that led from the shelter into the town of Oswego. Note the high chain-link fence topped by three rows of barbed wire. (Photo by Gretchen Van Tassel, May 1945. National Archives, RG 210, CFZ-226.)

Regina Gal and her children, Charlotte and Albert. (Photo by Hikaru Iwasaki, August 1944. National Archives, RG 210, CFZ-106.)

Jakob Waksman and his son Andre. (Photo by Hikaru Iwasaki, August 1944. National Archives, RG 210, CFZ-71.)

Looking to the future: Artur Hirt and his son Joseph. (Photo copyright by Leni Sonnenfeld.)

First taste of ice cream. The Weinstein family: Marcella, 19,
Miriam, 17, Bernard, 14, Lea, 12, Jack, 10, Nathan, 9. (Photo
copyright by Leni Sonnenfeld.)

The shelter's first wedding. *Left to right:* Rabbi Sidney Bialik of
Oswego, Gussie Gruber (Ruth Gruber's mother), Marianna
Hartmeyer, Fradl Munz, Ernst Breuer, Rabbi Mosco Tzechoval.
(Photo copyright by Leni Sonnenfeld.)

Lighting Hanukkah lights in the shelter. Hanna Hendel, Tamar Hendel, Vilko Kremer, Eisig Hendel. (Photo copyright by Leni Sonnenfeld.)

Sculptor Miriam Sommerburg shows one of her works, a head of shelter director Joseph H. Smart, to Rela Liban and her soldier son. (Photo by Gretchen Van Tassel, May 1945. National Archives, RG 210, CFZ-116.)

Max Sipser, cartoonist for the *Ontario Chronicle*. (Photo by Gretchen Van Tassel, May 1945. National Archives, RG 210, CFZ-201.)

SEVEN

Persistent Problems

Occupational displacement is bitter for the
manual worker; it is tragic for the professional
man.[1]

THE PROBLEM OF filling those menial jobs needed to maintain the
shelter set the refugees against the administration and against each
other. A persistent and volatile source of tension, exacerbated by
different WRB and WRA perspectives and the lack of clearly defined
policies when the refugees arrived, it was never resolved satisfactorily.

The National Refugee Service advised the WRA and WRB to
arrange for the refugees to maintain their own camp because, psychologically, they needed to assume responsibility for themselves. The
government agencies, needing to minimize costs and to avoid criticism
of government "largesse," readily agreed. Thus expecting to rely on
refugee workers, the camp opened with only 45 permanent and 165
temporary employees. The first group transferred from other WRA
camps. The second included medical and social workers borrowed
from the WRA's Washington office and from private agencies, as well
as 150 Oswegans who performed secretarial, skilled, and unskilled
work that refugees were expected to assume within a few weeks.

The refugees were to maintain their own camp, but how this was
to be done was not yet clear. How should work be assigned? Should
there be compensation, and of what sort? What would the government's responsibilities be? Smart explained to the newly elected Advisory Council that shelter residents would have "full responsibility"
for camp maintenance, that issues such as wages had not yet been
decided, and that the government "wisely" preferred "to let policy
grow out of experience" rather than to make arbitrary decisions in
advance. He asked refugees to work voluntarily during the first few
weeks of "tentative and temporary" arrangements.[2]

96

The first month, while many still suffered from the effects of malnutrition, 150 volunteered, a "remarkable" showing.[3] Five refugee physicians, two dentists, and two nurses began work in the hospital/clinic. Office and activity positions filled readily. But most jobs required physical labor in kitchens, warehouses, and on the grounds, and, as soon as residents learned the nature of the work needed and realized that administration policies remained flexible, the early burst of volunteerism fizzled. Both physically and psychologically, the refugees were not prepared to perform manual labor. Many were too old or still unfit for strenuous work. All had come from cultures that associated such work with social inferiority. And those who were willing wanted to earn wages, an issue first raised aboard the *Henry Gibbins*. In the absence of clear policies, workers staged demonstrations and protests to make their needs known.

Joseph Smart urged the WRA to exert influence on policy decisions and to give shelter residents "the greatest possible measure of freedom." Acknowledging the WRA's role to be "largely custodial," he argued that it would be "impossible" to manage the camp's internal affairs if that were to be taken literally.[4]

Smart lobbied for free enterprise and earned wages within the camp and for work opportunities outside. Several refugees already enjoyed "preferential economic status" because they had funds or sources for assistance, and this created resentment among those less privileged, many of whom had skills capable of earning them income within the fort. Two shoemakers, both in their thirties and both made deaf and dumb in Dachau, had already asked Smart for permission to resume their trade. Others capable of finding employment in Oswego or elsewhere would also suffer unfairly if barred from doing so. Camp restrictions would not prevent writers, scenarists, poets, playwrights, artists, and composers from selling their products through the mail. Smart thought handicrafters "should be given the same opportunity." Finally, refugees deserved compensation "the same as POWs and other internees."[5]

Wages loomed as the principal issue and led, in early September, to the resignation of the Advisory Council after it lost credibility with workers and faith in the WRA. The unfortunate chain of events began after Smart jumped the gun and told the Advisory Council that he expected a wage system to be introduced retroactively on September 1. WRA Director Dillon Myer had said only that wages might become retroactive if the budget allowed, in which case the value of clothing and cash grants already received might be deducted. On September 7 wages still had not been approved and the Advisory Council submitted its resignation. Smart persuaded the council to continue but tension increased.

The Advisory Council wanted both unencumbered wages and wage differentiation, that is, bonuses for jobs deemed least desireable. Wishing to overcome growing resentments, it hoped that private organizations would fund an immediate bonus system and would continue to do so unless the government assumed the responsibility. Smart had to explain that if the refugees received such outside funds they would lose their government allowances.[6]

The government introduced a wage system in late September, but one that increased refugee frustrations. All full-time workers were to earn $18.50 monthly but this income would make them ineligible for cash allowances, which amounted to $8.50 for those eighteen years old or older, $7.00 for adolescents, and $4.00 for children younger than twelve. Regardless of the nature of the work, full-time workers would receive only $10.00 more than nonworkers. The wage was in line with worker earnings in the Japanese Relocation Centers, which paid $12.00–$19.00 monthly, but it was only one-fifth the average earned by domestics working in Oswego. The WRA had hoped to base Japanese-American wages on those paid by the Works Projects Administration, but an unauthorized statement to that effect by a WRA employee provoked a storm of public demands that Japanese-Americans not earn more than "the minimum wage of an American soldier."[7] Wanting to avoid a similar outburst, the WRA hesitated to pay refugee workers anything but agreed to do so when public criticism did not arise.

Shelter wages offered insufficient incentive for unattractive work and they seldom arrived on time. Late payments caused such hardship and feelings of insecurity that in November 1944 Joseph Smart used a personal bank loan to advance partial salaries. The shelter administration blamed the "confusion" on the WRA's having to quickly train replacement personnel for its Washington office.[8] But the problem occurred long before. "Slow pay" had provoked continual complaints in the Japanese Relocation Centers.[9] When promised shelter goods such as overshoes had not arrived by the time deep snow fell, the problem of late wages became even more critical.

Charged with producing needed workers and frustrated in its efforts to provide incentives for them, the Advisory Council introduced its own, unofficial bonus plan. The WRA agreed to permit fifty refugees to take temporary outside harvesting and canning jobs at fifty cents per hour. Two hundred fifty people applied and Smart left the selection to the council. It called a meeting of all workers or would-be workers and, on September 22, they agreed, on a vote of 300–7, that those selected for the outside jobs should "kick-in" 20 percent of their wages for inside bonuses.[10] This meant that outside workers would still earn nearly 40 percent more than those working within the camp. No sanctions existed and compliance was estimated at not more than 50 percent. Nevertheless, this and other "kickback" schemes produced funds for bonuses. Some staff thought the practice "vicious," but Smart understood its logic and practicality and did not interfere.[11]

Smart's relaxed approach permitted several circumventions of internment and employment restrictions. Edith Semjen, whom Oswego High School principal Ralph Faust nicknamed the "Blonde Bombshell," broke the first month of quarantine to go jitterbugging and see a movie in Oswego with Stanley Smart, Joe's son. Covering her with a blanket on the floor of his father's car, he drove easily through the guarded gate.[12] Crawling in and out of the fort through holes dug under the chain-link fence, shelter boys and town girls were sneaking kisses in the back rows of movie theaters and in empty barracks long before the quarantine was lifted.

Traffic through the fence increased after six-hour passes to Oswego became available. Young men such as David Levy and Sam Romano exited through the fence and hitchhiked to New York for "fun" weekends with friends. Slim Elise Neumann (Liesl Newman) remembers having to help free a heavyset woman who became stuck, but the main hole soon grew sufficiently large to accommodate two-way traffic. Thirty-two-year-old Mrs. Neumann, interned with husband, Karl (Carl), and six-year-old Peter, crawled under the fence rather than walking through the gate every Monday, Wednesday, and Friday, when weather permitted, because she did not want to be discovered working illicitly as a maid, at fifty cents hourly, for an Oswego physician.[13] Most refugees chose not to break the rules, but the more adventurous and ambitious had little to fear. Joseph Smart conducted no bed checks and lodged no charges for absenteeism or illicit work.

Shelter residents had come from Italy, where severe shortages meant that survival, both in and out of camps, depended on individual initiative and the black market. The group included a number of "entrepreneurs," none more successful than sixteen-year-old Paul Bokros, who had made liquor for British soldiers stationed near the Bari Transit Camp. He took partners to help him meet the demand and, although he and his family remained official camp residents, they had acquired an apartment in town.[14] The American camp offered no such opportunities. Nevertheless, forty-four-year-old Karl Bader, an electrical engineer, devised makeshift electric hotplates for sale throughout the barracks, a professional photographer sold portraits in Oswego as well as in the fort, and Zlatko and Milica Hirschler, a Yugoslav couple in their thirties, earned twenty dollars each time they strung a shipment of beads for a woman in New York. Others did tailoring, shoe repair, laundering, barbering, and even window-washing for fellow residents.[15]

Private entrepreneurship undoubtedly drew workers from camp jobs. Refugees who had lost everything often felt driven to use internment time to earn and save money for an uncertain future. After her day's work as a maid in Oswego, Elise Neumann washed and ironed for bachelor internees. Husband Karl washed windows for fellow residents. However, Elise also worked part-time in a shelter kitchen and Karl helped maintain camp furnaces. Determined to accumulate a nest egg, they sacrificed other activities. In Kansas City, where they made their home after the shelter closed, the Viennese couple joined an Orthodox synagogue. But they were surprised to learn recently that an Orthodox congregation existed in the shelter. They remembered only a Passover seder. The Neumanns took time from work only for an occasional movie or guest performance. But their hard work in Ferramonte and in Oswego enabled them to start life in Kansas City with four thousand dollars.[16]

A few refugees had property and bank accounts still safe or thought to be safe, but most had lost everything. Those who had currency were required, before leaving Italy, to turn it over to the Allied Control Commission, which promised to return it in converted American dollars soon after the group arrived in America. However, problems with improper receipts, cumbersome procedures, and Anglo-American disagreements over conversion rates caused a seven-month delay. Smart repeatedly protested and the NRS offered to extend 50 percent of the entire sum on credit, an offer the WRA refused. When the money was returned—$85,983 to 585 recipients, an average of $146 apiece—it fell $5,000–$15,000 below the total claimed.[17] Both the delay and the shortfall aroused considerable bitterness and dissatisfaction.

Concerned about an "undercurrent of feeling" against the refugees among clerks and working-class Oswegans, Smart feared that the $86,000 would be used on a spending spree for "luxury items," which would exacerbate resentments. He concluded that the shelter needed an "aggressive" United States War Bonds campaign.[18] Using suggestions from Smart and the Advisory Council, the WRA devised a plan that promoted three savings options. The funds could be left with the Joint Distribution Committee, which made the conversions for the Allied Control Commission; they could be used to buy bonds; or they could be placed in savings accounts in Oswego banks. If the latter option was chosen, the WRA would reduce cash allowances in the same amount as all withdrawals over twenty-five dollars. All but 2 percent chose to buy bonds, in which they invested 71 percent of the transferred funds.[19] Eager to support the war effort and to save for the future, most would have done so even without such pressure.

The labor problem remained the central issue and the Advisory Council continued to insist, without success, that bonuses were the key to resolving it. Finding the council ineffective, workers in early November 1944 elected a Labor Committee to speak for them. It proposed funding bonuses with a fifty-cent monthly tax on every resident over twelve. The following week, the season's first winter storm revealed that the problem was even greater than had been imagined, that keeping furnaces stoked with coal and keeping snow shoveled would pose major challenges. The Yugoslavs voted for a monthly tax of $1.50 on all nonworking refugees and agreed to prorate bonuses among three worker categories, with physicians and heavy laborers receiving the most. Smart had to warn that the government would cut cash allowances if it found the refugees able to afford either tax proposed.[20]

The Advisory Council continued to press for bonuses but increasingly focused on ways of improving working conditions. It called for prompt wage payments, government-provided work clothes, more serviceable tools, and sanctions such as loss of recreational activities for people who refused to work. Smart could not provide work clothes, he managed to obtain some improved tools, and he struggled to make partial wage payments when Washington delayed. He also made half-hearted efforts to apply sanctions but did so neither uniformly nor consistently.

Winter hardships brought the labor problem to a head and forced the Advisory Council to resign once again, this time permanently. A mass workers' meeting on December 4 exploded in angry denunciations of the Advisory Council and of compulsory work requirements. Smart attributed it to three or four "agitators" and fifty to seventy-five malcontents who either refused work outright or claimed unverified disabilities. He concluded that they did not object as much to his labor plan as they did to the Advisory Council. They opposed "any group" appearing to cooperate with the administration and this meant that "the Council pattern does not work at the shelter."[21]

The Advisory Council aroused resentment from the start. The Yugoslavs had argued for proportional representation, which all other groups opposed without being able to agree on a specific alternative. The WRA wished to use the council to counter the influence of national groups and agreed to rely on national representation only if representatives were equally apportioned among the five major groups (Yugoslavs, Germans, Austrians, Poles, and "minority" groups) and were elected at-large. The council quickly found itself caught between an administration that viewed it strictly as a conduit to the refugees, and an increasingly resentful population that wanted to influence policy. Unable either to keep the refugees in line or to influence policy, the council frustrated staff and residents alike, gaining neither's confidence. Similar problems had arisen in the Japanese Relocation Centers, and there too representative councils became lightning rods for labor problems. So long as they deflected hostilities from camp administrators, however, the WRA insisted they were useful.

The Advisory Council's resignation in early December mollified dissidents, and labor tensions eased, in part because a new job rotation system found wide support. Introduced by Morris Burge, Smart's new administrative assistant, it divided all able-bodied men between the ages of eighteen and fifty-five into ten groups of twenty and assigned each to heavy outdoor work two days each month, a plan similar to proposals refugee groups suggested earlier but rejected in favor of bonuses. Rotation succeeded "beyond" Burge's "own expectations," and the Labor Committee disbanded because it no longer felt needed.[22]

Six weeks later a tragic accident threw the camp into its most serious labor crisis. On February 20, a huge frozen coal pile suddenly broke apart and crashed down on a seven-man crew, crushing forty-two-year-old Arpad Buchler. The quiet, well-respected Orthodox leader had just returned to relieve a friend after taking a break himself to visit his ill mother. Once a wealthy merchant in Zagreb, Yugoslavia, he left a young widow and four children under ten. Having brought his family safely through the emotional and physical terrors of Nazism, Buchler now left them destitute and stranded, without relatives, in America. Many attributed his death to his willingness to perform difficult work for which he was untrained and ill equipped.

Demands for proper safety measures and fair compensation swept the camp. Four days later a special *Ontario Chronicle* supplement called on the government to restore "faith in American justice and democracy" by heeding both demands. Workers called for mass protests and camp-wide strikes, which Smart averted with a conciliatory speech that drew a standing ovation. The lack of proper help and supervision with difficult tasks had long stirred resentment. Coal crews supposedly had been trained by an Oswego expert, but refugees spoke "bitterly" about his incompetence and sadistic humor—he found amusement in watching men strain to shovel coal from the tops of trucks that had gates to release it from the bottom.[23] The WRA feared that acquiescing to refugee demands would amount to "acknowledging guilt," but it bowed to Smart's demands for an experienced, permanent foreman.[24]

Compensation presented the crucial issue. Even with proper supervision, the work would continue to hold dangers for inexperienced men, and, fearing permanent disability or death, workers insisted on financial protection for their families. Evacuees in Japanese Relocation Centers received workmen's compensation. But the WRA learned that, because Attorney General Biddle held that the refugees technically were not in the United States, such benefits were "not applicable" in the fort.[25] This condition was open to challenge in the courts, but that procedure would have taken months, even years, so the WRA turned instead to Congress for redress. Sponsors of pending National War Agencies Appropriations legislation added riders extending the United States Employees Compensation Act, as amended, to cover the refugees, retroactive to August 4, 1944.[26] Four months later, in June 1945, shelter residents became eligible for workmen's compensation.

The refugees had to work through the winter without any assurance of protection, and their benefits, like their wages, remained considerably below minimum standards. There were no federal guidelines for computing payments. Smart wanted to use New York State formulas, but the United States Employees Compensation Commission insisted that, as in the case of evacuees in Japanese Relocation Centers, camp earnings should be the determinant. That meant that work-related death payments would total only $3000–$4000, a sum hardly sufficient to alleviate fears among the shelter's poor but middle-class population.

Because of work exemptions and the refugee group's age, sex, and health profile, relatively few people bore the burden of the more difficult physical jobs. Excluding women with small children and people deemed medically unfit, potential adult workers numbered nearly five hundred, but one-third could do only light work and nearly fifty had exemptions because they held "essential" leadership positions such as Advisory Council member, house leader, or religious functionary. Furthermore, the younger and more physically fit generally were also best suited for clerical, recreation, and community activity jobs or for work in the plumbing, carpentry, electrical, and mechanical workshops. This left fewer than 200 men and women for unskilled labor and meant that stocking warehouses, shoveling coal, stoking furnaces, and collecting garbage fell to fewer than 100 men, most of whom were over forty-five and had never before performed manual labor.

Most refugees, including many on whom the most onerous tasks

fell, willingly accepted work assignments, but administrative vacilla-
tion and the lack of clear policy worked in favor of people who
refused. Holdouts suffered little, and complaints that "nothing is
done against non-workers" exceeded all other gripes.[27] At the same
time, those who did more than their share met rejection and ridicule.
Tagged "quislings," they often "succumbed" and refused to continue
working.[28] The administration added to the problem because it often
did not know how many workers it needed and inflated its demands to
compensate for no-shows, a practice that led to complaints that people
sometimes showed up for work, had nothing to do, and were used for
personal chores.

Both residents and staff turned to Curt Bondy and Rudolph
Dreikurs for help with labor problems. Bondy agreed on the need for
wage differentiation and recommended using coercive tactics as well.
Dreikurs did not propose specific measures and insisted that using
punishments and penalties would only increase antagonisms. However, Dreikurs noted that the administration concerned itself primarily with camp maintenance whereas the refugees most wanted
vocational preparation for future readjustment. He urged the WRA
to give the latter more thought. Smart wanted both wage differentiation and more vocational preparation, but the WRA introduced neither during his tenure.

Joseph Smart lacked experience in Washington and enjoyed little
influence in the WRA's Washington office. A worker in western agricultural resettlement, he joined the WRA and headed the Denver
office responsible for five Japanese Relocation Centers before taking a
position with the Institute for Inter-American Affairs in Peru. Dillon
Myer called him home from Peru to assume responsibility for the
Emergency Refugee Shelter. A man who took with him a thick scrapbook of personal mementoes when he resigned ten months later to
work privately on the refugees' behalf, he maintained "excellent rapport" with shelter residents but did not earn high marks as an administrator.[29]

Smart's staff found him likable but difficult to work for. Reuben
Levine, chief of the Administrative Management Division, thought
Smart spent too much time "on matters unrelated to the actual administration of the Shelter" and failed to delegate responsibility.[30] Edward
Quigley, head of the Fiscal and Personnel Section, blamed "all" staff
tensions on cliques that developed in the absence of a specific line of
authority and resulted in low morale.[31] The situation improved somewhat in December 1944, when Morris Burge arrived to serve as
assistant director for administrative duties, for he tended to details
and left Smart to meet with various individuals and groups. However,
Smart continued to overlook rule infractions that did not reach Wash-

ington ears and he hesitated to impose sanctions against recalcitrant workers. His style failed to win support either among his shelter staff or in the WRA home office.

Three directors succeeded Smart, each of whom came directly from the Washington office and had more influence there. Malcolm Pitts, a WRA troubleshooter particularly adept in dealing with staff problems, reported not to WRA Refugee Officer Edward B. Marks, Jr., but directly to Dillon Myer. A man whose influence went "beyond the definition of his job," he served as acting director from May 20 to July 2, 1945.[32] Ed Marks left the National Refugee Service to join the WRA as its principal refugee officer. He met the *Henry Gibbins* in Hoboken, accompanied the refugees to Oswego, remained a frequent visitor, and served as acting director from July 2 to July 20. Clyde E. Powers, WRA chief engineer for camp construction and maintenance, became acting director on July 20 and director on August 19, remaining until the camp closed on February 28, 1946. A cautious bureaucrat, Smart thought him "well-meaning" and "amiable" but "unsuited" to the job.[33]

Reassigning responsibilities, clarifying lines of authority, and tightening procedures, Pitts quickly reshaped the camp's entire administrative structure. He made it clear that "we have a Shelter here and not a hotel," and that people physically capable of working would do so.[34] He resumed rotation, introduced staggered hours, and made changes such as better kitchen ventilation to improve working conditions. At the same time, he promised to ban nonworkers from classes and activities and to withhold their passes and privileges so long as they did not work. The threat of not being able to attend beauty culture classes immediately produced fifty female kitchen workers. Refugee leaders cooperated but refused to discontinue illicit bonuses. According to Reuben Levine, "within a few days some of the fog cleared away."[35] And Edward Quigley reported that even long-smoldering tensions faded.

Pitts's success hinged on his ability to establish control over camp discipline. He repaired the holes in the fence, had it checked regularly, and conducted occasional bed checks. The front gate became the only means of exit or entry. And gatekeepers now recorded all pass violations. Depending on the weather, the camp gave 1000–3000 daily passes each week. During the last seven months, when such records were kept, there were only 211 violations, an average of one a day. Each resulted in temporary suspension of privileges.

There were rule infractions but there was no crime. During the entire life of the shelter the guardhouse was used only seven times, six of them during Pitts's brief tenure. Smart used it only once, to make an example of two men who engaged in a fist fight. He incarcerated them for two days, released them on fourteen-day suspensions, and warned that another incident would find them in jail for the remaining two weeks, a threat he did not carry out. Pitts jailed a frequently disruptive woman for three days, and sentenced five men for four to ten days each because of unauthorized trips to New York, after which he mended the fence. Those found working in Oswego were confined to the fort for a few weeks and had to pay income taxes. Their employers lost other privileges—a dairy owner who supplied products to the fort henceforth required special permission to enter the camp. At the same time, no refugee was accused of a crime either in the fort or in Oswego.

Pitts put the shelter's administrative house in order and Ed Marks maintained the new discipline but created a more humane environment. Staff-resident tensions typified the "basic split" common to all live-in institutions in which a small supervisory staff manages a large confined population. Such a facility is a "social hybrid, part residential community, part formal organization." Its "central feature" is the dissolution of barriers that normally separate work, play, and sleep. [36] This disrupts ordinary social patterns and makes it necessary for people to rely on artificial barriers, such as stereotypes, a situation that further increases tensions. Marks persuaded Reuben Levine and Betty Schroeder, staff dietician, to assign themselves temporarily to regular kitchen work. They found it difficult to continue to think of the refugees as lazy ingrates, and refugee workers saw them less as Gestapo-type figures.

Marks was acting director only eighteen days, but he understood camp dynamics, improved communication, and extended refugee freedoms. He formed a National Board of Representatives, the first official representative refugee body since dissolution of the Advisory Council seven months earlier. The board consisted of eighteen voting members elected on a proportional basis and eighteen nonvoting members elected at large. Several had served on the Advisory Council but now they acted as a legislative body and enjoyed greater responsibility and acceptance.

The board also formed smaller administrative and judicial bodies. It elected a nine-member Executive Committee from among its own members. And it organized a standing Complaint Settlement Committee to consider gripes otherwise sent to the director, and temporary courts of arbitration for occasional problems requiring mediation. The latter consisted of three members of the Executive Committee, one selected by each of the disputants and the third selected by the two first chosen. Punishments included a demand for a statement of apology, an order to repair damages, and/or a fine, which was never more than five dollars and which was used by the National

Board for community welfare. Court rulings could not be appealed. National group rivalries had declined and the five national committee chairmen sat on the Executive Committee, which meant that the entire structure did not face rival power bases as had the Advisory Council.[37]

Clyde Powers maintained Pitts's administrative procedures and Marks's refugee programs and managed the shelter on a "businesslike" basis.[38] Each of Smart's three successors served as "acting director," partly because Germany surrendered before Smart resigned and the WRA expected that it would soon be able to close the shelter. From the start, that expectation obstructed long-range planning.

Only a few days before Marks arrived, Samuel Dickstein, the Democratic chairman of the House Immigration and Naturalization Committee, opened subcommittee hearings on the shelter. He raised hopes that the refugees would be released to live freely in the United States. Before Marks returned to Washington, the full House committee dashed those hopes. It called on the Departments of State and Justice to investigate the practicability of returning the refugees to their homelands. Now the WRA and the Department of the Interior worked not only for the refugees' release from internment but for their admission as immigrants. The issue of freedom overshadowed all camp problems.

EIGHT

Liberty's Struggle

Release us from the fence, which grieves our mind;
Give free our will to life, to work, to truth;
Cut with your sword the knot, that keeps us bound;
Melt with your breath the hate against us Jews![1]

OSWEGO'S NEW RESIDENTS resented internment from the start, and their expressions of dissatisfaction alarmed nearly everyone who had direct contact with or responsibility for the shelter. The War Relocation Authority and National Refugee Service tried to keep the problem from becoming a public issue; at the same time, however, they lobbied strenuously on the refugees' behalf. Until Germany surrendered on May 6, 1945, the campaign called for internment-at-large, also called "sponsored leave." After V.E. Day, the struggle increasingly became one for immigration status.

Refugees, relatives, and friends showered Washington with petitions and letters seeking both special consideration for various individuals and greater freedom for all. One broadly supported refugee petition insisted that Sir Clifford Heathcote-Smith gave "binding" assurances that the group would not be placed in "a closed camp" and would be able to visit American relatives within" a short time."[2] It also held that Rome selectees had good reason to expect only those restrictions placed on all wartime resident aliens. NRS attorney Ann S. Petluck personally delivered to the WRA offices her organization's plea for a relaxation of all restrictions. An army sergeant who turned to the Veterans of Foreign Wars for help noted that "if a serviceman may marry a foreign girl and gain her admittance," surely he "should be able so to serve his mother." After all, "how much more meaning" would his sacrifice have "when his mother too becomes part of America."[3]

The former MGM scenarist who expected to disembark and head

for Hollywood deluged friends, organizations, and officials with requests for help. Sixty-three-year old Ernst Wolff sent Eleanor Roosevelt a personal plea and an essay, which she forwarded, as she did most Oswego mail, to Secretary Morgenthau. In "Storm in the Shelter," Wolff wrote of gratitude for safety and for life's necessities but of hunger for freedom. How had "guests" become prisoners? How was it that "we exist in a legal vacuum, under a sentence more cruel than that of a common criminal—the sentence of uncertainty?" Could it be that we "were foolish to believe that human compassion and decency and liberty were the law in America?" "I want only to be a man," he cried, "as I was before." And that meant having "free will, equality, world-citizenship," and being on "an equal footing with other men on earth who are . . . useful members of human society."[4]

All such pleas to Mrs. Roosevelt, Henry Morgenthau, Jr., Harold Ickes, the WRA , and the WRB elicited responses similar to that which Morgenthau gave Wolff. The secretary reminded Wolff that he had come to this land outside regular immigration procedures, that he would not be permitted to leave the shelter before the war's end, and that he would then return to Europe. Anything else "would not be consistent with the publicly announced conditions under which you were brought to Oswego."[5]

Petitioners could not know that, despite uniform replies, administration figures strongly disagreed among themselves. Oswego's internees saw a seemingly monolithic policy emanating from a government directed by a great humanitarian. They could not blame their confinement on Franklin Roosevelt, the personal benefactor whose picture graced most shelter apartments. It had to be a bureaucratic error, an anachronistic legality, or an unfortunate oversight. If the last, they thought Jewish organizations to blame for suppressing complaints rather than obtaining a correction. The government meant well but blundered. But organized Jewry had retreated.

Journalist Marie Syrkin visited during the euphoric days just after the quarantine was lifted and shelter children entered Oswego schools and found that one month in America had worked a "transformation." The refugees now looked as healthy "as any group of similar numbers elsewhere." They remained exceptional only in that they included "a large percentage" of refined, intelligent and cultured people and had children still "markedly below par" because of stunted growth. But, whereas the government owed the refugees only bare subsistence and was doing "its utmost" on their behalf, the Jewish community owed them "a tolerable life," comparable to that of Jews "living comfortably in New York," and it offered "too little and too late." The refugees expected American Jews to meet them "with flowers" and instead felt "further pauperized" by being left to rely on donations from strangers.[6]

Syrkin's criticism reflected the feelings of many shelter residents but did not recognize organized Jewry's vital involvement. Groups across the country offered assistance as soon as FDR announced the project. The widespread eagerness to help prompted the NRS, in early August, to conduct a meeting in Syracuse with area Jewish Federation and social service agency staffs. They discussed means of avoiding counterproductive competition and wasteful duplication. Two days later an expanded group met in New York to form a Coordinating Committee, which offered extensive aid before the government had a policy on private participation.

The Coordinating Committee included Oswego Jews, Jewish communal representatives from Syracuse and Rochester, and officials from ORT (Organization for Rehabilitation and Training), B'nai B'rith, the Jewish Welfare Board, Agudat Israel, Agudat Harabonim, the Synagogue Council of America, the National Council of Jewish Women, HIAS (Hebrew Immigrant Aid Society), and the National Refugee Service. The last three assumed financial responsibility. Groups added later included the American Jewish Committee, the American Jewish Congress, the Association of Yugoslav Jews in the United States, and the United Galician Jews of America. The American Council of Voluntary Agencies for Foreign Service channeled aid from its constituent organizations through the Coordinating Committee, as did the YMCA, Polish War Relief, Tolstoy Foundation, American Friends Service Committee, Unitarian Service Committee, American Committee for Christian Refugees, Catholic Refugee Committee, and the United Yugoslav Relief Fund.

Initially the Coordinating Committee both lobbied in Washington and functioned as a social agency in Oswego, with the NRS dominant in both efforts. But it soon limited itself to social services. Getting the refugees settled in the camp became the task of half a dozen social workers on loan from the NRS and other private organizations. Shelter children gained acceptance to Oswego schools in part because the Coordinating Committee assumed financial responsibility for texts, materials, and lunch milk. Soon the NRS provided extensive medical and dental care, everything from corrective surgery to hundreds of eyeglasses and fillings, as well as teachers and supplies for dozens of English and vocational classes. The private role was crucial but this help received little recognition because the government insisted that the organizations maintain a low profile and dispense all services through the shelter administration.

Refugees took Jewish organizations to task both for insufficient material assistance and for inadequate political support, particularly the latter, a charge on which organized Jewry, especially the NRS, remained vulnerable. On the one hand, the NRS worked with welfare organizations to achieve major improvements in life within the camp. On the other hand, it worked with Jewish "defense" groups to discourage private political initiatives. They feared arousing anti-Semitic and antirefugee sentiment and so warned friends and relatives of the refugees. By late December the NRS could assure the WRA that it had checked most independent efforts.[7]

Most early reactions to the new arrivals were favorable. Every major New York and Washington paper, and dozens throughout the country, carried sympathetic stories. The August 1944 editions of *Life* and *Mademoiselle* magazines included photographic essays that brought Edith Semjen several marriage proposals, including one from an army private who tried to have her released to his mother in Denver after he was transferred overseas.[8] The publicity prompted such an avalanche of mail and packages that even Dillon Myer, who had encouraged widespread coverage, found the attention "totally out of proportion" to the camp's significance.[9]

Criticism by three public figures created considerable consternation in WRB and WRA offices and in the White House. On August 10 the *New York Post* reported that Senator Robert R. Reynolds (D., N.C.) would soon launch a campaign to prevent Oswego from becoming "the entering wedge" for additional free ports. The next day Reynolds inserted into the *Congressional Record* a lengthy attack on FDR by American Coalition leader John B. Trevor. It argued that the president had no legal or moral justification for such an "extraordinary" circumvention of American immigration law. Trevor claimed that Middle East camps could take them, that their presence was not analogous to POWs because they had no equivalent statutory recognition in international agreements, and that, in effect, they were public charges. Reynolds thought it "reasonable" to assume that the refugees were Nazi or Fascist subversives, in which case FDR had acted traitorously and they should be "mandatorily" excluded.[10]

Ohio Governor John W. Bricker, the GOP vice-presidential nominee, accused FDR of intentional deceit. Not only had the president overstepped his constitutional authority by lifting immigration restrictions in his "usual hush-hush" manner, but he had given Congress false assurances that the group consisted primarily of women and children when in fact it included a majority of males, most of whom were "not laboring men" but "writers, lawyers, artists and intellectuals."[11] Reynolds was an ardent restrictionist but Bricker had endorsed the Alfred E. Smith petition for "free ports" only five months earlier. His attack stunned the administration, particularly since

Dewey, who had called for the admission of 100,000 refugees and had also signed the Smith petition, did not repudiate him. The WRB was on the defensive.

Westbrook Pegler, the third critic, was the most hostile. In his syndicated column of September 26, he accused the president of outright "fraud." On November 14 he suggested FDR's motive. Suspecting "a plot to let in all the Communists of Europe," Congress had recently "turned down cold" a request from Attorney General Biddle that it suspend all immigration laws. Pegler accused Roosevelt of exploiting American compassion and acting unilaterally to "let this batch in," thereby circumventing the law he had been unable to change.

Reynolds, Bricker, and Pegler struck sensitive administration nerves but did not arouse broad support. Neither, however, did they stir rebuttal except among liberals who could be expected to react. On October 26 a *New York Post* editorial labeled Bricker "the nationalist, nativist side of the 'liberal internationalist' Dewey campaign." It pictured him gathering Coughlin supporters while Dewey fished for Willkie votes. Two weeks later FDR won an unprecedented fourth term and the refugees stirred little postelection interest. Nevertheless, stinging criticism during the campaign encouraged future caution.

Another series of critical comments aroused consternation of a different sort. The Yiddish daily regularly carried a column "News and Views," written in English by its editor, Samuel Margoshes. Having visited the shelter at the request of World Zionist leader Nahum Goldman, Margoshes on August 13, 1944, described unsatisfactory camp conditions that provoked two schools of thought among the refugees. The first wanted to take "drastic action," and the second, those with "cooler heads," insisted on "caution and patience." He thought the problems had gotten out of hand in part because Jewish organizations had been inadequately involved. The refugees felt "deserted." "Only" the World Jewish Congress and Agudat Israel had their religious leaders in the camp.

The following day Margoshes wrote, "The honeymoon is definitely over . . . a grey reality begins to rear its ugly head." The right to work had become as important as freedom. "Many refugees dread the prospect of sitting idle behind the wire entanglement . . . the querulous mood . . . is intensified by the feeling that they have been deserted by the national Jewish organizations." He found tempers "hot" and "likely to flare" but thought that, "with prudence and courage," Jewish organizations could prevent a serious problem from developing. However, on August 15, declaring that he had decided "to tell all," he described the conditions and results of internment—inadequate clothing, a lack of recreation facilities, an absence of news sources, and beggary induced by poor quality and insufficient food. Jewish organizational representatives were working on the scene but were not known to the refugees. "It all adds up to a picture of sullen disappointment."

The NRS and other groups sought but failed to obtain a retraction. Rabbi Stephen S. Wise publicly denied the Margoshes charges and assured Ickes that "no sensible person" would encourage the refugees "to seek admission to this country at this time."[12]

Unbeknown to the refugees, however, their demands for freedom led quickly to actions on their behalf within the administration. Less than two weeks after the shelter opened, at the WRA's urging, Interior Secretary Ickes asked Attorney General Biddle to approve a program of camp leaves. One month later, Biddle vetoed any changes in the internment policy. He noted assurances he had given to Senator Reynolds, chairman of the Senate Military Affairs Committee, warned that any relaxation "might affect" additional government rescue efforts, and suggested that postwar immigration could be damaged "generally." The attorney general claimed "legal considerations" but offered only political reasons for his action.[13]

The Biddle letter opposing any internment changes came to be seen as a statement of official policy but did not deter either the WRA or the Interior Department. Three days later, Myer asked Pehle to approve a "modified type of leave parole arrangment," and Pehle passed the request to the White House.[14] Pehle had approved Oswego school enrollments and six-hour passes without presidential permission, but he had in hand requests for both from Oswegans. In view of FDR's promises to Congress and sensitivity to criticism, the WRB director would not act similarly in the matter of releasing them from Oswego. Special Assistant James Abrahamson prepared a WRB memorandum that advised the submission of a request to the president worded so as to elicit a reply stating the Oswego refugees had the same rights as any other refugees in this country. Such a statement could then be used as a "start" toward release.[15]

Biddle took an inflexible position, the refugees continued to clamor for freedom, and clear divisions appeared within the administration. Ickes, who had little direct contact with Roosevelt, spoke for the WRA. Biddle and Morgenthau, who had considerably more contact, controlled the WRB. The task of justifying the WRB's position to the WRA fell to James Abrahamson.

Forced to do an about-face, Abrahamson explained that the WRB policy might appear "harsh" but that there were factors "of more overriding importance than individual desires." Chief among them, he explained at a joint November 17 meeting, were "the integrity of the Administration in the eyes of the public" and "the establishment of a liberal postwar immigration policy." He noted that "one of the refugee agencies [NRS?]" had even informally warned him restrictionists would capitalize on "any misstep."[16]

Pehle had hoped to open additional temporary havens but this was no longer possible. Hungary had held the last major Jewish community and it was now decimated. The exigencies of the presidential campaign and news of the Hungarian deportations led him to announce on October 16 that sufficient facilities existed in the Mediterranean area and additional refugees would not be brought to the United States. Thereafter, he lost interest in Oswego. Months later he sat passively and watched Morgenthau tell a Jewish delegation that they should "keep faith" with their dead president's wishes and not seek to revise the internment rules.[17]

Franklin D. Roosevelt opposed all efforts to alter the conditions under which he brought the refugees to Oswego. A direct appeal for sponsored leaves from the NRS to the president in late 1944 prompted him to write to Biddle on January 17, 1945. That note, the single recorded presidential statement regarding the campaign on the refugees' behalf, declared that he "definitely" wanted them to return to Europe as soon as this could safely be arranged. In the meantime, he wanted them to remain confined to Oswego.[18] Thereafter, Biddle and, to a lesser extent, Morgenthau, managed the opposition. Biddle did not, however, reveal the president's instructions to Ickes until mid-March. He did so at that time to alleviate the pressure on William O'Dwyer, who had succeeded John Pehle as WRB director.[19]

Idealistic and pragmatic, imaginative and calculating, Franklin D. Roosevelt understood subtleties of power and nuances of policy better than any president before or since. He had an uncanny ability to stand aloof from the fray and attract accolades for humanitarian impulses that he did not translate into actual policy. It was enough to know that this president, engaged in a deadly Zoroastrian battle with evil incarnate, had his heart in the right place. The Oswego refugees shared this attitude with most Americans, especially Jews and other minorities whom the New Deal made room for in the councils, if not the seats, of power.

The NRS and WRA did not know that their true opponent resided in the White House. The NRS had found common interest with the WRB in the effort to obtain temporary havens, and it found common interest with the WRA in the effort to reduce camp tensions. One week before Biddle responded in the negative to Ickes's initial request for a leave program, WRA Director Myer turned to the Coordinating Committee for its help in formulating a specific leave proposal. The Coordinating Committee soon limited itself to social services and the request fell to the NRS. The NRS, which operated both as a welfare agency in New York and as a voice for refugees nationally, did not form a second organization to deal with political questions but worked closely with the American Jewish Committee, the Joint Distribution Committee, and others.

In early December, the WRA gave Ickes an NRS proposal that suggested three paths to greater refugee freedoms: (1) short-term leaves for specific periods of time; (2) internment-at-large for the entire group, an economy measure that would permit closing the camp; and (3) immigration visas for those who could qualify. Nearly 31,000 unused quota spaces remained for 1943–44 from the five countries represented by 890 of the Oswego refugees.[20] However, until hostilities ceased, the WRA thought the second option, now referred to as "sponsored leave," most achievable. The NRS would arrange transportation from Oswego to places of temporary resettlement and would be responsible for housing, welfare, medical care, and, where possible, job placement. The refugees would report regularly not to the Immigration and Naturalization Service of the Department of Justice but to district WRA offices. The plan did not address questions of ultimate destination; the NRS would return the refugees to Oswego for ultimate disposition.

The "Latin American Internees" offered the WRB a precedent for temporary havens and they now served equally well as a model for sponsored leave. In the spring of 1944 it had not served WRB purposes to mention that one group among the Latin American Internees, Jewish refugees indiscriminately picked up as "enemy" aliens, now lived as "internees-at-large" throughout the midwest.

Seventy-nine hapless Jews had been included among enemy aliens rounded up throughout Central and South America in 1942. The NRS learned that they were imprisoned, along with Nazis and Nazi sympathizers, in United States Army camps and succeeded in having them transferred from the jurisdiction of the State Department to that of the Justice Department, which then gathered them as a group and moved them to an Alien Control Center at Camp Algiers near New Orleans. The Justice Department also agreed to conduct case-by-case investigations and hearings. They continued to be classified as "excludables without visas," subject to warrants of deportation drawn but not served for the duration of the war. However, after individual clearances, the Justice Department paroled them to the NRS, which arranged for them to live freely, under local agency supervision, in midwestern communities.[21]

Release from Oswego would require either paroles or visas. The WRA focused initially on the former. However, prospects for the latter appeared to improve by late 1944, when Edward Stettinius, Jr., succeeded Cordell Hull as secretary of state. Breckinridge Long had left the State Department but aides such as Howard K. Travers remained. WRB Special Assistant James Abrahamson expected Stettinius to remove Travers as Visa Division chief and either create an assistant secretary for refugees or move the department's refugee advisor into the office of Assistant Secretary Dean Acheson, where the WRB had found allies during its campaign for free ports. Abrahamson felt confident that Stettinius wanted a "humane" and "fairly administered" refugee policy.[22]

Members of the Immigration and Naturalization Service offered additional encouragement. Edward J. Shaughnessey suggested that, although theoretically the refugees did not reside within the United States, they might still be considered eligible for preexamination, which in turn would make immigration possible. Shaughnessey met with Professor Joseph P. Chamberlain and Joseph E. Beck (NRS), Mrs. W. P. Schiefflier (American Friends Service Committee), and Isadore Asofsky (HIAS). The immigration officer advised them to raise the subject of preexamination with the WRB and to give them "the most appealing" cases first.[23] One-third of the refugees were stateless and would pose a special problem, but, he assured them, the State Department could, if it chose, waive document requirements or accept substitutes.

Preexamination offered a little-known means of circumventing the requirement that visa applicants reside outside the United States. Used primarily to arrange immigration for aliens who had entered the country illegally or overstayed temporary visas, it relied on an unofficial arrangement with the Canadian government, which permitted approved individuals to cross the border for a few hours in order to complete necessary paperwork with an American consulate in Canada.

The WRA had other options if it wished to divide the refugees into separate groups. Pehle thought special consideration might be given to the fifty-one refugees who qualified for nonquota or preference visas because they had spouses living as resident aliens or citizens in the United States or had sons serving in the Armed Forces. The NRS raised the possibility of making special arrangements for all who already had quota numbers or could otherwise qualify for immigration. However, the WRA insisted on treating all the refugees as one group.

The WRB remained officially responsible for shelter policy but, from late 1944, increasingly left administrative matters to the Department of the Interior and questions of internment regulations to Attorney General Biddle. It expected to close its offices by June 30, 1945 (the actual closing did not occur until September 15), and began to reduce both its staff and its commitments. Between mid-December

1944 and late February 1945 all but three of its thirteen nonclerical Washington staff left, most, including John Pehle, to return to full-time Treasury work. Ed Marks reported that neither General William O'Dwyer, Pehle's successor, nor Florence Hodel, his special assistant, could get excited about the shelter when there were "too many other important things."[24] Viewing it as a political burden, O'Dwyer expected UNRRA to accept responsibility for it and, in the meantime, was relieved to rely on Biddle.

The attorney general quickly repudiated Shaughnessey. He firmly opposed "any arrangement" that would permit shelter residents to gain immigration without first returning to Europe. Using preexamination for the Oswego refugees would draw attention to its use, threaten its continuance, and, most important, would "breach faith" with Congress.[25] Ickes continued to press O'Dwyer to show "leadership," but to no avail.[26] The struggle over the refugees' current dilemma and future disposition increasingly became a tug-of-war between Ickes and Biddle.

A loose coalition of Jewish and non-Jewish groups—NRS, American Council of Voluntary Agencies for Foreign Service, American Friends Service Committee, Unitarian Service Committee, American Committee for Christian Refugees, Catholic Refugee Committee, YMCA, and the United Yugoslav Relief Fund—discussed bringing public pressure to bear and seeking cabinet-level meetings. Interior and the WRA shared their frustration but vetoed using outside pressure on the administration. Both Ickes and Biddle refused to meet with a private delegation. The NRS understood "fully" and agreed to use restraint.[27] Frustrated by the lack of clear authority as the WRB became increasingly inactive, the Interior secretary never managed "to call the score."[28]

Ickes's anger temporarily shifted from Biddle to the refugees after he received the Bondy, Dreikurs, and Gruber reports. The feisty, long-time liberal, an early supporter of Peter Bergson, concluded in mid-March that the shelter was "a mistake" and those who could not adjust to internment might be better off returning to Europe. As if to justify his apparent capitulation, he added, "I can imagine nothing better calculated to add fuel to the anti-Semitic sentiment in this country than to permit almost a thousand foreign-born citizens, most of them Jews, to come and go at their pleasure in this country."[29] That same day, however, Ed Marks informed Joseph Smart that Ickes was giving serious thought to making a direct appeal to the White House.[30] The secretary had learned of FDR's January 17 letter to Biddle.

Prospects for release from Oswego seemed dismal but there arose the possibility of limited leaves for a special few. The attorney general "seemed to admit," at a March 16 meeting with Abe Fortas and William O'Dwyer, that questions of sponsored leave and preexamination involved political rather than legal issues and, in view of the evidence of growing deterioration within the camp, he appeared ready to consider temporary leaves for a limited number on medical grounds.[31] He indicated, however, that this would have to be done surreptitiously; the Justice Department would look the other way. Fortas persuaded him to accept a formal proposal in order to protect his credibility. Four days later O'Dwyer passed six WRA cases to Biddle for immediate attention:

> One family of three had, during six years of flight, suffered experiences that were severe even when compared with those of other refugees. The wife and mother seemed to be all right when she arrived but developed threatening paranoic behavior that caused her to be labeled "crazy" and led to the ostracism of her husband and eleven-year-old daughter. The WRA wanted to parole her to family members in New York who would arrange out-patient psychiatric treatment for her.

> A sixty-one-year-old man, alone in the shelter, had seen his wife deported to Poland, had been tortured in both Dachau and Buchenwald, and had lost the use of one foot. He suffered a paralytic stroke on the way to Oswego and could not care for himself. His three children, now all American citizens, included two sons in the Armed Forces and a daughter who wanted to care for him at her home in Philadelphia.

> A seventeen-year-old girl, orphaned by the Nazis, had joined another family in order to be accepted for Oswego. Emotionally the age at which she had been separated from her parents, she had no close attachments within the shelter and remained withdrawn. A paternal grandmother and two uncles, both physicians, lived in the United States and wanted very much to care for her.

> A thirteen-year-old boy lived in the shelter with his mother and two illegitimate infant sisters. The refugees cruelly rejected them and he developed antisocial behavior. Shelter welfare workers thought him intelligent and in need of a supportive and structured environment. They concluded that he would be better off in an institution for emotionally disturbed children.

> A nearly blind, diabetic widow had an especially difficult time in Oswego's harsh climate. The WRA wanted to release her to a daughter and son-in-law on Long Island who were eager to care for her.

> A forty-four-year-old man had grown despondent and withdrawn because he feared not being able to support his wife and nine-year-old son, who now lived in New York. He had lost considerable weight and could not work. The WRA asked that he be reunited with his family in New York.[32]

Biddle did not respond to these first six cases, but throughout late March and early April the WRA maintained a steady stream of requests. Some children needed foster homes. Others needed a vacation from the fort and their parents and the WRA had offers of summer camp scholarships. The WRA also asked that shelter residents having to be hospitalized outside Oswego be allowed to have their closest relative in the shelter accompany them.[33]

Franklin D. Roosevelt's death and Harry S. Truman's inauguration did not mark any change in policy. The succession on April 12 marked the end of an era but did not spell a new beginning. Saddened bureaucrats conducted the affairs of government as usual. The refugees did not know that the benefactor for whom they deeply grieved was responsible for the restrictions against which they chafed. Neither did they know that Francis Biddle and Henry Morgenthau, Jr., who preferred to maintain a low profile on Oswego matters, would continue to insist on faithful adherence to Roosevelt's wishes.

Two developments in late May brought the campaign for more freedoms a change of cast and of tactical priorities Shelter Director Joseph Smart resigned to introduce a public drive on the refugees' behalf. And Samuel Dickstein (D., N.Y.) threw his congressional weight behind their cause. Germany's surrender on May 6, only twenty-four days after Roosevelt's death, made continued internment increasingly difficult to support. But the camp could not be closed until the question of the refugees' ultimate disposition could be resolved. Much to the dismay of the NRS, both Smart and Dickstein began a public campaign for immigration.

Smart and Dickstein thought Oswego separate from other refugee and immigration questions, but the NRS, fearing that a special campaign on behalf of the Oswego refugees would obscure the larger problem and thus jeopardize possibilities for displaced persons generally, thought them publicity hungry and irresponsible. It wanted to postpone the question of ultimate status and continue instead to lobby for a program of sponsored leaves. Seventeen thousand aliens without permanent visas lived in the United States and it seemed unlikely that they would be deported. Congress would undoubtedly grant them permanent visas and such legislation could easily "blanket in" the Oswego refugees as well.[34] However, the NRS could not halt the public campaign and it seemed likely that restrictionists would soon pick up the challenge. The NRS felt compelled to act.

President Truman would have to intervene, but how could he be approached? The NRS, American Jewish Committee, Jewish Labor Committee, and Anti-Defamation League of B'nai B'rith agreed to seek administration support for a direct appeal to the White House.

Their representatives, along with Ruth Gruber and an officer of the American Friends Service Committee, held separate meetings on the morning of June 5 with Ickes, Morgenthau, and O'Dwyer. Ickes objected to the Smart-Dickstein initiatives but saw no other course if Biddle remained adamant. He warned, however, that restrictionist sentiment remained strong on Capitol Hill, "particularly [regarding] Jews."[35] Dispirited and pessimistic, he urged them to press Biddle. However, Morgenthau insisted that any violation of his "promise" to the dead Roosevelt would mean, "I could not sleep with my conscience."[36] He insisted that only Congress should choose to disregard FDR's instructions.

Whereas Ickes seemed defeated and Morgenthau intransigent, O'Dwyer was now enthusiastic and eager to help. The WRB director revealed that he would soon propose sponsored leave to his three-member board, and he expected to take the issue directly to Truman. That same afternoon, William O'Dwyer announced his candidacy for mayor of New York. The following day he transferred official responsibility for shelter policy to the Department of the Interior, along with a strong recommendation for sponsored leave. And four days later the *New York Times* quoted him as saying, "It doesn't make sense in a land of freedom to keep these people confined as though they were in a concentration camp." O'Dwyer intended to turn what he had considered a political burden into a political asset. The delegation could only hope that the ebullient candidate wielded influence sufficient "to get results."[37]

That same week Harold Ickes took the Oswego question directly to Harry Truman. Speaking informally, he asked the president for permission to implement sponsored leave within thirty days. Truman respected Ickes as "an able administrator" who "was not a special interest man." But he also considered him "a troublemaker," someone "difficult to get along with."[38] The secretary had had little influence in the Roosevelt administration and lost even that under his successor. Truman agreed only to forward Ickes's request to Biddle, whose resignation as attorney general had already had announced.[39]

Biddle answered Truman's inquiry only two days before Thomas G. Clark succeeded him as attorney general. He indicated there were no legal obstacles to sponsored leave. He continued to have only two objections and each could be overcome. First, Roosevelt's original promises should be honored, which could be done with "measures calculated to satisfy" Congress and assure that "no breach of faith would be involved."[40] Second, immigration laws needed to be upheld, which required only that the attorney general exercise his authority to waive grounds for inadmissibility and that the secretary of state exercise his power to waive required documentation. Biddle noted that

Ickes proposed to discuss sponsored leave with key senators and representatives and recommended that he obtain approval from the Senate and House Immigration Committees. If Truman agreed to sponsored leave he should notify Congress and indicate the committees' approval. HST asked Ickes to proceed accordingly.

It was becoming increasingly clear that the refugees' future would have to be decided soon. All interested parties preferred to close the camp as quickly as possible. But they disagreed on the fate of its occupants. Should they be returned to Europe or permitted to stay? If permitted to stay, should they be given sponsored leave or regular immigration? Dickstein announced that he would soon open congressional hearings on the Oswego issue.

NINE

Freedom Achieved

I would rather die than go back.
> Jacob Ernest Kahn, February 25, 1945

Would I like to stay in America? I don't know what I would like. What is good for a Jew? What is a Jew in Europe? Nothing!
> Henry Macliach, April 8, 1945

I will never go back to Germany. I can't. The agreement? Just a formality.
> Miriam Sommerburg, April 8, 1945

None of us intended to stay in the States. . . . My dad said, "Let's get out of Italy, at least the kids will eat for a while. We'll get out of the war and get back on our feet. Then, when the war is over, we'll come back."
> David Hendell, October 31, 1979[1]

RETURN OR ADMISSION—that was the issue. It colored thinking during the campaign for temporary havens, it influenced the selection in Italy, and it dominated the struggle to ease internment. Theoretically, everyone agreed the refugees would leave at the war's end. But contradictions existed from the start.

Restrictionists opposed every scheme for temporary admissions because they believed American-Jewish organizations would make it nearly impossible to removed from the United States any refugees temporarily admitted. The State Department used this argument to oppose half a dozen bills for temporary admissions, the last introduced only two months before the WRB was announced.[2]

Rescue advocates preferred to minimize or postpone dealing with the political and practical problems inherent in a policy that would return victims to the places of their trauma in wartorn Europe. They preferred to note merely that the policy complied with international agreements made in April 1943 at the Bermuda Conference. No one challenged FDR's unequivocal promise to Congress on June 12, 1944, that "upon termination of the war they will be sent back to their homelands."[3] Each family head signed an agreement to that effect. Still, return was not legally binding. FDR's statement had only political import and, as noted earlier, the refugee agreement, intended only to have psychological significance, presented problems in translation that rendered it ineffective.

The selection itself offered concrete reasons for believing the commitment to return a mere "formality." Sir Clifford Heathcote-Smith, seemingly speaking for the American government, promised the Rome group that they would be able to stay. Nearly one-third came from the camp at Fiermonti and they had less obvious reasons to expect the same. Ackermann and Korn had delegated the Fiermonti selection to American Service Committee representatives. Wishing to be most helpful, they divided applicants into four groups, ranked according to immigration prospects, and selected the best prospects first. On learning this, Pehle feared it might discredit his efforts to establish additional shelters. He flirted with the notion of expelling "the entire group to Canada" immediately after the November 1944 presidential election.[4]

Most Oswego refugees wanted to immigrate. Sixty percent had active immigration cases pending. Many others had been refused on technicalities used during the Depression and war years to hold immigration far below legal limits. Some saw Oswego as a short-cut to immigration. Others thought it a second chance. When they found themselves interned indefinitely and facing an uncertain future, for reasons they did not understand, they fell victim to wrenching mood swings. People "either bathed in gloom" or grew feverish with "elation and optimism."[5]

Roosevelt's death and rumors about the pending dissolution of the camp created grief and hysteria. The rumors took on new meaning in late April, when Smart informed several refugee groups that he had been informally advised of plans to return them to Europe. News of Hitler's death and a series of German surrenders that climaxed in the unconditional surrender of all German forces on May 6 brought both relief and trepidation.

Two days later Joseph Smart announced to a large crowd in the shelter theater that he would resign as director to campaign for their freedom, a campaign he expected to culminate in congressional action. The resignation, effective May 31, took the WRA by surprise. Smart recalls that he conferred with Eleanor Roosevelt but not with Dillon Myer, an "uncharacteristic rudeness" that he later regretted.[6] Ostensibly, he acted in response to a petition drive organized by the camp's national groups. In actuality, refugee leaders working under his tutelage had to resurrect the national bodies in order to strengthen the petition. When the Council of Jewish Federations refused his request for $25,000—NRS officials objected to his tactics and questioned how the money would be spent—Smart again turned to the refugees, and they raised $10,000 from friends and relatives.[7]

Smart gave refugee activists opportunities to work on their own behalf and attracted new supporters. Noting that there remained 125,512 unused quota numbers for the five largest nationalities in the shelter during the previous three and one-half years, the Oswego Citizens' Advisory Committee also identified shelter residents as "unique" and separate from other refugee groups. It sent petitions to Truman and Congress, the latter presented May 28 by Republican Representative Hadwan C. Fuller of the Oswego-Oneida district, calling for freedom of movement for the entire group and immigrant status for those who wanted it.[8]

Smart also found support among prominent Americans. People who agreed to be listed on the letterhead of his "Friends of Fort Ontario–Guest Refugees" included Eleanor Roosevelt, Thomas E. Dewey, Albert Einstein, UNRRA Director Herbert H. Lehman, labor leaders David Dubinsky and John L. Lewis, historian Charles A. Beard, theologian Reinhold Niebuhr, broadcaster Robert St. John, writer Katherine Anne Porter, and singer Sophie Tucker. William O'Dwyer joined the list after announcing his entrance into the New York mayoralty race. More than three thousand Americans joined the "Friends" and many wrote to Washington on the refugees' behalf. Smart also hired a lobbyist who was formerly legal counsel for the Department of Labor and specialized in immigration.

The public campaign, not coincidentally, opened on two fronts. That same week Samuel Dickstein, chairman of the House Immigration and Naturalization Committee, announced congressional hearings on the Oswego question. Disregarding Attorney General Biddle's efforts to dissuade him, Dickstein turned to Smart and obtained, in confidence, summaries of likely testimony from suggested witnesses.[9]

Assuring the WRA that he had a "friendly" subcommittee, the frequently flamboyant congressman appeared confident that he could get results.[10] The refugees did not need legislation to obtain immigrant status, but there were precedents for such a course of action—several thousand aliens who had entered before enactment of the National Origins Quota System could not get quota numbers and found themselves with illegal or questionable status until legislation in 1929 and 1934 made it possible for them to become immigrants. Restrictionists might still block such an effort, in which case a strong subcommittee report could be used to force action in the attorney general's office. Such a report would recommend closing the shelter, granting immigration to the qualified, and arranging sponsored leave for the rest.

The Dickstein Hearings brought forth fifty-nine witnesses with not one dissenting voice among them. Held in the fort on June 25 and 26, 1945, the two-day show presented stirring evidence that continued confinement was unnecessary, unhealthy, and unconscionable. William O'Dwyer set the tone with a strong plea that the congressmen "open the door" and make it possible for the attorney general to act. Ed Marks noted the refugees' close ties to America and the assistance available to them through family and private organizations. Malcolm Pitts reported government costs, occupational patterns, and the group's low incidence of camp violations. Ruth Gruber stressed that the refugees had been selected carefully and cherished deep commitments to democracy.[11]

Fourteen Oswego citizens testified to the refugees' desirability. Educators felt especially enthusiastic. Oswego School Superintendent Charles R. Riley thought shelter students "definitely superior," a "specially selected group." Principal Ralph Faust reported that, after only one year back in school, eight of forty refugee students qualified for Oswego High School's chapter of the National Honor Society. Campus Elementary School Vice-President Eric Brunger summed up the general feeling. He felt "rather selfish" because only Oswego was privileged to add such a talented and highly motivated group to its student population.[12] Others told of the refugees' suffering in Europe and their ability to integrate readily in the United States—forty-one wished to enlist in the American Armed Forces but could not do so because they did not reside in the United States (see App. 2). Only one internee expressed a desire to go elsewhere—thirteen-year-old Vlado Arnstein wished to settle in Palestine.

The subcommittee voted unanimously to close the camp—no one wished to see Uncle Sam spend $600,000 to maintain the facility for another year—but they could not agree on the disposition of its population. Congressman Fischer warned, one day before the hearings, that everyone did not see eye to eye, and it would not be "as easy as Sam Dickstein expects."[13] He insisted throughout that the refugees' future should be left entirely to the discretion of the Department of Justice.

Dickstein ignored Fischer's opposition and Lowell Stockman's reservations and promised the refugees freedom. In an exclusive interview with the *Ontario Chronicle,* he called for their release even if it cost "one million dollars," a reference to the bond that might be necessary.[14] Such a bond, he felt certain, could be raised no matter what the cost. The refugees could also be released on their own recognizance or be declared to be in the United States illegally, in which case they could obtain preexamination and enter Canada to apply for American visas. The congressman preferred the last but viewed all three possibilities as steps toward immigration and indicated he expected a decision in thirty to sixty days.

Having the refugees declared illegal residents meant repudiating the notion of free ports, an issue not yet tested in the courts but one that had aroused academic interest. In an article offered as evidence at the Dickstein Hearings, legal scholar Albert G. D. Levy reasoned, "free ports for humans do not exist."[15] Levy argued that the refugees resided in America and the talk about free ports merely confused the issue. Biddle was avoiding the issue, as evidenced by his refusal to make a judgment regarding the citizenship of children born in the camp. Even if the shelter was analogous to Ellis Island, its residents would be deemed to be on American soil and under American jurisdiction.

Neither the subcommittee nor the full House Immigration and Naturalization Committee lived up to Chairman Dickstein's assumptions and expectations. Two members of the subcommittee and a majority on the full committee clearly favored return, and this seemed explicit in a resolution passed by the latter. It asked the departments of State and Justice to determine, "at the first opportunity," the practicability of return and requested that the attorney general, "in accordance with the provisions of existing laws and procedures," declare those unable to do so to be illegal aliens subject to immediate deportation proceedings.[16] Interior Secretary Ickes noted that continued delay would interfere with efforts to formulate a postwar immigration policy and urged both the attorney general and the secretary of state to proceed.

Ickes and the WRA did not see such action as precluding immigration. The resolution offered something for everyone and rejected nothing. Subcommittee Counsel Thomas Dooley assured Ruth Gruber that declaring the refugees illegal aliens subject to deportation also made them eligible for preexamination. Nothing had been gained but nothing had been lost. Dickstein had merely drawn public attention to the issue. The matter still rested with the departments of State and Justice. Neither was ready to act.

An investigation would most likely lead to one of three courses of action, each of which could still lead to immigration. First, the refugees could be preexamined and apply for immigrant visas. Preexamination could be given after a six-month residency or, if the attorney general chose to contradict earlier statements, he could rule that they had already been in residence within the United States and were thus immediately eligible. In either case, the secretary of state and attorney general would have to waive required documents. Second, they might refuse to waive documentation, in which case the refugees would be subject to deportation but might also be placed on parole, which could also lead to preexamination. Third, deportation proceedings might actually occur but these would be lengthy, open to challenge, and could still lead to preexamination. Deportation hearings would stigmatize the group and create a public relations problem but not necessarily preclude admission.

The public relations question had international as well as national consequences and loomed larger as the enormity of the displaced persons problem in Europe became more apparent. Oswego could not be treated in isolation. Other nations with far more refugees looked to the United States for direction. Earl Harrison, the dean of the University of Pennsylvania Law School who had been United States commissioner of immigration and now served as American representative to the IGC, pleaded for thoughtfulness. With "the streams of displaced peoples in Europe so swollen and overflowing," it was essential to "preserve the status quo" until the flow subsided.[17] The refugees should remain, interned or free.

Forcible repatriation would complicate overseas problems but it would also contradict international and American commitments. UNRRA opposed using any coercion to achieve repatriation.[18] Marks informed Myer that, with the single exception of Russians returned to the Soviet Union because of special arrangements with Stalin, United States policy had strictly followed a War Department declaration issued on July 7, 1945, which stated that no one "will be compelled to return to his former domicile except to stand trial for a criminal offense."[19]

American commitments made forced repatriation unlikely, and the House Committee on Immigration and Naturalization resolution indirectly raised possibilities for immigration, but this situation was not understood within the fort. Ed Marks blamed much of the growing dissension within the camp on Smart's continued involvement, particularly his contention that the Friends of Fort Ontario represented the refugees' "only hope of salvation."[20] Smart did not visit the camp until late July, but Doris Smart, his wife, continued to live there and met regularly with a small "Freedom Committee" to report on his activities and solicit financial support. The Smarts may have contributed to refugee strife over strategy, but disagreements sharpened because the debate had become public, because internees still had little concrete information, and because some began to fear that time was running out.

The refugees wished to live freely in the United States and most hoped to remain permanently, but initially a significant number had expected to return, particularly Yugoslavs. Sixty-six Yugoslavs did choose repatriation, thirteen in May 1945 and fifty-three the following August. A few dozen others hoped to find and join family members in other parts of Europe or elsewhere. However, by late summer few still clung to "the illusion" that they had homes and businesses to which they could return.[21] Europe no longer offered them a future. They became desperate to remain.

Bernard Guillemin felt desperate from the start. In mid-May he took action. On May 16, in the *Oswego Palladium Times*, the forty-seven-year-old German, Roman Catholic journalist criticized internment as contrary to American ideals. His letter elicited a flurry of responses for and against the refugees' cause and sent shivers of fear through the shelter. The newly formed Executive Committee feared that the commotion would "further complicate" chances for immigration.[22] They solicited refugee letters that expressed proper gratitude and asked the WRA to refute Guillemin publicly.

Three months later, despite Acting Director Clyde Powers's warnings against similar outbursts "anywhere," the *Ontario Chronicle* cautiously moved toward a critical stance.[23] Many refugees viewed the camp paper as a house organ. It had barely survived a vote calling for its dissolution at a meeting the previous winter of over four hundred residents angered by Arpad Buchler's death and by the paper's unwavering support for the administration. Few refugees continued to read it—it was in essence a public relations effort directed toward friends on the outside. But four months had passed since V.J. Day, and freedom seemed no closer.

The *Ontario Chronicle* shifted toward a new assertiveness when, on September 13, it also published a Guillemin letter calling for America to live up to its ideals by granting the refugees freedom within its borders. Remembering the three-month debate Guillemin's previous letter had provoked in the Oswego paper and recalling repeated incidents of violence in Japanese Relocation Centers when dissent got out of hand—a phenomenon due in part to the high percentage of young people among the evacuees—Powers saw this new development as "potential dynamite" and soon closed the paper.[24] Like the Advisory Council, the *Ontario Chronicle* tried to serve both refugee and government interests. And, like the council, it went down in defeat.

After the presidential election, the WRA fear of arousing significant public opposition proved unfounded. Except for glowing accounts of Christmas and Hanukkah celebrations, the camp attracted little attention. In late February *PM* ran a series of human interest features on the refugees and their hopes. On March 8 the *Christian Science Monitor* called such efforts "the opening gun" of a drive to gain permanent entry for 15,000–25,000 aliens here on visitors' visas. It warned of an even bigger problem. The need for asylum would continue after the war, when the IGC would need homes for at least one-half million to two million stateless. The *Monitor* did not want them in the United States—"just transferring a race problem from one country to another does not solve it." Six days later the *New York Herald Tribune* ran another sympathetic feature. Such articles remained rare. Whether friendly or unfriendly, the press remained distant.

The Dickstein Hearings stirred new interest in Oswego and in the larger issue. *Survey Graphic*'s June issue featured a four-page essay on Americanization at the fort. Writer Ruth Karpf also noted that only 28,000 quota and nonquota immigrants had been admitted the previous fiscal year, although 158,000 numbers were available and a total of one million numbers remained unused. On August 6 *Time* observed that Europe counted its displaced persons "in the millions." America had fewer than one thousand but could thus "glimpse" the larger problem. How could we refuse to accept so few and expect nations shattered by war to do so much more?

The larger refugee issue would soon directly affect the fate of the Oswego group. In mid-May, word of terribly unsatisfactory conditions in American DP camps prompted several initiatives. Emanuel Cellar (D., N.Y.) led Jewish congressmen in a protest to the War Department. Stephen S. Wise and Nahum Goldman sought "urgent" help from George Warren, the State Department's advisor for refugees and displaced persons. And, after Truman refused Henry Morgenthau, Jr.'s, request for a cabinet-level committee on DPs, the Treasury secretary pressed the State Department for an "immediate" investigation.[25] Acting Secretary of State Joseph C. Grew accepted Morgenthau's suggestion that Earl Harrison conduct the inquiry. Harrison traveled to Europe in mid-July, accompanied by Joseph Schwartz, an American Jewish Joint Distribution Committee official who knew what needed to be seen.

Harrison exposed shocking camp conditions and reported the number of Jews unable to return to their homes as 100,000, most of whom wanted to resettle in Palestine. Indicating that few wished to emigrate to the United States, he also insisted that America had to set an example by opening its doors. Harrison reported to Truman on August 24. The following week the president, in a message released to the press, urged Prime Minister Clement Attlee, Churchill's successor, to open Palestine to 100,000 Jews.

That same week the departments of State and Justice broke their silence on the three-month-old congressional committee resolution pertaining to Oswego and notified Harold Ickes that they would, after assessing European political conditions and the practicability of return, make the necessary arrangements for temporary admissions.

Attorney General Clark and Secretary of State James F. Byrnes indicated that House and Senate Immigration Committee approval
should be considered but was not essential. They agreed, "where
possible," to uphold the integrity of American immigration law and
proposed that a twelve-member panel make the necessary determinations.[26] State and Justice would each provide four representatives,
and Ickes was invited to appoint four as well. The twelve representatives were divided into four panels:

Panel 1:	E. L.Freers (State)
	S. A. Diana (Justice)
	Janet Margolies (Interior)
Panel 2:	Philip F. Cherp (State)
	Thomas P. Galvin (Justice)
	Frieda Reifer (Interior)
Panel 3:	J. L. Tochey (State)
	J. Auerbach (Justice)
	Edward Huberman (Interior)
Review Panel:	Marshall Vance (State)
	Joseph P. Savoretti (Justice)
	Edward B. Marks, Jr. (Interior)

The WRA thought that the panels were to identify those who wished
to return. It expected a welcome solution to be "forthcoming" and
asked the NRS to prepare a comprehensive plan for resettlement.[27]

Interior representatives realized that they had been too optimistic
as soon as the twelve panelists gathered in the fort. During their first
meeting, on September 12, Marshall Vance indicated that he considered the refugees lucky to have lived in the United States for a year
and thought that they deserved no special advantages over millions
whose wartime experiences had been more harrowing. Philip Cherp
said he would "get rid of" the refugees by removing them from the
country as soon as possible. The State Department officials re-
preatedly remarked, "Jews have just as good a position in Germany
and are as well treated as anybody." They thought "all Germans,
including Jews" were obligated to help restore Germany.[28]

The panels were to interview each family and determine the
"practicability of return" for each, based on the following guidelines:

I. A. Practicable and willing to return to country of nationality or
domicile.
B. Practicable but unwilling to return to country of nationality or
domicile on the ground of:
1. Fear of religious persecution.
2. Fear of political persecution.

3. Extermination of family members.
4. Economic hardship.
5. Personal preference.

II. A. Willing and presumably able to go to some country other than the United States or country of nationality or domicile.

B. Willing but presumably unable to go to a country other than the United States or country of nationality or domicile.

C. If not permitted to remain in the United States, willing and presumably able to go to some country other than the United States or country of nationality or domicile.

III. A. Impracticable to return to country of nationality or domicile because not recognized as national or resident of that country.

B. Impracticable to return because of a clear showing of danger to the individual's safety.

C. Impracticable to return at this time due to a serious physical or mental ailment making it dangerous to travel.

D. Impracticable to return because within non-quota or preference quota class on basis of family ties in the United States.

E. Impracticable to return because of exceptional circumstances [such as, rabbis who possess nonquota status; aliens in possession of expired immigration visas which were not used for reasons beyond the control of the possessors; fiancées of United States citizens in the Armed Forces of the United States].[29]

State and Justice representatives thought return should be judged impracticable only if returnees would be in clear danger or if their return would put undue hardship on American wives and children. Visa Division Chief Howard K. Travers noted that this narrow interpretation had support in the White House and in Congress, where half a dozen bills to curb immigration were pending. He indicated that Richard B. Russell (D. Ga.), chairman of the Senate Immigration and Naturalization Committee, and most members of the House Immigration and Naturalization Committee remained "determined" to uphold "the return commitment." According to Justice Department representatives, the attorney general knew that the narrow interpretation would place many refugees in a "controversial" category, and he expected to make individual determinations in all such cases.[30]

This paneling stirred both joy and terror in the camp. In preparing its resettlement plan for the WRA, the NRS had asked everyone for names and addresses of potential American sponsors. The appearance of the panelists appeared to confirm that immigration visas were "in the bag."[31] However, those interviewed by the second panel met with such hostility that they began to panic. Thomas Galvin asked questions like a "case-hardened Immigration inspector interrogating a suspect." And Philip Cherp repeatedly accused interviewees of trying "to evade their responsibilities and break faith" with the United States government.[32]

State and Justice representatives on the other two principal panels tended to agree personally with Ed Marks and the three shelter social workers who represented the Interior Department. They treated interviewees with obvious sympathy, but only Joseph P. Savoretti, who conversed privately in Italian with several refugees, voiced dissatisfaction with his department's intentions.

The panelists reached agreement on only 223 of the 814 refugees still in the camp: 32 seemed willing to return to their homelands, 72 preferred to emigrate to other countries, and 119 who wished to remain won everyone's approval. State and Justice representatives insisted on repatriation or emigration for 695 and thought that this should be done forcibly if necessary. Interior representatives insisted that 738 should be permitted to remain, a figure that included people who opted for emigration but did not have necessary visas. Unable to agree, the panelists did not issue a set of recommendations. Interior continued to press for preexamination, but State and Justice seemed to disassociate themselves from the entire problem.

Two months elapsed and the refugees' prospects suddenly dimmed. On November 21 the State Department notified Interior and Justice that James Byrnes, who had succeeded Edward Stettinius, Jr., as secretary of state, would issue temporary visas and turn the entire matter over to the Immigration and Naturalization Service. Two weeks later the Justice Department notified Interior that it had accepted Byrnes's offer and would grant preexamination to 106 Oswego refugees, thirteen fewer than State and Justice panel representatives had agreed upon. The rest would receive temporary visas and would become subject to immediate deportation if they failed to arrange "voluntary departure."[33] Furthermore, with or without WRA approval, within four days Justice would notify the Senate and House Immigation Committees of its intent. Attorney General Clark wanted evidence of support from Capitol Hill before Congress adjourned for its Christmas break.

The Justice proposal never reached Congress. Interior Undersecretary Fortas persuaded Clark to delay so that the WRA could offer an alternative. The WRA approved the use of temporary visas, agreed that the Immigration and Naturalization Service should exercise jurisdiction on a case-by-case basis, and accepted the notion of "voluntary" departure for those found to be inadmissible. It opposed forcible repatriation for those not ruled inadmissible. Such action would repudiate UNRRA, IGC, and American Armed Forces policies; it would totally contradict Truman's effort to have 100,000 Jewish DPs accepted for Palestine; and it might be "physically impossible." The millions uprooted by war included 100,000 Jewish and 700,000 non-Jewish "hard-core" displaced persons, who would not or could not return to their homes. In view of such "present-day actualities," the WRA insisted that the United States should grant preexamination to all Oswego refugees still in this country six months after the camp closed.[34]

The WRA's counterproposal also never reached Congress. Justice and State still seemed reluctant to accept the fact that international circumstances would not permit them to act as they wished. It was mid-December 1945, the refugees had been in Oswego sixteen months, and they faced a second treacherous winter. It had been seven months since Germany surrendered, six months since Dickstein held hearings, four months since World War II had officially ended, and three months since Interior, State, and Justice representatives had interviewed every family head in the shelter. All means of preventing forced repatriation had been exhausted but one. Presidential intervention had brought the refugees here; only presidential intervention would enable them to remain.

Truman was noncommittal when first approached by Ickes. Four days after their June 14 discussion, the NRS turned for help to its Kansas City affiliate, the United Jewish Service. The UJS arranged for NRS representative Fannie Steiner to meet separately in Kansas City on November 22 with three Truman intimates, Eddie Jacobson, Tom L. Evans, and Clarence Decker. She reported that each agreed to take NRS proposals to the president. Their contacts remained off the record. However, after Truman acted, he felt the NRS did not show sufficient appreciation, feelings Eddie Jacobson conveyed to the NRS through the UJS.[35]

Help also came from within the White House itself. Only two members of Roosevelt's White House staff remained throughout the Truman years, David Niles and Stephen T. Early. Under Roosevelt, Niles worked largely on labor rather than minority issues. FDR avoided addressing the Jewish problem, but Truman could not. Niles, the elusive but omnipresent Roosevelt advisor who had ordered a Gallup Poll that turned up widespread public support in April 1944 for temporary havens, served as Truman's principal advisor on Jewish questions and this became his major task.

Niles thought State Department influence might be decisive on the Oswego question. American Jewish Committee correspondence reveals that in mid-October he advised Judge Nathan Perlman of the American Jewish Congress that it was "most important" for a nonsectarian delegation to approach Secretary Byrnes.[36] Non-Jewish organizations became involved later but officials of the NRS, American Jewish Congress, American Jewish Committee, National Council of Jewish Women, and the National (Jewish) Community Relations Advisory Council (NCRAC) determined the strategy. They wanted to resolve the Oswego problem within the context of the larger displaced persons issue.

The Niles-Perlman meeting occurred the same week that Britain moved to relieve pressure on its Palestine policy by suggesting a more active role for the United States. London proposed a joint Anglo-American Committee of Inquiry, and Truman quickly accepted. One month later, on November 13, the *New York Times* reported that Britain would admit "distressed persons" into the United Kingdom and expected other nations to act accordingly. Now, forcibly repatriating Oswego refugees would weaken Washington's position on the Anglo-American Committee of Inquiry, and the State Department moved to transfer the problem to the Justice Department.

Justice, increasingly isolated, remained adamant, but the case for permitting the refugees to remain grew stronger. Smart reported that Senator Robert Taft (R. Ohio), House Speaker Sam Rayburn (D. Tex.), and House Majority Leader John McCormack (D. Mass.) each promised to speak within the administration on the refugees' behalf. More important, Senate Immigration Chairman Russell withdrew his opposition and agreed to a "total solution" allowing for regular immigration.[37]

Restrictionists such as Russell could no longer avoid the consequences of Hitler's human destruction. The Nuremberg trials, in progress, addressed only crimes of war but revealed horrifying atrocities. Congress had already approved $550 million for UNRRA and Truman's request for an additional $1.35 million was pending. In view of the enormity of the problem, how could the United States avoid utilizing available visas? Russell much preferred to admit refugees already in good health and already Americanized.

Resistance to the admission of the Oswego refugees crumbled. In mid-December New York Archbishop Francis Spellman notified the NRS that he had been told, "on good authority," that the fifty-one refugees eligible for preferential treatment would receive regular visas and the rest would be granted preexamination, a report confirmed by the New York Office of War Relief Services.[38] Two days later, Clarence Pickett (American Friends Service Committee) and Bruce Mohler (National Catholic Welfare Conference) accompanied Judge Perlman (American Jewish Congress), Joseph Chamberlain (NRS), Isiah Minkoff (NACRAC), and Ruth Gruber to the State Department. Secretary Byrnes was out of the country and they met with Dean Acheson. The undersecretary indicated he would discuss the issue with Truman the following day.[39] The next day, December 15, Justice Department Counsel Philip Glick asked Clyde Powers for additional information on cases requiring extensive outside medical care. He thought it possible that "negotiations" had begun.[40]

Chamberlain notified Harrison that the Oswego question had reached "a critical stage" that would soon force White House action.[41] He believed Attorney General Clark still favored forced repatriation and asked Harrison to make a direct appeal to Clark and send a copy to Acheson. That same day, December 19, presidential counsel and speechwriter Judge Samuel I. Rosenman phoned NRS Executive Director Joseph E. Beck in New York from the White House. The next day they met in the White House.

Sam Rosenman and Joe Beck drafted the Truman Directive. It ordered government offices to use "every possible measure" to facilitate the full immigration allowed by law and to give preference to both the Oswego refugees and displaced persons in America's European zones.[42] Beck acceded to the president's request that the NRS begin the Oswego resettlement while Congress remained in adjournment for the Christmas break and complete it "as soon thereafter as possible."[43]

The Truman Directive broke new ground in immigration history, not because it granted preferential treatment to refugees but because it established regular use of the corporate affidavit. Would-be immigrants without sufficient means previously needed individual American affiants to guarantee that they would not become public charges for at least five years. The State Department had accepted a corporate affidavit only once before, in 1940, for two thousand children brought temporarily from England by the United States Committee for the Care of European Children, one of several nonsectarian organizations that the NRS hoped might obtain administrative and legislative help for refugees. The 1940 group included few Jews and few refugees; they were "simply British children living in the war zone."[44] Truman legitimized guarantees from responsible welfare organizations for large groups of refugees, thus establishing an alternative to the device used most widely to cause delays and disqualifications that held immigration below what the law allowed.

The State Department agreed to accept an NRS affidavit for the Oswego refugees before it resolved questions concerning how the corporate affidavit should be used and to whom it should apply. State wanted it to cover the entire Oswego group but Justice thought it unnecessary for those who could show that they need not become public charges. State's view prevailed. And that meant that all shelter residents had to relocate in new communities under the auspices of the NRS or cooperating organizations—the Catholic Committee for

Refugees and the American Committee for Christian Refugees, which took responsibility for Protestants and Greek Orthodox. HIAS did not participate in the affidavit but, under the NRS, continued to serve those whose families had asked it for assistance and most who chose repatriation or emigration.[45]

People who wished to make their own arrangements could not do so and a significant number chafed at having to accept assistance of any kind. Many insisted on using their own funds to pay the ten-dollar visa fee and other expenses. A sixty-three-year-old Polish woman without American relatives and with only limited funds accepted help under protest. A large woman who walked with a cane, she had a crippled hand and limited sight but looked forward to working as a dressmaker at an agency hostel in New York and to maintaining her "enthusiasm" for living and independence.[46]

The scramble to close the camp quickly caused the NRS to compress into twenty days a task expected to take three months. Ten NRS workers interviewed every family head at least twice. More than twenty government workers also arrived to take photographs for visas, distribute ration cards, perform health checks, and register eligible males for the selective service. Both groups worked seven-day weeks, often late into the night. Some were inexperienced and had to learn on the job at the same time that hastily devised procedures were undergoing revision.

The entire task of processing took only six weeks. And, beginning January 17 and continuing through February 6, three buses left every two or three days for the four-hour bus ride to Niagara Falls, Canada. Fifty-three percent went from there to homes of relatives or friends and required only the paperwork necessary to satisfy the Immigration and Naturalization Service every six months until they were totally self-supporting. A number of those resented having to relocate under organizational auspices and insisted on paying their own visa fees and other expenses. But many of the 22 percent who listed unidentified addresses on the closing roster and all of the 21 percent who went directly to local welfare agencies needed temporary financial assistance and help in finding jobs and housing.

Most national groups entered on the January quota, but Austrians were distributed over both January and February, Greeks and Rumanians had to wait until February, and Yugoslavs had to be spaced over four months. This did not become known, however, until State Department quota numbers arrived. By then, half had been processed and scheduled for departure. Some families had to delay, even after having sent their baggage, and accept temporary visas. Many feared deportation and several panicked. Local receiving agencies, who faced the same shortage of trained personnel as did the

NRS, found some still fearful after arriving in their new communities.[47]

WRA staff feared the persistence of institutional dependency, and the idea of actual freedom did stir conflicting emotions, but when it arrived elation quickly overcame fear. Announcement of the Truman Directive initially created greater anxiety, evidenced in the rise of psychosomatic complaints. But nervousness soon subsided and medical complaints quickly declined. The Medical Department became the first to close. Whether people faced the uncertainties ahead with trepidation or threw themselves joyfully into preparations, they discovered increased energy as freedom drew nearer. A WRA community analyst compared them to "an eager football team" approaching the field just after "the coach's last pep talk" before "the big game."[48]

Despite blizzard conditions, people rose at dawn to bid farewell, sometimes to folks with whom they had stopped speaking. Only one man did not want to leave. Nikolas Gedroyce, a forty-seven-year-old White Russian who claimed direct descent from the former kings of Lithuania, had refused from the beginning to make friends, learn English, or adjust in any way. From the beginning, he demanded to return to Italy. But that remained impossible. He chose instead to emigrate to Canada and left on the last bus.

Oswego immigrants bore little resemblance to the ragtag refugees who had arrived eighteen months earlier. Most had regained their health and many now struggled to maintain their figures. All had baggage, which included modest but complete wardrobes. Most spoke at least a little English and many spoke it well. They knew how to shop in American stores, celebrate American holidays, and observe American customs.

Promising never to forget the many Oswego friends who had entertained her in their home, Fortunee Levitch wrote to the *Oswego Palladium Times* on January 19, 1946, "We shall carry with us the pleasantest memories that will remain unforgettable in our hearts." Gloomy times could now be left behind. She, and many like her, wished only to focus on a better future.

TEN

Toward Renewal

THE ROOSEVELT ADMINISTRATION had expected to provide only minimal maintenance but the refugees arrived with specific goals. All wanted American medical care. Those with children sought American schooling. Many anticipated family reunions. And several had occupational plans. Most obtained the desired treatment and education and, after an eighteen-month delay, reunion with American relatives. Their achievement indicates their resiliency and determination and that of friends in both the public and private sectors.

The government assumed that the refugees would organize whatever classes they wished for their children and teach them themselves within the confines of the shelter, but the newcomers arrived with plans under way to expedite American school enrollments. During the Atlantic crossing, to facilitate placement in American schools, forty-four-year-old Erich Wittenberg, a former Czech coal-mine operator, had made a file giving each school-age child's educational history. Parents had already tried to educate their children as best they could and "it was not enough." Only in American classrooms would youngsters "make up the lost time."[1]

Students as well as parents clamored for American schooling. Reporter Naomi Jolles asked a group of newly arrived boys what they most wanted and heard a chorus of "school, school, school." Ambitious yet fearful, they were old beyond their years. Blond thirteen-year-old Erik Levy hoped that teachers would realize they had fallen behind and would "take care of us a little." Fourteen-year-old Joseph Hirt wondered how American children, "ever lucky and happy," would accept them. They would not understand him on those occasions when memories would cause him to "think and speak like an old man."[2] Still wearing his GI uniform, Hirt spoke six languages and had seen much while working as an interpreter at Allied airbases in Italy. Parents and children persisted, Joseph Smart acted, the Coordinating Committee and Oswego leaders responded, and shelter youngsters sat in Oswego classrooms when schools opened on September 5.

One hundred twenty-five Oswego families included children seventeen years old or younger. The school enrollment as of September 15, 1944, was 193 students, of whom 172 were five to seventeen years old. The remaining 21 were older students, eighteen to twenty-one years old, who had not completed secondary school.

Nine young adults sought admission to Oswego State Teachers' College, but the WRA did not permit them to enroll until second semester, after it had determined that their presence would not provoke criticism. Two college and several high-school students took courses during the summer of 1945 at the Oswego branch of the Rochester Business Institute and four girls who graduated after one year from Oswego High School enrolled there as regular students. The Coordinating Committee provided tuitions and supplies. The restriction against attending schools outside Oswego most affected Aca and Rajko Margulis, both medical students, and several Orthodox youngsters wishing to enter New York *yeshivot*.

As with American school enrollments, the refugees insisted on and obtained extensive medical services. The government intended to provide only care needed for survival or for conditions such as contagious diseases, which, if left untreated, would be detrimental to the health of the entire group. It intended to provide maintenance and essential care but not rehabilitative or elective treatment and service, vague distinctions that acquired meaning only when the WRA and NRS groped for solutions to needs.

The dental story offers a case in point. The Army equipped the shelter with a dental office sufficient for routine work and the WRA temporarily provided an American dentist to familiarize the two refugee dentists with American equipment. However, unlike Japanese-American evacuees or enemy POWs, the refugees had not received proper care for years and needed far more than routine dental work. Nearly everyone had cavities, and five hundred needed bridgework or dentures. Many had lost all their teeth. Surprised and overwhelmed, the WRA accepted responsibility only for those with limited or no mastication.

The National Refugee Service provided dental care the government considered elective. Amid wartime shortages of personnel and materials, it tried to do so as quickly and economically as possible. Mass-produced dentures proved to be ill fitting and uncomfortable and individual impressions had to be taken so that appliances could be made to order. The bulk of that work was given to one of two refugee dentists, a skilled but highly nervous man who had difficulty coping with the pressure. New York and Oswego dentists, paid by the government with NRS funds, periodically assisted. They included a pediatric specialist who worked during the summer and two dentists who lived at the fort for several weeks during the fall. Nevertheless, a serious backlog persisted. After one year one hundred residents still needed dentures and more than four hundred waited to complete other work. All dental work was not completed until shortly before the camp closed.[3]

As with education and dental care, the government wanted the camp medically self-sufficient. In addition to dental offices, the Army prepared a thirty-bed hospital and an out-patient clinic, facilities deemed sufficient for a general community of comparable size. Dr. Reece Pedicord and a WRA nurse-consultant supervised final preparations and remained long enough to familiarize the refugee staff, which included five physicians, two pharmacists, and six nurses. One physician performed limited laboratory work; the Oswego hospital took all X rays and several tests. In the camp, thirty to forty refugees filled support jobs.

The refugee staff desperately needed a permanent, full-time American administrator. Unable to escape the debilitation, paranoia, and national-group tensions that afflicted the entire camp, and reviled by patients who wanted "American specialists," they needed an outsider to coordinate medical services and represent them in dealings with both patients and WRA personnel. An Oswego physician and a hospital superintendent on loan from a Japanese Relocation Center each served briefly as hospital superintendent, the first only part-time, but the medical staff did not have an adequate administrator until Dr. Ronald Loeb arrived nine months after the camp opened. Another three months passed before he obtained a medical secretary and a medical social worker. The camp never had a hospital dietician, especially unfortunate because nearly ninety refugees had diabetes, ulcers, hypertension, and other conditions requiring special diets.

The camp hospital was underutilized but demands on the outpatient clinic and pharmacy proved overwhelming, as did unanticipated needs for various appliances (see table 8). Hospitalizations within the shelter numbered 336, but an average of only twelve beds per day were occupied. However, outpatient visits totaled almost 19,000, an average of thirty-two daily but often as many as seventy or eighty a day when the weather permitted. Hundreds of residents needed additional services the government had not anticipated—eyeglasses, hearing aids, surgical appliances, orthopedic devices, and, in the case of

TABLE 8
Shelter Medical Statistics

1. SHELTER HOSPITAL
   Total admissions   336
   Average daily census   12
   Major operations performed   40
   Minor operations performed   47

2. OUTSIDE HOSPITALIZATIONS (Oswego, N.Y., Syracuse, Philadelphia)   44
   Total outpatient department visits   18,819
   Average daily medical and surgical visits   31
   Average daily dental visits   26

4. SHELTER PHARMACY
   Total prescriptions filled (approx.)   15,000

5. VITAL STATISTICS
   Births   23
   Deaths   14
   Stillbirths   1

6. ADDITIONAL OUTSIDE SERVICES
   Eye examinations   749
     Eyeglass fittings   over 400
   Eye, ear, nose, throat treatments (inc. minor surgery)   731
   Skin and allergy cases   6
   Diathermy (skin treatment)   8
   Electrocardiograms   7
   Basal Metabolism Tests   8
   X Rays   315
     (105 performed outside prior to April 1945)
     (210 performed inside after April 1945)

SOURCE: Loeb Report, Appendix, "Hospital Statistics"

two young men, prostheses. A dozen patients received electric shock treatments in Syracuse and nearly four dozen required outside hospitalization. Ostensibly, the government provided all.

In reality, after shelter residents pressed for more extensive medical care, the government turned to the National Refugee Service. An agreement negotiated on October 23, 1944, stipulated that the WRA would make the proper determinations and recommend individual cases to the NRS. The private agency arranged and paid for nearly all medical and dental services obtained outside the shelter and many performed within. Many individual cases had to be negotiated because specific guidelines and criteria did not exist. This resulted in frustration and delays that led Dr. Loeb to wish either that the government accept "sole" responsibility or that the NRS station a medical social worker at the shelter to expedite decisions and arrangements. He regretted the lack of "careful planning" before the refugees arrived, which could have avoided many problems.[4]

The NRS worked directly with camp officials to provide medical care, but it arranged for most other goods and services through the Coordinating Committee. These provisions included subscriptions to various English and foreign-language newspapers and magazines, materials for the *Ontario Chronicle,* and furnishings and equipment for the camp's religious and recreational facilities. The latter included a library, gymnasium, bowling alley, youth center, playhouse, movie theater, music room, two arts and crafts centers, and four recreation rooms. The Coordinating Committee also provided "supplemental" clothing such as winter hats and gloves, bath robes and slippers, and raincoats.

The Coordinating Committee found it much easier to organize private aid than to resist what it viewed as excessive government reliance on private generosity. Learning that it could call for additional assistance "at almost every point," the government began to define its own responsibilities much more narrowly than it did in either POW camps or Japanese Relocation Centers. The NRS and its partners feared that Oswego might become "a yardstick" in other cases where private support might not be "so readily forthcoming."[5]

Ironically, the role of the Coordinating Committee and its constituent organizations greatly increased, but their visibility declined. Government recognition of the Coordinating Committee included the stipulation that the private organizations not publicize their work, an effort to avoid the charge that too much was being done for them.[6] Smart also feared that private involvement would undercut his authority. He never succeeded in halting appeals to outsiders or in deterring outside encouragement for refugee grievances, but he did severely limit contact between the refugees and their principal benefactors. At his request, Coordinating Committee Executive Director Joseph Berger delivered all aid through either the director's office or the Welfare Department and limited his personal appearances within the camp. Berger also cooperated by discouraging contact with refugees except through "official" channels and tried to be "scrupulous in avoiding discussions on questions of policy."[7]

As with rehabilitative health care and children's education, refugees had specific ideas about community activities. First and foremost they wanted to learn English. Fifty-eight-year-old Jacob Ernest Kahn was unusual because he spoke English so well that only his "precision" suggested it might not be his mother tongue.[8] Formerly an iron dealer in Germany, he had been a frequent traveller to America and had lived briefly in England. Others such as Zdenka Ruchvarger (Ruchwarger), Fredi Baum's twenty-year-old sister, had picked up enough words to engage in simple conversation. Dr. Abraham Ruchvarger (Avram Ruchwarger), her thirty-two-year-old bride-groom of two months, agreed to work without pay aboard the *Henry Gibbins,* the only refugee physician willing to do so. The young couple received a private cabin and an invitation to take all meals with the ship's American medical officers. Others immersed themselves in English dictionaries and newspapers, considered treasured posses-sions.

The refugee experience created a passion for English. Dozens flocked to English classes Ruth Gruber conducted informally aboard ship. Some, like forty-four-year-old Berthold Gunsberger, who had a wife and son in New York, showed interest in little other than English-language study. Ten part-time teachers, recruited from Oswego and the surrounding area and paid with NRS funds, arrived in early October to offer five levels of instruction for two months to five hundred pupils. It is unlikely that any other community in America could boast of a class enrollment that included more than 50 percent of its adult population.

At the same time, ORT provided equipment and teachers for six-week courses in beauty culture, carpentry, machine-shop work, and auto mechanics. Later, sewing and tailoring were added. Like the WRA, the NRS and ORT did not plan for a long internment. The classes ended, two months elapsed, and, in response to refugee de-mands, the courses were repeated. This established a pattern, with courses being repeated after shorter intervals as internment con-tinued. NRS and ORT classes proved so popular, despite erratic attendance and organizational problems, that Malcolm Pitts suc-ceeded in easing the labor problem by predicating enrollments on willingness to work. Smart had tried similar tactics but only half-heartedly because, like the NRS and ORT, he saw the classes as vocational and did not wish to undermine this. Most refugees, middle-class business and professional people, viewed ORT classes as avoca-tional.[9] However, several did use skills gained in them to move into new occupations such as manicurist or hairdresser.

Shelter residents enlisted considerable outside support, but they also contributed greatly themselves to community life. "A people who lives, sings; a people who sings, lives." That maxim, noted in the May 17, 1945, *Ontario Chronicle* in recognition of Jewish Music Month, celebrated striking achievements. The Fort Ontario Chorus made its debut on an NBC Christmas show broadcast from the camp less than five months after the group arrived. The Fort Ontario Orchestra had already given the first of many concerts and the Fort Ontario Chamber Trio appeared soon after. The impressive array of musical talents was matched by a sophisticated and appreciative audience.

Leo Mirkovic, a forty-one-year-old baritone formerly with the Zagreb Opera, had to refuse professional inquiries from opera companies in Boston and in New York. He served as cantor for the liberal synagogue and performed frequently and graciously both in the fort and in Oswego. The Chamber Music Trio included thirty-seven-year-old Vera Levinson, a concert pianist from Russia who did not perform until learning that older children still in Europe were safe; thirty-three-year old Albert Schimel, a concert violinist from Austria; and thirty-four-year-old violist George Steinberg, a Polish-born electrical engineer held hostage by the Germans after World War I and expelled with his wife in 1940. Their son was a captain in the United States Army. Popular singers included thirty-five-year-old Eva Bass, a double for Edith Piaf, and Marianna Hartmayer Breuer, the lovely twenty-two-year old whose voice attracted rescuers in a camp in France.

Two musicians provided organizational skills. Forty-two-year-old Charles Abeles, a music director from Austria, organized and conducted the camp orchestra and formed a school that offered instruction in composition and theory as well as instrumental music. The Roman Catholic bachelor also composed skits and operettas, one of which, presented in December 1944, included such numbers as "The Captain Korn March," "Miss Gruber's Fox Trot," and "I Have a Girl in Springfield, Mass." The latter referred to a heart-warming romance between Artur Ernst, a sixty-year-old Roman Catholic attorney from Austria, and an American concert violinist he had met in Europe. It became a theme song, along with the Hit Parade tune "Don't Fence Me In." Fifty-seven-year-old Polish-born Sally (Solly) Schnaymann had served a Berlin synagogue for thirty years as choirmaster and organist. A former leather merchant interned with his wife, he created and conducted both the Fort Ontario Choir and the liberal synagogue choir.

The refugees also included several professional theatrical people, especially among the Russians and Austrians. Most outstanding among several Russian entertainers were circus performers Michele and Olga Mikhailoff and their twenty-year-old son, Vadim. Michele, also a stage designer, supervised shelter theatrical productions. The Austrian national group organized its own drama corps and staged several shows.

Forty-two-year-old Siegfried Kuttner, a German-Jewish professor of theatrical set design and former member of the Prussian Ministry of Education, staged two one-act Chekhovian dramas and several playlets, made and exhibited models of operatic sets he had created in Europe, and painted surrealistic watercolors depicting previous prison experiences and life within the fort. In the camp with his actress wife, Lotte, and their eleven-year-old son, the scenarist, lecturer, and painter also reluctantly accepted the job of community activities supervisor for all classes and programs organized and conducted by the refugees themselves. The task was enormous and would normally have required a professional group worker to organize a comprehensive program of classes and activities and to mediate between various groups. Each Japanese Relocation Center had such a person, but the shelter had a smaller population and fewer staff. The WRA persuaded Kuttner to accept the position and did not add a group worker to the staff until March 1945, when the Bondy, Dreikurs, and Gruber reports revealed that need.

Forty-five-year-old Miriam Sommerburg headed the list of professional artists in the camp. New York philanthropist Adolph Lewisohn had financed her studies as a young sculptor and she enjoyed a considerable reputation in France and Italy as well as her native Germany. During her refugee years she lacked proper tools and turned to watercolors and carvings. In Italy, she published a book of woodcuts. Interned in Oswego with five of her six children, she resumed sculpting. Fifty-one-year-old Max Sipser, a graphic artist and caricaturist from Austria, resumed work with a cartoon in each week's *Ontario Chronicle*.

The refugees also included two distinguished German-Jewish portrait painters, sixty-one-year-old Vladimir Zabotin and seventy-two-year-old Herman Bruck. Zabotin, interned with his wife, Adelheid, and sixteen-year-old son, Konstantin, painted the portraits of numerous refugees and Oswegans. However, Adelheid, a sculptor, and Bruck did not resume their work. Bruck, having to hold his head next to the canvas to work without eyeglasses, arrived determined to take up his work again but was known to have painted only a self-portrait, which he insisted on continuing to improve.[10]

The camp teemed with musical, theatrical, visual, and literary artists, and they adapted to camp life in strikingly different ways. Performers fared better than writers, composers, and artists; musicians fared better than theatrical figures. Returning to the stage before appreciative audiences meant releasing and sharing pent-up emotions, often a "lifesaver."[11] However, staging a theatrical performance required far more planning and preparation time than arranging for a recital or concert, and, since everyone hoped to be released soon, producers limited themselves to one-act plays or skits.

Performers could pour their emotions into words and notes that others had created, but people who produced original material had to be able to hear their inner voices. The lack of quiet and privacy, coupled with the uncertainties of an indefinite internment, made it extremely difficult to use the time in Oswego creatively despite the availability of studios, instruments, and materials. Some writers and composers made little effort. Others tried but produced incomplete works or nothing at all. And a few worked "feverishly," expressing a compulsiveness that proved to be equally "abnormal" and unproductive.[12]

Refugees and volunteer Oswegans conducted all community activities. These ranged from musical, theatrical, and artistic endeavors to Boy and Girl Scout Troops, a nursery school, and Zionist youth activities. However, the NRS made the programs possible. The WRA considered only clerical, medical, and laboring tasks to be wage-earning positions, but the NRS insisted that community activities required paid workers and agreed to finance the program. It persuaded the WRA to grant community workers the $8.50 allowance given nonworkers, and it contributed an additional $10.00 so that they received pay equal to those in wage-earning positions. As with medical care and other subsidies, NRS funds went directly to the WRA and remained unknown to residents.

Camp life was made bearable by a combination of extraordinary private assistance and individual initiative. Teenage boys built a simple radio system linking various barracks, fun at all times but highly practical when winter severely restricted movement for many. Fifty-eight-year-old Margareta Ehrenstamm formed a Ladies Service Committee to provide parties for "lonesomes" and meals and cheer for shut-ins. Fifty-eight-year-old Milan Kastle, a former chocolate manufacturer, installed a piano in his living quarters and had to limit the number of visitors at any one time.

Such individuals strove to look on the brighter side. Energetic Mrs. Ehrenstamm regretted, "Now that things are better we seem to show less patience. When it was harder, we just had to hold on to keep going.[13] She felt keenly, however, that it was much easier for her because she and her husband, once a prosperous silk manufacturer in Germany, were together and they knew that their children were also safe.

Until group worker Edward Huberman arrived in March 1945, the Community Activities program lacked overall planning and continuity. Huberman helped residents address needs not yet met. Zdenka Ruchvarger (Ruchwarger) began to hold gymnastics and dance classes for girls. Forty-four-year-old Fortunee Levitch, a frequent guest speaker in Oswego, organized a Girl Scout Troop. Fortunee and Zdenka worked together to create a summer children's theater. Indefatigable forty-two-year-old Ferdinand Kaska, a bachelor and former railroad clerk who sponsored a Boys Club and worked with the Boy Scouts, organized the Austrian Theater Group. Leon Levitch formed a Youth Orchestra. The Russian entertainers became more active.

Playlets, operettas, concerts, and stage shows began to appear at the playhouse at least biweekly. The demand for many performances necessitated their being offered on two or three successive evenings. Huberman scheduled movies five nights weekly and frequently filled the two-hundred-seat theater. He also scheduled a weekly educational film and lecture series, both of which focused on aspects of American life. The music school added courses in music appreciation. Fredi Baum had access to government vehicles and taught himself to drive, but many others learned in classes that Huberman added. Other new courses included arts and crafts, drawing and painting, fashion design, and boxing.

Huberman introduced activities meant to relieve stress, but, even more important, he stimulated and encouraged ventures that fostered a feeling of community. An arts and crafts exhibit on April 30–May 5 occupied 250 refugees of all ages and drew hundreds of visitors. A July Lawn Festival found dozens participating in sack races, egg tosses, and rope pulls, all organized by refugee committees. During the summer, weekly baseball games, square dancing, and song fests were also introduced, the result of a much-loved unit of the American Friends Service Committee.

Ten women and two men training at Haverford College for Quaker relief and reconstruction work in Europe asked to do summer fieldwork at the shelter. And they quickly ingratiated themselves as "the mothers of the youngsters, the clever guides of the grown-ups, and the sincere friends of the adults." The Quaker service unit refused to accept monotony or apathy. Fortunee Levitch thought that they made "every single minute of every day" count.[14] Former residents who know little of the NRS and the Coordinating Committee continue to feel immense gratitude to the Quakers. Ralph Manfred Kuznitski (now Ralph Manfred) remains grateful to them for teaching him, as a sixteen-year-old, to "relax and find peace."[15] Children's activities proved mutually satisfying for leaders and participants, but the Quaker team felt disappointment at not being able to attract more than a few dozen adults on any regular basis to its recreational programs.

The story of the Emergency Refugee Shelter is striking in its disclosure of refugee initiative and private participation, but nothing distinguishes it more than the freedom and support given religion. The kosher kitchen served more than one-fourth of the camp's Jewish population. Jews and non-Jews worshiped as they wished, non-Jews in

Oswego churches or the fort's chapel, and Jews in two synagogues within the camp, one Orthodox and one liberal. Religious holidays drew camp-wide participation. The camp allowed for every expression of religious identity, including indifference. It was not, however, conducive to the outright rejection of religion. A few Jews had apostasized in an unsuccessful effort to avoid victimization. Most again identified as Jews. Those who truly wished to erase all connection to their Jewish past waited until after being released from the camp to do so.

Two dedications soon after the shelter opened clearly signaled a new beginning. Jews in Fort Ontario gathered on the evening of September 17, 1944, not only to observe Rosh Hashanah for the first time in several years but to celebrate the Jewish New Year by consecrating two synagogues. Two months later, on Saturday evening, November 18, a large crowd gathered to dedicate two flags, the American Stars and Stripes and the Jewish Star of David. Placed side-by-side in the shelter theater as "a sign of friendship and brotherhood" between "two nations," the flags symbolized renewed and restored Jewish dignity.[16]

A sense of ecumenism characterized the holiday season. Hanukkah, the gift-giving, eight-day Festival of Lights that marks an ancient recovery of Jewish independence, arrived Sunday evening, December 10. The shelter celebrated with candle-lighting ceremonies, children's playlets, songfests, and a distribution of parcels of clothing, candy, and toys for the entire population. Less than a week after the holiday concluded, the camp turned to Christmas festivities. Features included a large, outdoor tree, several parties, and gifts from St. Nicholas.

The highlight of the holiday season, a fifteen-minute NBC Christmas special broadcast from the shelter on December 23, featured the Fort Ontario Choir singing Christmas carols. Intended as a "demonstration of goodwill," it included an address by journalist Dorothy Thompson, who referred to the refugees as "a Christian message . . . that the people who sit in darkness may yet see a great light," and personal comments by two Roman Catholic residents, one of whom had been imprisoned by the Nazis because of her marriage to a Jew.[17]

Unfortunately, the discovery on December 29 of Karolina Bleier's tragic suicide caused the upbeat mood of Hanukkah and Christmas to turn quickly to gloom. A long wintry depression set in and lasted until Passover heralded the arrival of spring.

Jews have a collective memory, quintessentially expressed in the Passover seder, which reenacts the three great experiences of enslavement, deliverance, and redemption that mark the historical birth of the Jewish people as a free nation consecrated to God. It is a unique memory, "not a matter of intellection but of evocation and identification," one that fuses past and present so that the experience is reactualized rather than merely recalled.[18] Reactualizing aroused new passions on March 28 and 29, 1945, in Fort Ontario for seder participants who saw themselves as slaves delivered but still awaiting redemption in the promised land.

Resplendent both nights in traditional white cassock and skullcap, Rabbi Mosco Tzechoval presided at the head table in the kosher dining hall. The first night, a mood of serious pedagogical discussion prevailed during the portion of the service that preceded dinner. Spontaneous merriment broke out only after the meal concluded, when men suddenly lifted Joseph Smart to their shoulders, carried him to an open area, and encircled him in swirls of men joined arm-to-arm in joyous song. The second night, passion exploded in exultation. This time all formality disappeared, and singing, whirling men interrupted the service to form human chains that wove among the tables in uninhibited "ecstasy."[19] In every dining hall, each transformed by red wine, festive foods, and white tablecloths, spirits temporarily soared.

Spring also brought the first small gains in the campaign to tear down government restrictions. Achieved in response to unrelenting refugee demands and deepening refugee needs, new privileges included foster home placement, overnight conjugal visits, and brief convalescent furloughs. Smart gained approval for the first shortly before he resigned. Pitts remained unmoved by individual needs but Marks continued Smart's efforts, under changed circumstances, and obtained several changes Smart had long sought.

Malcolm Pitts replaced Smart shortly before the Welfare Department sent the Bleier infants, Ronald and George, to a foster home in Rochester, the first such placement. He refused to allow Geza Bleier to travel beyond the twenty-mile restriction to visit them, and the department did not make additional placements until Ed Marks arrived and approved such travel. The department clashed with Pitts on several issues, most notably his refusal to permit the department to transfer families severely needing privacy to empty bungalows on Officers' Row and to permit the conversion of one such home into a hotel for conjugal visits.

Pitts insisted that he would not sanction "favoritism," and when the wife of sixty-three-year-old Feibish Koppelman traveled from California to visit him, the acting director refused to allow her to remain within the fort past 9:00 P.M. and refused to allow Koppelman to remain in Oswego longer than the prescribed six hours.[20] Made deaf and feeble by torture in Dachau and Buchenwald, Koppelman rapidly deteriorated. The WRA released him on November 26 on indefinite leave. He died in California six weeks later.

The same week that Ed Marks replaced Malcolm Pitts, William O'Dwyer transferred overall responsibility for shelter policy from the War Refugee Board to the Interior Department, and Attorney General Biddle approved brief convalescent leaves justifiable on medical grounds. Marks granted emergency leaves of one week or longer in cases of family illness or death, introduced conjugal visits, allowed residents with family members placed outside the camp to visit them overnight, permitted people granted leaves to travel unescorted if able to do so, and initiated two to three week convalescent leaves. Biddle approved leaves only for transfer to an institution, but Interior extended them to include home visits.

Geza Bleier and Renee Buchler, both pushed to the brink of total exhaustion by the loss of their spouses and the demands of youngsters, traveled regularly to Rochester and Buffalo, respectively, to visit their children while they regained their stamina. Walter Lowitt had exhausted efforts to gain his wife, Regina's, release from the shelter. He made the trip from New York biweekly to spend weekends with her. Ingenious Chaim Feffer married the childhood sweetheart he located in Montreal with the help of Lisbon postal workers. He checked in daily while they honeymooned for a month in Oswego before she returned to Canada to await his release. Sixty-two-year-old Norbert Bass, the father of two sons in the United States Army, had escaped a train that carried his wife to Dachau, fled across Europe with a permanently stiffened left foot, and suffered a paralytic stroke soon after disembarking in Hoboken. The once wealthy Austrian manufacturer experienced severe headaches and insomnia. He visited a daughter in Philadelphia.

The group profile of the thirty-one people given medical leaves reveals a fairly equal balance of men and women and of different age groups but an unusually high proportion of Jews of Polish origin and of people separated from their spouses. The former constituted 15 percent of the total population but 42 percent of the furloughed group. Most had lived for some time in Germany. The first to be made stateless and to be deported, they had been refugees the longest. Adults unaccompanied by spouses constituted 28 percent of the population—no distinctions were made between those never married and those widowed, separated, or divorced—but 74 percent of those selected for convalescent leaves. People without a confidant tended to interact the least and to become the most depressed.

Convalescent leaves both reduced and exacerbated tensions. They permitted the temporary removal of people suffering the greatest stress, but they created intense competition and resentment that turned to "hysteria" when home visits became possible.[21] The WRA increased the monthly number from three or four to ten, but only word in late December that the camp would soon close quieted the clamor.

ELEVEN

Conclusion

ABOVE ALL, America's lone Emergency Refugee Shelter in Fort Ontario, New York, stood as a tragic symbol of political and diplomatic failure. Could it have been otherwise?

By 1944, victory loomed on the horizon and Franklin D. Roosevelt still had time to demonstrate that the leader of the free world would no longer stand aloof from the destruction of European Jewry. That appeared to be his intent in January, when he established the War Refugee Board. Four million Jews had been murdered but the Hungarian community, swollen to one million, remained intact, as did pockets of Jews in Rumania, France, and elsewhere. And the United States now had an agency within the government, an agency with cabinet status, charged with rescuing them and finding temporary havens for them.

The War Refugee Board responded to the challenge with a grand scheme to establish such havens within the United States. In proposing that tens, perhaps hundreds, of thousands be brought to this country it intended neither to revise nor circumvent American immigration law. It wished only to implement a temporary program and, in order to do so, to postpone the question of ultimate resettlement, just as Roosevelt was postponing decisions on postwar boundaries and governments. Most important, the WRB did not expect enormous numbers because it hoped to use the American program to persuade other governments to take similar action. Proximity, availability, and costs made Mediterranean sites more practical. The board hoped to persuade Britain to establish temporary camps for Jews in Palestine.

152

By settling some refugees, the United States would set an example for the world.

The evidence suggests that, despite continued anti-Semitism and restrictionist thinking, by spring 1944 revulsion at Nazi barbarities had created widespread support for the establishment of interim refugee camps in the United States. This attitude is indicated by the results of the April 1944 Gallup Poll commissioned by David Niles, resolutions passed by both major political parties and by the AFL and CIO, broad church support, and the impressive list of public figures marshaled by Alfred E. Smith and Peter Bergson. It is evidence that offers the tantalizing possibility that Congress was out of step with the country and the cabinet did not act because of unfounded fears.

The Oswego story suggests that the Roosevelt administration, with the help of supportive congressional figures, could have used the WRB to marshal broad public support for the temporary admission of large numbers of European Jews. The issue here is not whether or not rescue was actually feasible but whether or not policy-makers thought it was and how they responded. No one in a position of influence stated that conditions in Europe made the scheme impractical. It appears that the administration failed to act in 1944 not because of naïveté or wartime conditions but because it considered the issue largely in terms of domestic politics and judged those incorrectly.

It took four months for the temporary havens proposal to reach the White House officially (although the president was already very much aware of it.) And John Pehle had to present it to FDR without an accompanying board endorsement. Another month passed before the president announced Oswego. By then the Hungarian community had been decimated. A large scheme was no longer needed.

The WRB had independent status, it had considerable influence, and it had an able and dedicated staff. Why did the temporary havens proposal, its most significant effort, fail?

Franklin D. Roosevelt structured the War Refugee Board in such a way as to be confident that it would not place him under undue pressure—he encouraged it to challenge Britain on its Palestine policy but did not wish to subject himself similarly. Formation of the WRB in effect marked a transfer of responsibility for refugee policy from a discredited State Department to a Treasury Department eager to save lives, but Henry Morgenthau, Jr., had to share membership on the board equally with the secretaries of state and of war. That arrangement, unique among government agencies, guaranteed that the irrepressible young Ivy League lawyers who staffed both Treasury and the new agency would be restrained when necessary.

Of the WRB's programs, only the temporary havens proposal threatened to embarrass the president politically, and only the temporary havens proposal opened a sharp gap between the WRB's members and its staff. Henry L. Stimson ran interference for Roosevelt and firmly blocked the Treasury Department firebrands. During the same weeks that he weakened and delayed the temporary havens proposal, he also killed in committee a Senate resolution favoring establishment of a Jewish state in Palestine. In both cases, he made it unnecessary for the State Department, which was far more vulnerable to criticism, to act. Speaking both as secretary of war and as an administration figure with an inside track on Capitol Hill, the venerable Stimson, a restrictionist at heart, enabled Roosevelt to stay on the high road and work both sides of the street.

John W. Pehle and his staff relied most heavily on Morgenthau, the cabinet member closest and most loyal to FDR, a man who took breakfast regularly in the White House. But the Treasury secretary offered from the start only qualified support for temporary havens. He deleted the original proposal from the Treasury report that convinced Roosevelt of the need for a War Refugee Board and, in the face of Stimson's warnings about the plan's political dangers for the president, he grew increasingly reluctant to give it his full support. No one in government knew more about Hitler's atrocities and wished to save Jewish lives more than the WRB staff. Yet, without Morgenthau's full support, they, Pehle in particular, grew more cautious.

Pehle remained a loyal bureaucrat. When he could not persuade, he did not persist. Neither did he innovate. The War Department brought over 400,000 enemy POWs to this country; congressmen clamored for them to help meet America's critical labor shortage. No one argued that refugees might prove equally useful. And, when the British stalled and prevented the opening of a promised, jointly sponsored camp for stateless persons in Tripolitania, the WRB continued to press the British. It did not consider opening a camp sponsored only by the United States. Rescue hopes rode on people who had good intentions but limited imagination, people who would not challenge Roosevelt.

Peter Bergson, a maverick unencumbered by bureaucratic habits and obligations, took the cause of Jewish victims to the American public and got a hearing for the temporary havens scheme within the Roosevelt administration. However, he could never gain the trust of the community he sought to represent and succeeded only in uniting them against him rather than enlisting them in his campaign for temporary havens. Peter Bergson remains a controversial figure. Nevertheless, he and his cadre of young revisionists are on their way to becoming mythic heroes. It is a bitter reward for the failure of their efforts and the abuse heaped upon them by American Zionists.

American Jewry consisted largely of third-generation German Jews and first- and second-generation East European Jews, disparate groups who united easily only in opposition to Bergson. "Old" Jews feared that public demonstrations and combative rhetoric would arouse an anti-Semitic backlash. "New" Jews thought it folly at best and traitorous at worst to insist that anything, even immediate rescue, should divert attention from the only ultimate solution for threatened Jews, a Jewish state. Stephen S. Wise and Nahum Goldman, like John Pehle, tried to meet a new challenge with old methods. American Jewry's most prominent leaders were well-meaning but worn-out and frightened elderly men who denied Bergson legitimacy but could not offer an alternative.

Timid and divided, rescue advocates did not give Roosevelt a clear message. Had they united and taken their cause to the American public, could they have made a difference? Such a campaign was not practical until formation of the War Refugee Board. Pehle and Bergson believed that they could still save as many as fifty to one hundred thousand Hungarian Jews and perhaps a few thousand from the Balkans and elsewhere. Had American Zionist leaders cooperated and had Pehle been willing to take his case to the American public, could they have generated support sufficient to overcome Roosevelt's reluctance in time to be effective? They had less time than even they realized. Systematic deportations began in Hungary in late April 1944 and within three months led to the destruction of three-fourths of that country's Jews. Perhaps they could have saved significant numbers but only if they could have opened temporary havens in March or April, something they did not realize until the fate of Hungary's Jews became known in the fall.

Had the president intended the War Refugee Board to fulfill its stated mission, had he lent his support instead of waiting to be persuaded, then unified action by rescue advocates might have attracted sufficient public approval by spring 1944. A unified campaign and a supportive president might very well have discouraged restrictionist opposition and minimized political risks. Oswego was not free of anti-Semitism but it accepted the refugees in its midst and demonstrated that able leadership could hold anti-Semitic sentiments in check. Had the United States shown such leadership, would Britain have followed suit and would Hungarian Prime Minister Miklós Horthy have honored his April 1944 offer to release tens of thousands of Jews? At the time, the staff of the War Refugee Board believed that both were possible.

What did Franklin D. Roosevelt intend? Clare Booth Luce once observed that "every great leader had his typical gesture—Hitler the upraised arm, Churchill the V sign, Roosevelt? She wet her index finger and held it up."[1] Created in response to private and public pressures, the War Refugee Board was another of his devices for testing political winds. Its members provided status and its staff gave it credence but its structure assured restraint. An instrument for applying pressure against the British but not against himself, it put the president in a position to act magnanimously if a groundswell for action developed, while enabling him to give the appearance of action without having to take political risks.

Britain adamantly opposed every WRB effort and protected its Palestine policy. So long as Roosevelt contented himself with mere gestures, His Majesty's Government did not have to act. Given the rescue advocates' ineptitude and British pragmatism, Roosevelt was never challenged to take more than token action. And tokenism produced the Fort Ontario Emergency Refugee Shelter.

The Oswego camp sprang from one failure and remained in existence because of another. The first was that of the War Refugee Board, which proposed many havens. The second was that of the War Relocation Authority, which sought the refugees' freedom. Philosophically opposed to maintaining people in camps and fully supported in that view by its superiors in the Department of the Interior, the WRA set out from the beginning to ease internment restrictions. By the time the refugees arrived, it had already resettled on an internment-at-large basis more than 30 percent of the evacuees in Japanese Relocation Centers. Its failure to do the same for the refugees occurred not because it made an inadequate effort but because it faced insurmountable opposition. First the War Refugee Board and later the Justice Department and Department of State opposed releasing the refugees. But Franklin D. Roosevelt was the real opponent.

FDR refused to incur political risks for temporary havens and would not do so for the token one thousand he brought to this country. As did the War Refugee Board itself, the Emergency Refugee Shelter's administrative structure protected him from undue pressure. With responsibility for overall policy belonging to the War Refugee Board and day-to-day management assigned to the War Relocation Authority, FDR again faced divided authority incapable of presenting him with a challenge.

Like the WRB members and staff, the WRB and the WRA had conflicting goals. The WRB wanted to keep the refugees confined to Oswego, wished to provide no more than minimal maintenance, and opposed outside jobs that might place them in competition with American workers. Pehle remained interested in the Oswego refugees only insofar as they might help him win support for additional camps. He had to demonstrate that refugees could be brought to this country without placing undue wartime demands on the American people. The War Relocation Authority saw the need for greater freedom, for meaningful work, and for rehabilitative care. Dillon Myer concerned himself not with larger refugee questions but with the one thousand in his charge. He knew the debilitating effect of internment on personalities and relationships.

The refugees did not see themselves as an experimental model for additional WRB camps and did not know of the WRA's campaign on their behalf. Having endured unimaginable loss and deprivation, they had somehow been invited to be the "guests" of the president of the United States and expected, or at least hoped, to be treated accordingly. Less interested in how the invitation came about than in how they could use it to begin rebuilding their shattered lives, they assumed that Oswego meant American health care and American schooling as well as improved living conditions and freedom. Freedom remained beyond their reach. Yet they were far from passive. Labor problems persisted in large part because the government could not respond adequately to their struggle for meaningful work and adequate compensation. Without refugee initiatives, camp maintenance might very well have become impossible. At the same time that they most wanted to resume normal life and never accepted internment, they demanded and obtained improvements in every area of camp life.

Oswego's refugees also obtained unprecedented outside help. Private organizations, Jewish and non-Jewish, supported the temporary havens proposal, donated goods and services to the camp, worked for the refugees' freedom, and assisted them in their new communities. But only the National Refugee Service, to whom the WRB turned even before the shelter opened, played a dominant role throughout. The WRA came to depend on the NRS for both material and political assistance. And President Truman called on it to help draft the directive and to assume overall responsibility for the Oswego resettlement. The latter continued for several years, until each of the nineteen inadmissibles won the right to immigrate or no longer needed temporary visas renewed.

From beginning to end, the shelter promoted new forms of cooperation between private organizations and the government. This was especially true in the delivery of social welfare services. Similar arrangements did not develop in either POW camps or the Japanese Relocation Centers, both because they did not attract comparable interest and because their numbers precluded comparable involvement. At the same time that the government relied increasingly on private assistance, thereby absolving itself of obligations that it might otherwise have had to assume, it placed severe restrictions on private participation. The NRS and cooperating groups relinquished control of their own programs and maintained a low profile. The arrangement did not become a prototype for refugee and immigrant aid, but it did open the door to increased private involvement.

Just as rescue advocates had been unable to agree on how to save Jewish lives, shelter friends could not agree on how to win the group's freedom. The National Refugee Service, like the American Jewish Committee and World Jewish Congress, strove to strengthen government ties and avoid arousing anti-Semitic opposition. Preferring private lobbying to public campaigns, it discouraged relatives and parochial organizations from seeking independent solutions and opposed public efforts by both Joseph Smart and Samuel Dickstein. It bore the brunt of refugee dissatisfaction but contributed to the ultimate outcome in such a way as to help thousands of additional Displaced Persons.

Until the enormity of the Displaced Persons problem made both return and continued internment an embarrassment, Harry S. Truman felt that he should not renege on Roosevelt's promises. He timed the directive and the Oswego resettlement to reduce the likelihood of congressional opposition—the State Department and, to a lesser extent, the Department of Justice had already acquiesced—but few on Capitol Hill still believed that America would be able to resist making unused quota numbers available to Displaced Persons. Furthermore, most thought Americanized refugees far more desirable than those still in Europe. Surprisingly, until the American Jewish Committee raised the question in a November 26, 1945, letter to Secretary Byrnes, no Jewish group even raised the issue of liberalizing America's immigration law.[2] Jewish eyes were turned to Palestine. A large Jewish immigration seemed unlikely at that point and restrictionists did not feel threatened.

Oswego directly influenced Truman's adoption of the corporate affidavit, which proved to be his single most significant act affecting refugees. The Oswego resettlement could not have been completed in record time had not the State Department accepted a blanket guarantee in fulfillment of the public-charge clause. The corporate affidavit provided an alternative to individual guarantees, the device used most often to hold immigration below the limit permitted by law. The Truman Directive remained in effect only two years and, because of administrative difficulties, facilitated the immigration of only half as many DPs as expected. But the corporate affidavit continues to be used.

As for the camp itself, what was American internment like and what did it mean? Contrary to complaints voiced by many at the time, Fort Ontario was far from a concentration camp. After the first month, everyone had freedom of movement within Oswego. Those who spoke English well, particularly intellectuals and performers, found acceptance and acclaim that compensated somewhat for the loss of status they incurred as refugees. The government made every effort to provide full religious freedom and to accommodate religious differences. Those who wished to live as observant Jews could do so freely, for the first time in many years. Families separated by varying immigration opportunities remained separated. However, during the last eight months, those who had spouses and children in the United States could enjoy unlimited overnight visits either within the fort or in Oswego.

Shelter residents had far greater freedom than the restrictions indicate, particularly during the first ten months, when Joseph Smart served as administrator. A few worked clandestinely in Oswego and took unauthorized trips to New York and nearby communities. Others, throughout internment, conducted small entrepreneurial activities within the camp. Thanks to their own impressive talents, as well as extensive private assistance, they enjoyed a wide choice of recreational, cultural, and educational activities. All had freedom to spend time in the fort and funds in Oswego as they wished. The WRA exerted pressure on people to perform manual work, but it did not force them to do so.

Oswego offered freedoms and comforts unavailable to interned refugees elsewhere, but it also brought debilitating frustration and uncertainty. For those who had lived in Italian camps, which emptied months before the shelter closed, as well as those who had lived in Italy in relative freedom, Oswego meant an excruciating delay in the resumption of careers and ordinary living. A few learned skills that led to later vocations, but most viewed ORT classes as avocational. Professionals missed opportunities to remain abreast of new developments in their fields. Creative artists felt stifled. The environment also promoted paranoiac behavior and fostered sexual dysfunction. The camp contributed directly to individual deterioration and social disintegration.

Internment disrupted traditional family patterns. The refugee experience entailed a struggle for survival that enlarged the parental role. But the shelter reduced parents to dependents with little control over their own children. Like all such facilities, it denied parents their role as providers, unwittingly made children privy to adult intimacies, and substituted communal meals and schedules for family activities. The shelter also permitted children to attend school with Americans while denying their parents comparable opportunities to work and live alongside Americans. All immigrant families experience generational differences in rates of Americanization. The shelter made the gap even greater.

The camp also encouraged children to form primary rather than secondary associations with their peers. Sharing the pain of childhoods brutally stolen, the frustration of early and uneven maturation, and the anticipation of discovery in a new world, they formed special bonds with each other, bonds that further separated them both from their parents and from their American classmates. A few who had special problems remained loners. Others, in families who tried to overcome destructive pressures through such measures as carrying meals back to their rooms to maintain family dining, developed less dependency on peers. Many, however, particularly among the Yugoslavs, formed intense friendships, which continue to the present day. Interestingly, they frequently cannot recall those schoolmates who were only one or two grades above or below them.

Most former shelter students also remember little of their parents' difficulties and recall the internment experience as a happy one. There they formed their closest friendships and learned to look to the future rather than the past. Loners found the experience more painful, but the majority who formed close bonds with peers made a smoother transition to America than they would have had they been regular immigrants. Because they constituted nearly 10 percent of Oswego's school enrollment, they drew far more attention and interest than they would have had they enrolled individually in schools across the country. Oswego mentors appreciated their ambition and talents, encouraged them to pursue dreams, and profoundly influenced their future careers.

Most children escaped the despair that afflicted so many of the older refugees, but the latter proved enormously resilient as soon as freedom became a reality. WRA staff had reason to fear that internment had made a considerable number institutionally dependent, unwilling to leave the security of the camp for the uncertainties of a competitive world. That fear proved to be totally unfounded. They left eagerly, neither beaten nor cowed. And they left with their pride intact, often refusing to remain welfare recipients for even a few more days.

The Emergency Refugee Shelter remained a unique and solitary act of tokenism. Politics pulled it from the wreckage of the temporary havens proposal, kept it in operation eight months after Germany surrendered, and enabled its refugee population to gain immigrant status. It served neither as a prototype for additional havens nor as a model for a new approach to immigration. It did, however, bring the NRS and other private groups into closer cooperation with government offices. And it led directly to the Truman Directive, which facilitated the admission of Displaced Persons and regularized use of the corporate affidavit. Above all, the Oswego story offers new insights into what might have been, a greater sense of the enormity of the loss, and a deeper awareness of how we could have been enriched.

Epilogue

The former residents of the Emergency Refugee Shelter in Oswego symbolize "the strength of the Jewish people . . . and (the) goodness of this nation." So New York Governor Mario Cuomo characterized them as he greeted more than three hundred former refugees, family members, and friends who gathered on August 2, 1984, for the fortieth anniversary of the group's arrival in Hoboken, New Jersey. Speaking at New York's Newman Theatre, a former HIAS shelter, Cuomo applauded his predecessor in Albany, Franklin Roosevelt, for making it all possible.

Those present agreed with Ruth Gruber: "We are the Oswego family . . . this is our day." She had planned the reunion and received much-deserved tribute. A few former Oswego refugees had gathered on other occasions, but publication of her book, *Haven,* the previous year enabled dozens to discuss, for the first time, their refugee experiences and to seek each other.

Adam Munz[1] spoke for the former refugees. It seems "as though it happened yesterday. . . . The stench of death was still in our nostrils. . . . How wanted were we? Hard to say. How much did we yearn to be wanted? We ached for it!" True, "so many more of us could have and should have made it." However, "the shame of it is not ours but Germany's and witnessing nations." He urged, "let us continue to help strive for a world where refugees will not have to be sheltered," a world better "than the one we came into."

Adam Munz was eighteen when he left Oswego and is today associate professor of medical psychology at Columbia University, director of psychological services of the St. Luke's Site of the St.

Luke's—Roosevelt Hospital Center in New York, past president of the New York Society for Clinical Psychologists, and current president of the clinical division of the New York State Psychological Association. Had he followed in his Polish father's footsteps, the tradition in Europe, he would have become a butcher. Psychology represented a "radical departure," the result of a "complusion to work with people" that grew from refugee experiences.[2]

Oswego gave young Adam Munz "a sense of what democracy is about." It influenced his choice of avocation as well as profession. Graphic artist **Max Sipser,** the cartoonist for the camp newspaper, taught him to paint miniatures in watercolor. He resumed painting a few years ago while recovering from heart surgery, has won prizes at several national and international art association exhibits, and plans to paint full-time when he retires. Munz is married to Lotte, a child psychiatrist, and they have a seventeen-year-old daughter, Robin.

Walter Grunberg, who characterized Oswego as "a bittersweet experience," also represented former internees. "We had everything but our freedom." Born in Italy of Austrian parents, he had been the last to celebrate his Bar Mitzvah in the camp. Now Walter Greenberg, he is a documentary filmmaker and communications expert. "The important thread" that Oswego refugees have in common is that "each one wanted to succeed and give back to society rather than take." He and his wife met at a Zionist training farm and lived on an Israeli kibbutz from 1953 to 1956. In Israel, "I wasn't part of a minority . . . I felt I was contributing to society . . . I felt productive. . . . I always knew that I was Jewish . . . the non-Jewish world let me know . . . in Israel I felt differently." But kibbutz life proved too confining. The Greenbergs moved to Cuba, where Celia had lived, and then back to the States.

Greenberg returned to Oswego on October 24, 1984, to attend a conference on university housing. A consultant to Rockman Community College, he found enormous satisfaction in resolving housing problems for others. "A kid who came hungry . . . without shoes . . . I had come full circle."[3]

Gruber called the reunion "a time for healing." That seemed apparent when **Marianna Hartmeyer Breuer,** the camp's first bride, led everyone in singing their old theme song. This time they sang "Don't Fence Me In" with affectionate nostaligia. The lovely soprano whose voice drew the attention of rescuers in a French camp has since sung with the Santa Monica Civic Opera Company, the American Opera Company, and the Beverly Hills Symphony. After terrors suffered at the hands of Gestapo men who tore her from her family, singing brought her "back to [her] senses." It remains her "biggest form of therapy."[4]

Manya—that was always her true name—Breuer's immediate family, German Jews, all survived: her father in southern Italy, her mother in southern France, her brother Zigi in Auschwitz, and her brother Willi in an Italian orphanage. Zigi returned to Italy to look for members of his family, met Ernst Breuer's father by chance in a synagogue, and learned that Manya had gone to Oswego, married, and was living in California. By the early sixties she was reunited with her parents and both brothers.

The reunion program also featured **Leon Levitch,** who played one of his own compositions, several of which have been recorded on the Orion label. He studied harmony with the renowned Isaac Thaler in Ferramonte and piano with **Frieda Sipser** and **Vera Levinson** in the shelter. The Yugoslav youth worked as a piano tuner in Los Angeles, a skill acquired during internments, and earned an M.A. in composition. In 1971 he helped create a department of piano technology at UCLA and in 1978 he was instrumental in developing a similar program at the Northridge Extension of California State University.

The reunion also featured taped vocals by **Eva Bass,** a waiflike songstress who entertained frequently but had difficulty coping with the rejection that her free spirit incurred. A Swiss-born former citizen of Poland, she died in 1971 at the age of sixty-two. **Yolanda Bass** Fredkove, an infant forty years ago, spoke movingly of her mother and played the tapes. Renamed Gloria because her mother wanted her to have a name that "sounded American" when the child enrolled in kindergarten, she briefly resumed the name Yolanda while searching for her "roots" but found it "too strange."[5] A paralegal in St. Paul, in 1985 she introduced a newsletter for former Oswego refugees and friends.

Roll Call

Charles Abeles, a forty-two-year old Roman Catholic interned in several Nazi camps because of his Social Democratic politics, the man who organized the camp orchestra and music school, returned to Austria, where a government pension awaited him.

Hermine Ackermann, seventy-three, died only two days before the **Arnstein** family (her daughter, son-in-law, and their children) left Oswego for Cleveland. Except for this, the boys, **Valdo** (Walter) and **Pavle** (Paul), view their adolescent years in Oswego as "a very pleasant memory," one that was even "exhilarating."[6] The next few years were much harder, for their parents, **Lavoslav** (Leo) and **Jelka,** had only two more years together. A former clothing manufacturer who worked in Cleveland as a clerk in a textile factory, Leo suffered a massive stroke at the age of fifty-one.

The brothers and their families live in Berkeley. Paul worked his way through Ohio State University's School of Veterinary Medicine and entered the United States Public Health Service. His research focuses on plague, rabies, and cancer. Walter, a Ph.D. in electrical engineering, designs computers. **Eva,** their younger sister, is married to an economist at Indiana University and operates her own art gallery.

Eighty-one-year-old **Eva Auerbach** explains that she and many in her generation "didn't realize how nice and good we had it" in Oswego until forced to fend for themselves after the camp closed. Her husband, **Jakob,** manufactured dresses before the war. In his mid-forties he had to accept menial work in New York until finally finding an office job with an import-export company. She became a seamstress for a fashionable milliner. If Yugoslavia had not become communist, they "might have returned."[7]

Karl Bader, the innovative electrician who made and sold electric hot plates, attended the reunion with his wife, **Magdalene** (Magdalena), and daughter, **Liesl Bader** Friedman. Karl found factory work in New York and his wife became a corsetiere. Now in their eighties, they live in a senior-citizen housing project whose gardens he lovingly maintains as a "paradise."[8]

Twelve years old when President Roosevelt died, Liesl felt sad but not sorry. She took the news to mean that "Maybe we would not have to go back where we come from as we agreed to with him."[9] A graduate of Queens College in sociology and psychology and of Columbia University's school of occupational therapy, she is married to Lawrence Friedman, a psychiatrist, and works as a clinical supervisor in pediatric occupational therapy in Manhattan.

Twelve-year-old **Joachim Bass** (Jack) spent the last four months of the shelter's existence in a foster home in Philadelphia along with his baby sister, **Yolanda.** WRA welfare workers persuaded their mother, **Eva Bass,** to give up for adoption an illegitimate daughter born in the camp. Today, Jack Bass owns a limousine service in Manhattan. He had mixed feelings about attending the reunion, which released bits of repressed memories. Meeting with this writer in Ruth Gruber's apartment, he discussed the experience "for the first time" and found that he wanted to use it to help others.[10]

Also very much on the reunion scene were **Fredi Baum** (Fred) and his wife, **Jenny Baruch** Baum. The shelter's official interpreter, viewed by other refugees as having official status, he became an assistant regional director for UNRRA and worked with Displaced Persons in Europe. When he returned to New York he found a job with a shoe-importing firm, and today he owns a chain of retail shoe stores. The Oswego group included very few men in their twenties, the prime age for military service. Twenty-five-year-old Fred had been ineligible for the military because he had lost a leg in a prewar accident. Tragically, the Baums lost one of their two children, a twenty-two-year-old son, in a mountain-climbing accident.

Having known several camps both as a refugee and as an UNRRA worker, Fred wants Oswego to be seen as distinctive. Compared to the other camps, "the only bad thing [about Oswego] was the climate."[11]

Geza Bleier attended the reunion with his two sons. Infants when their mother committed suicide and the WRA placed them in foster homes in Rochester, they lived in and out of New York orphanages while Geza struggled to earn a living and find a wife and mother. Two marriages to refugees, the first to **Rachael Ovadia,** ended in divorce. Happily married to his American-born fourth wife, he is, at seventy-two, erect and handsome and carries his years and his difficulties with dignity. "In spite of all that happened to me . . . I considered myself a winner because I was alive, I had two healthy children . . . other people had bigger losses."[12] A shoe merchant in Yugoslavia, he is now a textile salesman in New York. His son **Ronald,** who served in the Peace Corps, now teaches high school. **George** is an elementary school counselor.

Ernst Bleier, a widowed jeweler born in 1899 in Vienna who was alone in the camp, died several years ago in New York. Geza reports that Ernst "never accepted his losses . . . could not acclimatize . . . became mentally ill and died." He notes that it is nearly impossible for those of us who have not known such trauma to comprehend fully the horror of the refugee experience. "To be displaced from your environment could crush a horse."[13]

Fred Bohm had lost contact with his parents and tried to get an emergency furlough immediately after learning that they had arrived in Oswego, but he was shipped overseas. He did not see them until after V.E. Day. An importer's agent in Austria, **Ignatz Boehm** found a job in New York with a former customer. As a young woman in the years before World War I, **Ester Boehm** had traveled to the Mideast to survey market conditions for the Singer Sewing Company. In her mid-sixties when the shelter closed, she applied to Singer for another job. "Surprised but cooperative," she was made a production line supervisor. Ignatz died in 1955 at the age of seventy-one, Ester in 1962 at eighty-one. Fred is an industrial designer. He and his wife have two daughters, one of whom, Rabbi Lenore Bohm, received ordination at Hebrew Union College in 1982.[14]

Paul Bokros attended the reunion with his sister **Nelly Bokros** Thalheimer. One of several young men deeply influenced by Oswego High School industrial arts teacher Tom Crabtree, the enterprising sixteen-year-old, who had run a thriving bootleg liquor business in Italy, became an electronics engineer. He served as an Air Force instructor during the Korean War and, as engineering director for a branch of General Dynamics, he has been involved in the development of several missile systems.

Paul never became a Bar Mitzvah and is ambivalent about Judaism. "I tried to go to Friday services. . . . I cannot bring myself to participate even in the least ceremonial services." Paul and his wife, Greta, spoke to me in their lovely poolside San Diego home in 1980, at a time when, to their surprise, their son was studying in a yeshiva in Israel. On a subsequent trip to Israel Paul found himself drawn first to the Wall, the only remnant of the ancient Temple Mount, to recite the Kaddish, the traditional mourner's prayer. And this past year, "for reasons that I do not understand," he fasted on Yom Kippur. He is not ambivalent about feelings of connectedness to fellow Jews. He and his family "took it for granted that Jewish organizations helped bring us over." They relied heavily on Jewish assistance when the camp closed, and remain deeply grateful.[15] Paul particularly remembers the Jewish country club where he lived with his parents and two sisters until Philadelphia's Jewish family agency found them an apartment.

Paul's father, **Filip Bokros,** who exported skins and lumber in Yugoslavia and became chief of the diet kitchen in Oswego, was already in his mid-sixties when the shelter closed. He worked at various menial jobs until his death of a coronary in 1953, two years after the death of his wife, **Alice.** She had worked in a sweatshop until becoming ill with leukemia.

Nelly Bokros, sixteen when the camp closed, obtained a B.A. in night school, has an M.A. in social gerontology, and works as a geriatric social worker. Married to Hans Thalheimer, a corporate vice-president, she is the mother of Philip, who is studying to be an industrial psychologist; David, a law student; and Jeffrey, an undergraduate. Oswego's friendliness and educational opportunities remain "special" for her.[16] Her sister, **Mira,** ten when she left Oswego, advanced from clerk to auditor in the civil service, married Myron Halpern, a professor of anatomy and physiology at Camden County College, New Jersey, and has two sons, both students.

I met **Bellina Boni** and her oldest son, **Raymond,** in August 1980 at Ruth Gruber's New York apartment. A Bulgarian widow, she lives with her middle son, **Claude,** a real-estate broker, and his wife, a librarian. **Sylvan,** her youngest son, recently earned his Ph.D. in philosophy and teaches the philosophy of religion to academically talented students. His wife is the principal of a Jewish Day School. Raymond, the family support for "several" years, earned an engineering degree in night school. The only one of the family no longer in

Philadelphia, he lives in Queens, where his wife operates a typing service.[17]

Ernst Breuer is a real estate broker in Los Angeles. He and Manya, the first to marry in the camp, divorced in 1965. They have three children. Diane is an airline stewardess, Gregory a pilot and air controller, and Marsha a hairdresser active in a support group for children of Holocaust survivors. **Alice Breuer,** Ernst's sister who traversed the Alps with Manya, is now Liesl (always her real name) Earle. She operates an imported knitwear shop in Toronto with Trudy, a sister who joined her from England.

Heinrich and **Elenora Bronner,** Orthodox Polish Jews, moved to Jersey City, where they had a sister and brother-in-law. A sixty-year-old former shoe designer, Heinrich never reestablished himself. Twelve years younger than her husband, Elenora worked in a sweater factory. Both died in their eighties. **Lily,** their oldest child, married a Post Office supervisor and had two sons, one a teacher and one a certified public accountant. **Jack,** the youngest, is a retired noncommissioned Army officer and works for NASA in Washington. **Edith** completed high school at night, became a keypunch operator, and married Murray Klein, released after the war from a Siberian labor camp. He is president of Zabar's, the New York gourmet shop, where he began as a delivery boy. Their daughter is an M.B.A. married to a physician. A son is a student. Edith is grateful for having come to a country whose opportunities are unequaled, but she wants it known that "we saved ourselves"—that the refugees were no longer in danger when the shelter opened. Oswego "doesn't wash [America's] hands clean."[18]

Undue stresses made it necessary for the WRA to find temporary foster homes in Rochester and Buffalo for the children of three families, the Basses, Bleiers, and **Buchlers**—each represented at the reunion. **Renee Buchler,** who lost her first husband in the coal accident, remarried in 1953 and is now Renée Tenenbaum. She attended the reunion with daughter **Hana,** a housewife like her sister, **Blanka.** Renée's son **Dan** supports himself with various jobs in order to devote himself to the study of Torah. His brother, **Pavle,** also a scholar and the father of five children, is a salesman for a metal stamping firm. Orthodox Sephardim from Yugoslavia, they have been "strengthened" by their trials. "We saw so many miracles. . . . Here in America, we were freer to be able to practice and be observant."[19]

Angelina Cicarelli and her twenty-five-year-old daughter, **Vesna Culic,** Yugoslav Roman Catholics, moved to Cleveland, where Vesna, an interpreter in Italy, worked as a bookkeeper until her marriage to **Rajko Margulis.**

Sari Danon, who had tears in her eyes when she heard "My

Country 'Tis of Thee," was fifteen when she moved with her parents, brother, and sister to Philadelphia. Now Sarah Meller, she and her husband, a luncheonette owner, have three children, a son who is a urologist, a son in the wholesale food business, and a daughter studying to be a pharmacist. Sarah's father, **Josip,** a Yugoslav merchant who deposited one of the larger sums of currency with the Allied Control Commission, never fully recovered his health. He worked in a variety store and died in his mid-sixties. His wife, **Hana,** sewed in a factory until the children were grown. She lives in Baltimore with **Ester,** her younger daughter. Her son, **Isak,** is a government auditor in Washington.[20]

A second Danon family, unrelated to the one above, included two brothers and their families. **Rafael Danon,** a confectioner from Yugoslavia, was initially ruled inadmissible because of psychiatric problems and may have spent some time in the Oswego County Sanitorium before obtaining a change in status. He and his wife, **Erna,** soon moved to California, where they established Danon Butter Cookies. Born in 1901, Erna died of a heart attack in 1963. Two years older, Rafael died in a convalescent home soon after.

Rafael's brother, **Sima Danon,** a leather worker in Yugoslavia and barracks leader in the shelter, was an existentialist who believed that you "had to do everything for yourself." The NRS sent him and his family to Cleveland, but they found it "too desolate" without their friends. Moving to New York as soon as it was possible, Sima borrowed $300 and opened a shop for seconds in ladies' underwear. Several years later he followed Rafael and Erna to California. Before his death in 1964, at the age of sixty-four, Sima owned a chain of fashionable dress shops in the Santa Monica area. Rasela, his widow, died in 1972 at the age of sixty-three. **Mika** (Mike), their son, manufactures draperies. **Ica** (Ike), his brother, is a real-estate investor.

Soon after **Irene Danon,** Sima and Rasela's daughter, joined the migration to California, she found herself a widow with three small daughters. Supporting her family by sewing in her home, she is today a successful real-estate broker living "the good life." Proud of her accomplishments, she is unabashedly patriotic. "Where else can a little refugee girl end up in a beautiful home, own apartment houses, drive a big car and keep going to school. Only in America."[21] The Danon family lost 190 relatives to the Nazis. "I'm a very positive person," says Irene. "Under the circumstances, [Oswego] was okay."[22]

A bribe got **Alexandra Deutsch** and her two daughters, both in their mid-twenties, out of the Sajmiste camp near Belgrade two weeks before its entire population of seven thousand women and children were deported. Alexandra, the widow of a leather manufacturer killed by the Nazis, is "still spry" at ninety. One daughter, **Elsa**

Deutsch Ceraldi, mother of a schoolteacher, died in 1981, when she was sixty-two. The other, **Gordana Milinovic Musafia,** wife of a bicycle shop owner, was until recently an administrative assistant to the president of an import-export company.[23]

Jakob Dresdner was born in 1901 in Satumare, Hungary, home of the Satmar sect of Hasidism, which argued that Hebrew was a sacred tongue not to be used as a vernacular, and which opposed creation of the secular State of Israel as an interference with the coming of the Messiah. Jakob, who served as cantor in the camp's Orthodox congregation, and his wife, **Ellena,** arrived with nine children, the oldest born in Czechoslovakia, the second in Belgium, and the rest in Rumania. They had eluded the Nazis by separating and hiding in various monasteries.

Elizabeta, the oldest, married a diamond merchant and emigrated to Israel. **Rudolf,** who operates a kosher fast and fancy food establishment, lives in Stanford, Connecticut. The others live in Brooklyn and the Bronx. **Francine,** a special education teacher, attended the reunion with **Salomon,** an insurance agent, and **Joseph,** who works in industrial diamonds. **Abraham** works in a lingerie shop, **Isidore** works in a knitting shop, and **Paula**'s husband works for a chemical firm.

Jakob died in 1982. Ellena, two years younger, died in 1983. The siblings remain close and gather with their families every four to six weeks. Oswego brought them to this country. "I felt I owed a debt," said Salomon. "Two years in the Army, I paid."[24]

Few are as willing to express their bitterness as is **Herbert Drucks** (Druks), who, as a youngster, watched his parents, **Chaim** and **Ada,** struggle while Chaim tried to resume sweater manufacturing. "I was sorry that we ever came here. This is a very hard country. It's a country that eats up people alive." The question "why?" haunted him. And his search for answers led him to earn a B.A. at City College, M.A. at Rutgers University, and Ph.D. at New York University. Associate professor in American diplomatic and presidential history at Brooklyn College, he says, "It's not all FDR and the scoundrels. There's a lot of American history that represents the better side of human nature. There's an ideal side—Jeffersonian democracy." As for Oswego itself, "it was an abomination. The United States Government owes us compensation for that imprisonment," just as it owes Japanese-American evacuees.[25]

Artur Ernst, a sixty-year-old Viennese Roman Catholic editor-attorney arrested for anti-Nazi editorials, married his "Girl in Springfield, Mass.," wrote for a German-language newspaper in New York, and lived in Springfield until his death in 1965. Lily, now eighty, made the eight-hour trip to Oswego nineteen times. She recalls, "He was enthusiastic . . . everything was as good as we could have hoped for . . . very friendly, nice, very good climate."[26]

Silvio Finci, who was working alongside Arpad Buchler when the coal accident occurred and refused to work thereafter, moved with his wife, **Rikica** (Ricki), and their two youngsters, **Mika** (Mike) and **Sonja,** to Baltimore. Silvio, a lumber mill clerk in Sarajevo, became a buyer for a larger lumber company. He died in 1983, two years after Ricki. Sonja, married to Theodore Setran and the mother of three children, is a secretary. Mike, a soccer star at the University of Maryland, is an independent insurance broker. He and his wife, Brenda, have two children, a son who is an attorney and a daughter who recently completed her undergraduate studies. His parents were active synagogue members but participation in various fund drives provides Mike's formal affiliation to the Jewish community.[27]

Oskar and **Lydia Finger** inherited a five-story brownstone on Seventy-Ninth Street two years after they moved to New York. Lydia opened a corset business, which her husband, a merchant in Czechoslovakia, soon joined. Would-be settlers in Palestine shipwrecked on the *Pentcho,* they never found time to visit Israel. Now eighty-six, Oskar is retired. However, at seventy-six, Lydia, a popular singer in the camp, still works seven-day weeks. Both attended the reunion. "I'm a very successful and very diligent girl. I don't want to get old." Having started "with eighteen dollars and two smart children," she says, "What we achieved is marvelous, [but we] got a lot of help." Their son, **Arnon,** is a mechanical engineer. **Susan,** born in the camp, is a single parent with a small daughter.[28]

Ernst Flatau, an attorney whose paternal grandfather had been one of the earliest Jews in California and whose clients in Germany once included the (American) Motion Picture Association, served as one of the camp's principal refugee leaders and wrote poetry that he recited on numerous occasions. Sixty when the camp closed, he found translation work in New York. **Anni Flatau,** eighteen years younger than her husband, a popular performer in the camp and one of the shelter residents selected to testify at the Dickstein Hearings, became a ladies' companion and waitress. Both died in the mid-1970s.

Ernst and Anni had three sons. Gerald, the oldest, was among a group of students in England sent to Australia during the war. Lung cancer took **Rolf Steven Flatau,** a corporate executive, in 1982 at the age of fifty-one. He left a wife and two children, a son who completed college and works for Swank, and a daughter still in school. **Fred Flatau,** his twin, is an internist in New York. He and his wife, a student nurse when they married, have two children still in school. A physician from a family of attorneys, Fred feels that the refugee experience did not influence his choice of professions but did cause him to become active in the politics of medicine. Remembering how it was in Europe, he opposes both restrictions against foreign physicians and the death penalty. Above all, he rejects absolutes. "I can never be as sure of things being right because I've seen noble experiments go bad."[29]

Hella Frajerman "wanted to live in New York with her friends," but, like many who had no connection to New York, she was persuaded to move elsewhere, in this case to Philadelphia. She became a cigar-factory worker, and **Icek,** her forty-one-year-old capmaker husband from Poland, learned how to be a furrier. Daughter **Rachel** is the mother of four youngsters and a recent widow. Her husband operated a dry goods store on Marshall Street. **Salomon** (Sam Fraserman), the oldest son, earned a B.A. in English literature from Temple University and is in management at the Industrial Supply Center, a government agency. His brother **Jacob** graduated from Philadelphia's Textile Institute and works for a division of Kodak in California. The youngest son, **Harry,** born in the camp, is a distributor for a Philadelphia dairy.[30]

Meant to be only for people who had no homes to which they could return, Oswego included only one family of Italian Jews. **Victor** and **Lidia Franco** had been born in the Dodecanesi Islands and their three children in North Africa. A merchant, Victor opened his own beer and wine store in Atlanta, where he died in 1981 at the age of seventy-one. The Francos lost their daughter **Rachele** to cancer in 1961 when she was twenty-four-years old. **David,** two years younger, has a wife and three children and works for a jeweler. **Miriam Mary,** who was the first baby born in the camp, and her husband work for insurance companies. All are observant Jews. Lidia says fervently, "I thank God I came" to the United States. About her refugee experience, there is "too much memory. [I] never talk." As for Oswego, "it was beautiful."[31]

Oton and **Elsa Froelich** chose repatriation to Yugoslavia, where their three children had remained with the partisans. Ironically, they sailed back to Europe at the very time that one son was flying to New York. Twenty-nine-year-old Ernest, a doctor of veterinary medicine, had been appointed an UNRRA Fellow and was on his way to a meeting at the United Nations. He never returned to Yugoslavia and never saw his parents again. The Froelich's daughter joined Ernest in the United States after both parents died, Elsa in 1959 at the age of seventy-two and Oton in 1968 at the age of eighty-five. Their brother continues to live in Yugoslavia.

Oton and Elsa listed themselves as Roman Catholics when they arrived in Oswego. Ernest, a Doctor of Veterinary Medicine who worked in research for thirty-one years, learned from his brother a few years ago that a "liberal" priest whom he knew well baptized his parents and younger siblings soon after Germany bombed Yugoslavia and predated the baptismal certificates so that the family might travel more freely from their home in Croatia.[32] Ernest was stationed with the Yugoslav Army at the time of his family's baptisms.

I met **Abe Furmanski** (now Abe Forman) in Ruth Gruber's apartment a few years ago and spoke with him and his wife, Regina, at the reunion. When he arrived at Oswego, he was a widowed tailor from Poland in his mid-thirties, who had seen the inside of several Nazi internment camps and worked with underground units in France and in Italy. In Oswego, he became a leader of the Polish group. In New York, he remarried and became a coin and metals dealer. Abe is "anti-religious" but sent his son, Armand, to a yeshiva "to learn what it is to be religious."[33] Armand died of Hodgkins Disease in 1970, when he was twenty-two.

Regina Gal, born in Poland in 1909, saw her husband and three brothers taken by the Nazis in France, where she had lived for some time and had borne two children. The former embroidery worker who fashioned a shirt and pants for each of her youngsters from a sailor's shirt became a seamstress in New York. She too "was not religious" but sent her children to yeshivot so that they would know "what it is to be religious." Her daughter, **Charlotte,** a bookkeeper, has returned to college to earn her B.A. Her son, **Albert,** who credits his love for music to the camp, became a computer programmer/analyst and married a social worker. They have one child.[34]

Clara Gaon, who attended the reunion, lost her husband, **Salomon,** to leukemia while in the camp and supported herself and seven-year-old **Zdenko** (Jack) in New York by working as a manicurist. Jack is a welfare worker for New York's Human Resources Corporation.

Nearly everyone in the shelter had dental problems, but few suffered more than **Vera Gross.** Ten years old when the camp closed, she endured years of severe migraines, ringing in the ears, and pain in the face, all induced by what was eventually diagnosed as a correctable dental condition. A one-time student of dental hygiene, she manages an orthodontist's office. Vera and her husband, the proprietor of a food store, have two daughters, one a computer scientist and one in dental work. Vera's parents, **Alexander** and **Jolanda Gross,** hoped to move with their daughter to Buenos Aires, where two siblings, their only remaining family, lived. However, by the time they obtained visas, they felt too settled in New York to move again. A coal mine expert in Yugoslavia, Alexander became a sales representative for

Gimbels. He died in 1960 at the age of sixty-three. Vera worked in an Ex-Lax factory and now lives in retirement in Miami Beach. She remembers that "The people in Oswego had never seen a Jew. They came to look at us." That part of her life was "very painful" because she "felt so different," even more different than in Europe.[35]

Chance brought the **Grunberg** family to Oswego and chance led them to settle briefly in Buffalo when the shelter closed. Viennese-born **Jacob,** a thirty-seven-year-old pastry chef, had lived in Italy for ten years when he and **Irma,** his Yugoslav-born wife, opened a hotel and hostelry in Fiume in 1930. **Walter** was born three years later. In 1940 an attempt to join the illegal movement of Jews into Palestine led to their internment in Libya and then in Italy. When the Oswego shelter closed, they were scheduled to settle in Newark. However, the Buffalo hotel in which their group stayed overnight on the return from Canada offered Jacob and Irma jobs. The family remained in Buffalo for six months, long enough to save the funds that enabled them to move to New York, another instance in which families not scheduled for New York insisted on living there anyway. Soon widowed, Irma eventually remarried and, for many years, operated a luncheonette with her second husband.

Lea Hanf, whose father was seized in 1941 and never heard from again, was nineteen when she moved with her mother to New York and began the long struggle that took her to the position of manager of a large textile firm. In 1965 she helped organize the twentieth reunion of the 1945 class of Oswego High School. Five years later she and her radio executive husband, Alexander Frank, died in a tragic car accident, three years after her mother, **Zlata,** died of a stroke. Denise Battat, their daughter, a graduate of the Fletcher School of Law and Diplomacy, continued her mother's correspondence with Oswego High School principal Ralph Faust and became one of my first leads to former Oswego refugees.

Hajim Hazan, a *shohet* (ritual slaughterer) from Yugoslavia, served a congregation in Cincinnati for eleven years and one in Sioux City for sixteen. Eighty-one and living in retirement in Miami Beach, he agreed four years ago to serve a Sephardic congregation as a "temporary" Torah reader and is still doing so. His wife, **Rika,** seventy-six, suffers a heart condition. They have three children. **Josef** is a photographer in Los Angeles, **Jack,** a dentist in Tampa. Linda, born in Cincinnati, is a homemaker with three small sons in Omaha. Hajim says of Oswego, "We were satisfied."[36]

David Hellner, a sixty-six-year-old merchant from Poland, was ruled inadmissible because of tuberculosis and died in a sanitarium in Perrysburg, New York. His wife, **Dina,** fifty-nine at the time, lived with daughter Judy Hellner Schatz and her family in Buffalo and died in the early 1970s. Married to a music teacher, Judy manages her own dress shop. Her daughter operates a cable station in San Francisco. Her sister, Ruthe Hellner Zogut, is married to a pharmacist and has two daughters, one a student and one who works for the Internal Revenue Service. The sisters attended the reunion. "My parents were very happy" in Oswego.[37]

David Hendel, the Yugoslav youth who traded Italian coins for a shirt and pants that he thought an American sailor gave away because they were soiled, attended night classes at City College, earned a B.A. in chemistry and biology, served in the Unites States Army, and returned to complete his studies in the School of Dentistry at Columbia University. He also changed his name to Hendell, thereby moving the accent from the first to the second syllable to order to discard the Germanic pronunciation. A specialist in the art of "bonding" to reshape and restructure teeth, he looks back on Oswego as "a dreamlike existence."[38] **Ruth,** David's younger sister, became a public school-teacher, married psychiatrist Jacob Robert Fishman, earned an M.A. in art therapy, and joined her husband in his Washington, D.C., office. The Hendels' parents, **Eisig** and **Hanna,** after years of struggle to reestablish themselves in the jewelry business, began to divide their time between New York and Bat Yam, Israel.

Eisig and Hanna also cared for their nieces, **Jetta** and **Gizella Hendel,** children of Eisig's murdered brother and sister-in-law. Jetta, married to clinical psychologist Myron Gordon, became fascinated with the South Pacific and served for ten years as the United Nations representative of the Southeast Asia Women's Association. Her daughter Tamar is an anthropologist, and her daughter Eve is preparing to become a clinical psychologist. Gizella earned a Ph.D. in anthropology from Columbia University and is an associate professor at the State University of New York in New Paltz.

Zlatko and **Milika Hirschler,** the Yugoslav couple in their thirties who earned extra money by stringing beads for a woman in New York, remained in New York only a few years before moving to San Francisco, where they operate a small business. He wrote an unpublished memoir, "Flight," which they share with friends, and they have also given me significant research help. Their friends, all Jewish and mostly former refugees, know their background. Yet the Hirschlers have taken Anglo-Saxon names, and Milika does not want to have their new names associated with Oswego. As for the experience itself, Zlatko wrote, "it was an excellent transition period for all of us . . . it was very beneficial to our inner well-being because instant free life might have ruined our inner equilibrium."[39]

John Hunter (he drove a taxi and waited tables at Hunter Mountain while an undergraduate) changed his name in 1960, when RCA accepted him as a management trainee. Few Jews were to be found in the board rooms of Fortune 500 companies, and he wanted to make himself more acceptable. In 1970 he founded a computer firm that employs 250 and annually grosses over $40 million. President of a subdivision responsible for acquisitions and mergers of Volt Science, Inc., the $400 million parent corporation to which he sold Delta Resources, he tells M.B.A. classes at Columbia University, his alma mater, "I really believe that our society is open to any level of achievement if one has the willingness and the commitment and the need to achieve."[40] Born **Ivo Hirschler,** he attributes his drive to insecurities stemming from the refugee experience and to encouragement he received in the elementary school of Oswego State Teachers' College.

A bachelor, John Hunter felt that he represented his parents at the reunion. **Julio Hirschler,** who died in the early 1960s before he reached seventy, had been a bank clerk in Yugoslavia and became a bookkeeper. **Ella Hirschler,** who died in the early 1970s at a similar age, made wigs for mannequins.

Raymond B. Harding ("David Harding, Counterspy" was his favorite radio program and he developed a special fondness for a cousin named Ray), like John Hunter, his lifelong friend, worked his way through school driving a cab and waiting tables. He graduated from New York University School of Law, served five years as a special assistant to Governor Hugh Carey, joined the law firm of Shea and Gould, and became the chief political strategist for New York State's Liberal Party. His parents wanted him to become an engineer, the profession most readily transferable from one culture to another. In college he switched to prelaw, an expression of his confidence in the future of America. The former **Branko Hochwald,** he views Oswego as the "best time" of his life, a "gift of a happy childhood . . . a carefree introduction to American schooling, and a time for forming lifelong friends."[41]

Ray Harding did not enter a synagogue for twenty years after his Bar Mitzvah. He thinks pride in one's background important but "never identified that with the rituals of Judaism." Nevertheless, he insisted that his two boys attend Hebrew School and each become a Bar Mitzvah. The sons, one an attorney and the other still a student, are both more traditional than Ray and his wife, Elisabeth, a former refugee who immigrated after the war.

In the summer of 1946 Ray's father, **Mane Hochwald,** a wood merchant in Yugoslavia and labor leader in the shelter, began work as a waiter in the Catskills, and **Jelka,** his wife, became a chef. Winters he waited tables at the Commodore Hotel and she made candy on an assembly line. She soon worked throughout the year as a chef, until taking a job with an insurance company. In their eighties and retired,

Mane and Helen Harding live in Forest Hills, next door to Irma Grunberg Liptcher, Walter Greenberg's mother. Says Ray, "My parents' generation acclimated extremely well with a minimum of feeling sorry for themselves. Their children's accomplishments became more important than ordinarily."[42]

Leon and **Sari Kabiljo** named their daughter, conceived aboard the *Henry Gibbins*, **Silvia Simcha,** to celebrate the joy they felt starting life anew. Leon, a revenue officer for the Yugoslav government for ten years, became a bookkeeper in a Baltimore lumber company. Sari remained at home with the children until they entered school and then worked eighteen years in a library. Silvia is a beautician. Linda, born in Baltimore, became a schoolteacher and married a podiatrist in Detroit. Says Leon, "We are very happy we came to the United States . . . here there is freedom like no other country."[43]

Eduard and **Margita Kaiser** and their sixteen-year-old son, **Bruno,** moved with Margita's parents, **Artur** and **Sida Bauer,** to Cleveland, where Artur, a Yugoslav cattle dealer and camp barracks leader in his mid-sixties, had three sisters and a brother. Edward, a former merchant, found work as a bookkeeper in a lumberyard. Margita was a cosmetologist. Bruno, now living in San Francisco, in an electrical engineer and manufactures burglar and fire alarms.

Moric Kamhi, twelve years old when the shelter closed, is now Maurice Kamhi, a New York television producer, who acted as Master of Ceremonies at the reunion. He and his wife, who were among a group that gathered with Ruth Gruber and this writer for a late lunch following the reunion, have two children, a son still a student and a daughter, Katherine, who is a regular on the daytime soap opera "All My Children." His mother, **Emica Kamhi,** left Oswego intending to return to Yugoslavia with her mother and son but she learned that her husband was dead and applied for immigration. In New York, she worked as a hairdresser, another of those who built a career from a skill acquired in the camp. Now Emica Agrimi, she and her second husband operated their own salon for many years. Expecting her to attend if "at all possible," they invited Eleanor Roosevelt to their grand opening.[44]

Branko Kaufmann, a portrait photographer who set up a studio in the camp using a camera borrowed from a professor at Oswego State Teachers' College and who represented the coal workers on the Labor Committee, tried to establish a studio in New York but was soon persuaded to return to Oswego. He, his wife, **Kathe,** and young Eva lived there until 1959 and then opted for sunny California. Branko died of a heart attack thirteen years later. **Eva Kaufmann** Dye and her husband, Robert, live in Millbrae, California; both are school teachers. Kathe (Kitty), who proudly showed Eleanor Roosevelt her barracks apartment, felt that people who complained in the shelter "had not suffered like we did" during the years they had survived by hiding in caves in Italy.[45]

The **Korner** family, Austrians of Rumanian origin, settled in Providence, Rhode Island, where they had a cousin. **Schlomo,** a sixty-five-year-old Hebrew teacher who had prepared shelter boys for Bar Mitzvah, again found youngsters to teach. He and **Schewa,** his wife, both died in 1962, five years after losing **Regina,** their oldest daughter, to appendicitis at the age of forty-nine. **Mina,** three years younger than her older sister, worked in a factory until her retirement. **Tina,** the youngest daughter, held an office job until marrying David Chernick, a partner in a family insurance company. Tina and David, whom cancer took in 1984, had four children, two sons and two daughters.

On May 11, 1982, the governor of Rhode Island signed into law the Act Relating to Emergency Medical Services, which authorizes personnel such as ambulance attendants and paramedics to assume responsibility for administering drugs without a physician's permission when they are unable to communicate with a physician. Tina considers the legislation, introduced thirty years earlier but not enacted until two months after the death of her older son, "a personal memorial" to both her boys. Less than two weeks after twenty-two-year-old, multilingual Russell died after not receiving medication in an ambulance whose communication system had broken down, she launched a vigorous campaign for corrective legislation. Six years earlier, she had lost Stuart, her younger son, validictorian of his junior high school. Victims of muscular dystrophy, both boys were confined to wheelchairs but remained indomitable and "lived life to the fullest."[46] They followed the example set by their mother, although she attributes her strength to their courage.

Liana Kramer and her mother, Regina, both of whom attended the reunion, prefer to be known by the names they took after leaving the shelter. After leaving the shelter, they remained in New York for three years, left for Italy to seek relatives, and returned to New York to join Liana's father. Regina worked as a furrier while Liana attended a Lubavitch school. Now "modern Orthodox," Liana teaches both elementary and Hebrew school. She and her husband, a building contractor, have three sons; the oldest lives permanently in Israel, the second studies at a yeshiva in Israel, and the third attends a yeshiva in New York.[47]

Suzanne Krauthamer Gurwitz looks back with "conflicting" views. She attributes her family's survival to "luck" but also believes that "God wanted us to be alive for some purpose."[48] A New York City schoolteacher, she has one son studying in Israel to become an Orthodox rabbi, a second who is a yeshiva student preparing to settle in Israel, and a daughter at Queens College. **Naftali** and **Resel Krauthamer,** Suzanne's parents, were both born in Poland soon after the turn of the century. Her older brothers, **Simon** and **Julius,** were born in Germany in the early thirties. She was born in France in 1939. When the shelter closed, the family settled in New York. Naftali resumed work as a furrier and died in 1979 at the age of seventy-seven, six years after the death of his wife. Simon is a stockbroker and Julius a government auditor. They remain observant Jews.

Berta Kremer and her two sons, sixteen-year-old **Hermann** and eleven-year-old **Vilko** (William) also moved to New York. She soon married **Sigmund Alster,** a fifty-year-old, Polish-born Viennese linen merchant who had been a property and building supervisor and a popular dramatist in the shelter. After Alster died of cancer, Berta, Eisig Hendel's sister, took a third husband and helped him expand his dry-cleaning store. They now live in Florida, where William is in the family business. Hermann is a civil engineer in Montreal.

Thanks largely to the Quaker unit that did fieldwork in the camp during the summer of 1945, seventeen-year-old **Rolf Manfred Kuznitski** "found peace" in Oswego. He and his parents lived in Toledo for several years and then joined the migration to California. **Berthold Kuznitski** died in Los Angeles in 1966 at the age of seventy-five. **Felicitas,** his wife, died six years later, at seventy-eight. Their son, now Ralph Manfred, still gets "goose-bumps" when he hears "God Bless America" or sees the American flag.[49] A chemical engineer and research analyst for Aerojet, he worked on the MX and other missile systems. He and his second wife are enthusiastic members of the Sierra Club. After becoming a concerned environmentalist, he now devotes his research to finding better and cheaper non-nuclear energy alternatives.

Joseph Langnas, the first Bar Mitzvah in the camp, settled with his parents and younger sister in Detroit. His father, **Ignaz,** a Polish-born Viennese merchant, spent his last years—he died in 1972—as a wine merchant after having struggled for many years at odd jobs. Joseph's mother, **Dora,** worked twenty years as a seamstress. Now Dora Stock, she is remarried and lives part of each year in Montreal and Miami. Joseph is a Doctor of Osteopathy and teaches pathology at Botsford Hospital near Detroit. He and his wife, a former refugee, have four children, two of whom are preparing to be doctors. Joseph's sister, **Bettina Langnas** Lis, educated in yeshivot as was Joseph, worked as a secretary. She and her husband, owner of a computer service, have three sons. Oswego was a topic freely discussed among the Langnases. It was for Joseph "one of those experiences by which we measure our lives."[50]

Ivo Lederer attended the reunion, as did his sister **Mira**'s husband, Howard Salomon, and their son, David. Mira was a remarkable woman. Twenty-one when the camp closed, she became a medical research bacteriologist, a junior high teacher, and the author of two books. She also wrote a moving article about her own mastectomy and hoped to write a book on Oswego. As with her cancer, she insisted on treating Oswego with absolute frankness. "To Americans, Jews included, it was a quaint, happy experience." But for those who lived it, "it was a mixture of pain, disappointment, frustration, and only faint hope that we might remain in the U.S."[51] Married to a third-generation American Jew, she thought the native-born incapable of fully understanding the pride she felt in seeing her son graduate from Princeton.

Ivo, five years younger than Mira, earned a Ph.D. in Russian and East European History from Princeton, taught at Princeton, Yale, and Stanford, and published extensively. Oswego represents for him a place from which "the dregs of World War Two" emerged and established an extraordinary record in "full and useful and rewarding lives." Unlike Mira, he regards the camp as a "positive experience." Like her, he believes that "only a foreign-born can truly appreciate what America is."[52] Their parents, **Otto** and **Ruza Lederer,** worked hard at various jobs. An attorney in Yugoslavia, Otto never reestablished himself in this country.

Eva Lepehne was seventeen when she arrived in Oswego with **Chaim** and **Julia Schlomowitz,** an Austrian couple in their fifties who befriended her after the Nazis killed her father in Germany and her mother during their flight. Traumatized and "emotionally immature," an assessment made both by camp authorities at the time and by Eva herself in correspondence with me, she managed, nevertheless, to advance within one year from the sixth grade to high-school graduate. Because her grandmother in Rochester, whom she hoped to live with, died before the shelter closed, Eva joined an uncle there. She became a licensed practical nurse. Married to Eric Rosenfeld, an industrial goods plant manager in Nashville, she is a synagogue bookkeeper and the mother of three children. David is a computer analyst, Vera is a special education teacher, and Ken is a student.[53]

David Levi wanted to remain at the shelter long enough to complete his studies at Oswego State Teachers' College—he feared not being able to resume his education once he had to support himself. Alone and ill after having lost his entire family, he recalls Oswego as a "memorable" experience to be cherished.[54] Fearing that he would get lost among the numbers needing assistance in New York, he selected Cleveland because it had large Jewish, Italian, and Yugoslav populations. The Jewish community helped him obtain work and complete his studies at Case Western Reserve University. A real estate broker for several years in New York, he is now a clothing salesman in San Francisco. Both his son, Robert, and daughter, Norma, are attorneys.

Stella Levi, who learned after the war that her husband was dead, supported herself and her nine-year-old son, **Jakov,** by working as a seamstress and beautician. When she remarried eight years later, her son took his stepfather's name and became Jack Wilson. Both Jack, who views Oswego as "a safe haven," and his mother attended the reunion.[55] A pharmacist married to a schoolteacher, Jack has two children and helped found a Conservative synagogue on Staten Island.

Fortunee Levitch, mother of Leon, the composer, had been a much-loved lecturer and dramatist in the camp. A popular guest in Oswego homes, she wrote on January 19, 1946, in the *Oswego Palladium Times,* "We shall carry with us the pleasantest memories that will remain unforgettable in our hearts." Gracious and witty, she met harsh tests after leaving the shelter. **Joseph Levitch,** her husband, a Yugoslav pharmacist with "artistic leanings," managed after several years to overcome American licensing obstacles and open his own small pharmacy. Soon after, armed robbers accosted him and re-awakened memories of Nazi brutalities. He fell into a depression that culminated in suicide. Debilitated by arthritis, Fortunee lives with daughter **Manon** in the San Francisco area. **Edward,** her older son, a building contractor inspired by Oswego High School industrial arts teacher Tom Crabtree, has in recent years suffered financial reverses and found new strength in Torah study.

Leo Levy (known as Juda) spent two years as a prisoner of the Fascists in Yugoslavia, during which time his family did not know his fate, until the Italians joined the Allies and freed him. An attorney, he applied for Oswego in order to give his teenage sons educational opportunities. Expecting to return to Yugoslavia, he led both the Advisory Council and the Yugoslav group and participated in several plays.

The NRS arranged for his family to move from Oswego to Philadelphia, but the family went instead to New York to be near friends. Juda's wife, **Irene,** a practical nurse in the camp, attended business school and worked for a manufacturing company until 1962, when they set out for the California climate in order "to prolong our lives."[56] The previous year Juda had retired as director of the treasury of Care, Inc. He died two years later and she moved to Israel, where she lived until poor health caused her to return to the United States in 1983. In attendance at the reunion, she lives in New York, where one son, **Silvio** (Robert Sidney Lee) is an attorney. His brother, **Erik Levy** Lee, a gastroenterologist, is a clinical professor at UCLA and the director of medical education for the Kaiser Permanente

Medical Group in Bellflower, California. Both sons served in the Korean War.

David Liban, and Austrian of Polish origin, never recovered from injuries suffered in a German concentration camp. He died in 1959 at the age of seventy-six. His wife, **Rela,** died in 1974 at the age of eighty-four. Their sons, Eric, a mathematics professor, and Jack, a heating and air-conditioning designer, supported them. Grateful to have them in this country after believing they had perished, Jack "always" assumed his parents would remain.[57]

Rafailo Margulis, a doctor who was dying of cancer, took his wife and sons back to Yugoslavia in the first group that chose repatriation but quickly regretted the decision and arranged for **Rajko** (Ralph) and **Aca** (Alex) to return on student visas. Harvard Medical School accepted both on scholarship. Ralph married **Vesna Culic,** who was then working as a bookkeeper to support herself and her mother, **Angelina Cicarelli,** in Cleveland. He is a gynecologist in Royal Oak, Michigan. They have two sons, one a physician and one an attorney. Alex married **Renee Reisner,** who died of systemic lupus in 1979. He heads the University of California Medical Center's Department of Radiology, which helped develop the CAT scanner, and is working on more advanced techniques for diagnosing cancer. Olga Margulis, their mother, joined her sons in the United States after being widowed and died of cancer several years later.

The Margulis family applied for Oswego in order that the boys, medical students in Yugoslavia, could complete their studies in this country. Dr. Margulis never wavered from that goal and chose repatriation after nine months because he could not accept internment. However, they prefer to forget old resentments. Remembering friendships and the absence of responsibilities, Ralph now views the experience as "very positive," and Alex as "one of my most wonderful experiences."[58]

The group at lunch after the reunion included **Olga Maurer,** her son **"International" Harry,** and his family. Harry, the baby born in the convoy on the way to the Naples pier, did his undergraduate work in philosophy at New York's City College, became a computer scientist, and worked for NASA and the Air Force before joining a private Canadian corporation. Harry's brother, **Walter,** fourteen when the family arrived, designs fur coats. **Leon,** their father, died at the age of eighty-six in 1982. Olga is eighty-two and a dynamic woman.

A fur merchant in Germany who became a bookkeeper in New York, **Jakob Merzer** died in 1962 at the age of forty-eight. His wife, **Sonja,** had gone to work the previous year, when he became ill with heart problems, as a floor lady in a garment factory. They had three daughters. **Yvonne,** thirteen when the shelter closed, is a widow and works for Singer Sewing Marching on Long Island. **Lillian,** nine years younger, married a businessman, as did Yvonne, and owns her own dress boutique in New York. **Beatrice,** born in the shelter, is a computer scientist in Washington, D.C., as is her husband. Sonja says of Oswego, "Today I know we had it very good."[59]

Leo Mirkovic, the baritone formerly with the Zagreb Opera, planned originally to return to the Opera as its director, but some colleagues there had become "big Nazis" and he chose not to subject himself to them. He sought to enter opera in this country but concluded that he needed a top agent and could not afford one. In 1951 he completed cantorial studies, a member of the first class to graduate from the Cantorial School of the Hebrew Union College–Jewish Institute of Religion. Having served congregations in Washington, D.C., and New York, he now lives in retirement in Miami Beach. Mirkovic's willingness to sing in Oswego and the surrounding area, and the government's eagerness to use him "for showmanship" gave him more freedom than most. He still serves on occasion as a cantor—"I'm an old man with a young voice." Now eighty, he says of Oswego, "The whole thing is best to forget. . . . I'm happy I came over, but a camp is a camp."[60]

Albert and **Bella Moschev** chose Philadelphia because of its proximity to New York and moved to New York in 1948, as soon as their daughter, **Rosa,** completed high school. A Bulgarian-born merchant, fifty-six when the camp closed, Albert first worked in a garment factory and then became a mustard factory foreman. Bella, who did crochet work, is, above all, happy to be in this country. "I'm so grateful to the government I don't have words." Rosa echoes her mother's feelings. When she thinks of Oswego she thinks of freedom. Children had it "better" than adults because they could cope more easily with the extreme cold and because they had more "freedom."[61] A stenographer, Rosa married Marcel Levy, a comptroller accountant. Joseph, their son, is an accountant. Linda, their daughter, is in advertising along with her husband.

With the help of friends, **Pesach Munz,** the butcher from Belgium, **Adam**'s father, became a diamond broker in New York. Eighty-four years old and partially aphasiac as a result of a coronary and a stroke, he still reports each day to the Diamond Dealers' Club. **Fradl,** his wife, died a few years ago of cancer. **Leon,** Adam's younger brother, manufactures fur coats in New York. He and his wife, Selma, have two children, Steven, an ophthamologist, and Rachael, who works in a bank.

Erna Neufeld supported her mother and six-year-old son in New York by working during the day as an interpreter for the health service of the International Ladies Garment Workers Union and by night as a beautician and pastry maker, the latter two skills both acquired in the shelter. **Georgio** (George), her son, an electronic engineer in Manhattan, reports that his mother, who died in 1970 at the age of fifty-eight, and his grandmother, **Irene Kabiljo,** who died in 1974 when she was eighty-five, "were ecstatic to have been part of the group."[62]

When **Karl** and **Elise Newmann** (Carl and Liesl Newman) and their seven-year-old son, **Peter,** arrived at the Union Station in Kansas City on a cold February day, a worker from the United Jewish Social Services welcomed them and took them to a poorly heated bedroom and bath on the second floor of an unkempt home in the inner city. They fashioned a makeshift kitchen and lived in the house in conditions far less comfortable than those in the shelter, for two years. Even so, they were more fortunate than most. Karl found work as a book-keeper for a grain company owned by Paul Uhlman, Sr., who had an exemplary record of assistance to refugees. And they had hot water. In early 1946 Americans suffered shortages of crisis proportions in both housing and jobs, and Jewish social service agencies chose to help as many as possible even though that frequently meant using substandard facilities. Carl and Liesl Newman live today in a comfort-able and spotless bungalow. Peter, a certified public accountant, and his wife, Bev, a congregation librarian, have three children.

Fifteen-year-old **Henny Notowicz** settled in New York with her parents, **Osias** and **Maria,** and, four years later, married a young accountant who became one of the principal officers in the Music Corporation of America. She worked twelve years as a braillist at the Braille Institute. Now divorced and living in Beverly Hills, she travels extensively abroad to buy art for commercial galleries. Daughter Gilda is an urban planner and daughter Linda an artist and pho-tographer.[63]

Ani Pick, a musical-comedy star in the camp, raised **Peter,** sixteen when the shelter closed, and **Geraldine,** born soon after the camp opened, alone and saw them both become Ph.D.'s. Peter is an art historian in San Francisco and Geraldine teaches at the Harvard Medical School. Anny found work in a card and gift shop in Hollan-dale, Florida, "to keep busy and to try to forget the past."[64]

Mrs. R., eighty-four, the wife of a wealthy manufacturer and real estate owner in Yugoslavia who died of cancer a few years ago, is the mother of two sons, one a high achiever now dead, and the other a man whose life has consisted of a series of personal disasters. All four were together in Oswego—the only survivors in their family. Her brother, "a beautiful person," a physician permitted to continue work-ing in Belgrade after nearly all Jews had been dismissed from their jobs, returned home one evening to find that his entire family had been deported. He took his own life. Of her life since the Nazis: "Oswego was the only place where I found peace. . . . we were not scared. . . . I didn't like to be dependent." Of her life since Oswego: "no relatives . . . really lonely. . . . we had so much property in Yugoslavia . . . here we don't have anything . . . it is so hard because it is so lonely."

Fritz Reisner, who had been the director of a railroad company in Vienna, found work in an export-import company. He died in 1969 at the age of seventy. **Stella,** his wife, worked as a bookkeeper for a glove factory. Now ninety-two, she lives in a nursing home in the New York area. Their daughter Renée, wife of Alex Margulis, died at the age of fifty-two. **Dorrit Reisner** Ostberg, three years younger than Renée, earned a B.A. in comparative literature and an M.A. in math. Her son is an attorney with New York City's Human Resources Administration. "Only recently" have they begun to discuss the past.[65]

Samuillo Romano, who hitchhiked to New York for fun weekends with David Levi, his best friend, entered the Army, returned to studies at Case Western Reserve University in Cleveland, and earned his B.A. in clinical psychology and M.A. in industrial psychology from New York University. At the time of his death from Lou Gehrig's disease in 1979, at the age of fifty-five, he was the account executive for the Eastern European Division of Marsh & McLellan Insurance Company. Sam and his wife, Renata, had two children. Karen is assistant director at Macmillan Publishing Company, Inc. Robert is an industrial real estate broker.

The Romano family accepted an NRS assignment to Cleveland but, like many others, moved to New York as soon as they were able, in this case two years later. Sam's father, **Sima,** the "Stocking King of Yugoslavia," was fifty-three and had been on crutches for nearly two years because of a bad fall in Oswego one month before the camp closed. He worked in the garment industry until obtaining a job, when he was over sixty, in the mail office of a bank. Always hard working, he died at eighty-four of cancer. His wife, **Clara,** now eighty-four and hard-working like her husband, retired at sixty-five but continued to work off and on in the garment industry. **Zarie** (Zachary), Sam's brother, became an insurance agent. Both his son and daughter work in banks, she as a cashier and he in public relations.[66]

Fifty-year-old **Moses Rosenbaum** moved to Chicago with **Fanny Heller,** whom he married while in the shelter, and found work in a luggage factory. He died in April 1978 at the age of eighty-two, believing that his first wife and all four children had been lost in the Holocaust. But one son, Morris, survived. Morris learned in 1965 that his father had been in Ferramonte and began an intensive search. Morris attended the reunion with his son, Mark. They continue to feel anger because, despite turning to location services, they did not learn of Oswego until 1983, five years after Morris's father had died.[67]

Josip Rothstein, a dry-goods manufacturer and wholesaler in Yugoslavia, had family in Washington, D.C., able to help him re-establish himself. **Sara,** his wife, returned to school. She had completed studies in dentistry in Germany and found herself unable to practice because of the Nuremberg Laws. After Oswego, she earned a degree in dental hygiene from Howard University. Josip died in 1970 at the age of seventy-four and Sara worked until her retirement in 1983, when she became seventy-four. They had three children. **Ralph,** the youngest, born in the camp, is a pediatric endocrinologist in Vancouver, British Columbia. **Lavoslav,** who was always known by his Hebrew name, Ari, and made it official when he became a citizen, and **Mirjam** both live in New York with their families. He is a business and tax attorney and she, the wife of a rabbi, teaches Judaic studies in a Hebrew day school. "If you're Orthodox and you want your children [Ari has five] to stay home [for their education], it is much easier if you live in New York." Fifteen when he left Oswego, Ari views the shelter and his entire refugee experience philosophically: "I've had a more interesting life than most of my contemporaries."[68]

Zdenka Ruchvarger (Ruchwarger), Fred Baum's beautiful sister, looks on the Oswego experience as a needed period of adjustment and transition to American life. But her husband, **Abraham Ruchvarger** (Avram Ruchwarger), "didn't integrate and never wanted to."[69] Sent to Italy by the partisans for rest and recuperation, he remained there in the hope of reaching Palestine and applied for Oswego only because his bride of two months and her family pressed him to do so. A surgeon, he went from Oswego to a job as a psychiatric worker in the American Legion Hospital in Belleville, New Jersey. Low-paying psychiatric hospital positions often offered the only jobs available to refugee physicians unable to resume their specialties because of restrictive licensing procedures imposed by state medical associations. The Ruchwargers later lived in Israel for a few years but returned to Washington, D.C., where he died of a heart attack in 1968 at the age of fifty-six. Zdenka, a nurse, has worked in doctors' offices since leaving the camp and continues to do so now in Los Angeles, where her son and daughter, both born in this country, live.

Adolph Schild, who had been a technical designer for the Electric Bell Company in Belgium, and his young son, **Ignace,** drew pictures for farmers in exchange for food and shelter while the family was hiding in the Italian mountains. In New York, after leaving Oswego, Adolph found work as a salesman for a graphic arts and photo engraving company. He died in 1956 at the age of sixty-six. His wife, **Fanny,** who became an electrologist, attended the reunion with both their children.

Ignace, now Irving, received a scholarship to the Cooper Union Art School, trained during the Korean War to be a Marine Corps combat photographer, and completed his education on the GI Bill. He is now full professor and chairman of the Department of Fashion Photography at Manhattan's Fashion Institute of Technology. His work can be seen on the back page of every *Mad* magazine and throughout such publications as *Glamour, Esquire,* and the German magazine *Stern.* "I'm very fortunate. . . . The yardstick I had . . . gave me the strength, the drive, to accomplish my goals." But "Jews overlooked by all governments should be recognized" through "memorials everywhere. . . . The world deserves to pay a price. . . . It has not paid the price."[70] **Florence Schild** Miller and her accountant husband have three children, one of whom is a traditional scribe in Israel.

Sally Schnaymann (Solly), the popular choirmaster of Fort Ontario, became a salesman for piece goods in New York and played the organ voluntarily for a Reform temple in New Jersey. Marta, his wife, cared for their five-year-old grandson, **Steven Schroeter,** while **Elsa** (Ilse) **Schroeter,** their daughter, worked as a milliner and model on 57th Street. Solly suffered a heart condition and died in 1956 at the age of sixty-eight. Marta had a stroke and died in 1971 at the age of eighty-four. Ilse, a widow three times, now semiretired, became a saleslady in the fur salon at Bloomingdale's. A proud, flag-waving patriot, she believes that the "most important" thing about Oswego is the "fact we were taken to America . . . one of the greatest gifts imaginable."[71] Her son, Steven Schroeter Kattan, is an independent producer, writer, and director of documentary films in Los Angeles.

Ferdinand Schoenwald, a widowed hosiery salesman from Yugoslavia, was seventy-four when the camp closed and he moved to New York with **Nada,** his forty-one-year-old daughter, and **Villi,** his thirty-five-year-old son. Nada married **Wilhelm Loewy,** who had owned a restaurant in Vienna and whose first wife had been interned in Teresienstadt. They made their home in San Francisco. Villi, who ran a dry-goods store in San Francisco, is now retired.

The **Selans,** sixty-eight-year-old **Serafina,** her two sons, **Carlo** and **Rudolf,** and their families all settled in Buffalo but also drifted back to New York. **Rudolf,** a coal mine owner in Yugoslavia, used ORT training in Oswego to become an upholsterer and interior decorator. He died in 1976 at the age of seventy-five. **Nada,** Rudolf's wife, started as a saleslady in a small dress shop in Buffalo and was for fifteen years a fashion coordinator for Bergdorf Goodman. Rudolf and Nada's son, **Branko** (William), seven when the camp closed, is an architect in New York.

Carlo Selan spent part of the late 1920s in the United States and returned to Yugoslavia to become the general manager in that country for Twentieth-Century Fox. In Oswego, he worked as film supervisor, helped organize the Spring Festival, and acted as a leader for Zionist activities. He and **Lotte** divorced soon after leaving Oswego, and she and **Mira,** their five-year-old daughter, moved to Switzerland. **Edna,** seven years old, remained in the United States with her father.

A Harvard Ph.D. in romance languages, Edna taught at the University of Illinois, married Wolfgang Epstein, an internist and professor of biochemistry at the University of Chicago, bore two sons, entered the University of Chicago Law School, gave birth to a daughter, served as an assistant prosecutor, and became one of the first women partners in the international firm of Sidley and Austin. A political activist who teaches and publishes extensively, she says, "I have a rich, full and happy life. This country has been good to me."[72]

Edith Semjen, the "Blonde Bombshell," moved to New York with her mother, **Elizabeth,** and, a few years later, married Bernard O. Starkman, a certified public accountant. Using "golden hands" whose only training consisted of the ORT classes in the camp, she began as a hairdresser in a "decrepit" old salon one flight up on a side street, moved and expanded, and, within a few years, had eighteen employees working for her in one of "the most successful beauty salons on the Upper West Side." Today, preferring less pressure, she works as a hairdresser in a salon off Broadway, where Ruth Gruber is one of her most "delighted followers."[73]

Sonja Sommerburg (Sonia Rabin), a member of the small group that gathered for a late lunch after the reunion, learned that she was Jewish only after coming to Oswego at the age of fourteen. Her mother, **Miriam Sommerburg,** had tried to spare her children, born of a non-Jewish father, rejection and suffering. In Italy, however, Sasha, the oldest, had joined the (Palestine) Jewish Brigade. He fought in Israel's War of Independence and continued to live in Israel with his wife, a Rumanian Holocaust survivor, until they emigrated to the United States in 1957. Of the four Sommerburg children in Oswego, two, including Sonia, married Jews and live as Jews. Sonia is an art director for a New York publishing company and administrator of her mother's estate. **Peter,** one year younger, served in the United States Army for three years as a paratrooper and is today an architectural engineer in Atlanta. **Dimitri,** one year older than Sonia, is a carpenter in Upstate New York. **Gioconda,** only nine when the family arrived, became both a dancer in the style of Isadora Ducan and a computer analyst.

Miriam Sommerburg, the sculptress who produced little of real value while interned, in freedom fulfilled the promise of her youth.

Seeking to convey "forever surviving wonder," she filled her Greenwich Village studio-apartment with soaring expressionistic wood sculptures, held nine one-woman shows, won numerous prizes, and saw her work added to the permanent collections of several museums, including New York's Metropolitan Museum of Art.[74] On her death in 1980, at the age of eighty, her body was cremated and the ashes strewn, at her request, over Lake Tiberius in Israel.

The **Spitzer** family relocated in San Francisco, where forty-eight-year-old **Filip,** formerly the principal printer for a Yugoslav newspaper, worked in a series of jobs but, like most in his generation, never regained his former status. **Mary,** his widow, met with me but could not discuss the past.

The Spitzer's daughter, **Margarita** (Margaret), eighteen when she arrived at the camp, needing to "overcome the fears I had of people," found it to be the best possible "in-between place" for recovering from recent traumas and preparing to start anew, a feeling shared by most of her contemporaries.[75] In San Francisco, she met and married Robert Fisse, a self-employed produce broker. Parents of Filip and Devin, they cleared their own land in the hills overlooking the city and, with their own hands, built a magnificent home that reflects their openness and their respect for nature. They grow much of their own food, make their own cereals, and create their own crafts. I was privileged to share their hospitality in 1980 and to have an opportunity to reciprocate in 1985.

Steffi Steinberg Winters also found that Oswego, where she graduated from high school and attended business school, meant "preparation for life." New York, where she "finally had to face" life, became the unhappiest place of all, at least for a time.[76] She found work as a waitress and as a secretary and, after a few years, became an administrative assistant to an exporter, a job she held for nine years. Married to Sam Winters, a scrap metal dealer, and the mother of three sons, she continued to correspond with Ralph Faust, her Oswego principal, and offered me early, crucial assistance in locating former camp residents.

Gertrude Steinberg, Steffi's mother, worked as a manicurist, practical nurse, kitchen helper, and doll-factory artist until obtaining a job as office manager. WRA group worker Edward Huberman helped place her in that position, which she held for seventeen years. Mrs. Steinberg, whose husband, a paper manufacturer in Berlin, died in Italian internment four years before his wife and daughter came to the United States, died in 1964 at the age of seventy-two.

The **Strauber** family moved to Brooklyn, where forty-five-year-old **Herman,** a Polish Jew who had been in the textile industry, had a cousin. He died in 1962. **Suzanna,** his widow, and their older daughter, **Elfrieda Strauber** Hendell, joined me for tea one afternoon in 1980 in New York. Thirteen when the camp closed, now divorced from David Hendell, Elfi is a social worker in New York. She attended the reunion with her sister, **Maria** (Marion). Seven when she arrived, Marion experienced her first "real" education in Oswego and has only "pleasant" memories.[77] She earned an M.S. in education from City College and is a school counselor in Ann Arbor, Michigan, where she lives with her husband, George Siegel, a physician and professor of neurology at the University of Michigan, and their three children. The family observed kashruth in the camp and continues to do so.

Thirty-six-year-old **Fanny Striks** and nine-year-old **Gertrude** moved to Brooklyn, where Fanny soon married Harry Saltz. She worked in the garment industry and he worked as a waiter, for many years at Katz's Delicatessen on Houston Street. Now widowed, Fanny lives in West Palm Beach, Florida. Trudy graduated from high school, married Michael Ehrlich, a textile wholesaler, and had three children. All are college graduates, one a computer programmer and one working in finance. "That we survived the holocaust is a miracle." Still fearful when she sees a policeman, her memories cause her "to try to be a better person."[78]

Eugene Svecenski, an internist, and **Lenka Svecenski,** an oral surgeon, both in their late forties when the shelter closed, worked in New York factories until they, like Dr. Ruchvarger, obtained psychiatric positions in a New York state mental institution. He died in 1962; she lives with her daughter, **Neva Svecenski** (Neva Gould), a pediatric pathologist at Chicago's Michael Reese Hospital, her son-in-law, also a pathologist, and their three teenagers. Neva, thirteen when she arrived in Oswego, already aimed to become a physician like her parents. She most remembers the camp for its "exceptional" people, particularly those always "willing to give." Her brother, **Ivan** Strong, is a New York attorney active in the Democratic Party. **Ernst Svecenski,** Eugene's brother, a former Yugoslav businessman, worked in a factory until his death in the early fifties. Their sister, **Yolanda Schlesinger,** died in New York in 1964.[79]

Not until attending the reunion did **Matilda Ternbach,** her son, **Rudolf** (Rudy), and daughter, **Lea Ternbach** Zierling, discuss Oswego. They moved to New York, where Matilda worked briefly as a practical nurse in a nursing home before entering the needle trades and becoming a fur finisher. Now seventy-six, she lives in retirement in Beverly Hills, Florida. "We went through very hard times, thanks God we survive, now we are o.k."[80] Lea, ten years old when the camp closed, is a housewife in New Rochelle, New York.

Rudy, an infant in the camp, is completing his doctorate in psychology at Boston University. Originally interested in basic research in neuropsychology, he works as a behavioral psychologist at Belchertown State School for the multiply handicapped near Amherst. Influenced by Anna Freud's work with children who survived concentration camps, he decided "to make science help" by serving "people who have the greatest need."[81]

The **Tusaks** moved to Dallas, where forty-five-year-old **Makso,** a machinist in Yugoslavia, found work with Airplane Instruments. Cancer took him in 1966. His wife, **Gizela** (Gisela), a teacher's college graduate, worked initially as a beauty operator and then took an office job, which she held twenty-five years. She has since lived in Florida, California, and Indiana, each time relocating to be with her daughter, **Edna.** Two when the camp closed, Edna earned a Ph.D. in economics, taught at the University of Florida, served as senior economist for SRI Industries in Palo Alto, and now teaches environmental economics at Purdue University. Proudly sharing with me her official release from the shelter, signed by C. H. Powers, Gizela said she feels "deep gratitude."[82]

Rumanian-born **Mosco Tzechoval,** the Oswego refugees' leading religious figure, had been professor of theology and ethics and director of a yeshiva and talmudic seminary in Antwerp, Belgium. His Polish-born wife, **Mindla,** had been a professor of theology and morals at a seminary for women in Antwerp. They settled in New York and he entered the diamond trade. It was a logical choice. Traditional European rabbis studied Torah for its own sake, not in order to serve congregations. And the Tzechovals had come from Antwerp, the capital of Jewish activity in the diamond trade since the late nineteenth century. In mid-April 1960 the bodies of the Tzechovals were found floating in a New Jersey lake. Speculation attributed their deaths either to suicide or to diamond thieves.[83]

Andre Waksman was born in France, took his first step in Italy, and showed his first tooth in the United States. He returned to France to study at the Sorbonne, married a French girl, and is a documentary film director in Paris. One daughter works for a magazine and the other is in art school. Andre's brother, **Samuel Waksman,** born eight years earlier in Belgium, earned a Masters in social work from the University of Michigan and works for the state of Ohio as an assistant director of forensic psychiatry. Their parents, **Jakob** and **Suzanne,** both Polish-born and in their early seventies, live in retirement in Miami Beach. A furniture manufacturer in Belgium, Jakob worked as a carpenter in Hoboken, New Jersey, where Suzanne became a jewelry saleslady. Suzanne says of Oswego, "quarantine . . . fence . . . zoolike . . . very beautiful people in Oswego . . . a big waste of time. . . . Oswego delayed us during our prime years but it was not like a concentration camp."[84]

Twenty-one-year-old **Tea Weiss** (Thea) settled with her parents, **Sandor** and **Wilhemina,** in Youngstown, Ohio, where Sandor had a brother. A textile merchant in Yugoslavia, Sandor worked in an electrical assembly plant until he found a job as a bookkeeper. He died in 1971 at the age of eighty-four. His wife died in 1981, when she was eighty-nine. Thea remained with her parents in Youngstown for five years and then joined an aunt and uncle recently arrived in New York from Brazil. A keypunch and clerical worker married to Samuel Sanders, a postal employee, she is the mother of two children. Arthur is an attorney and Shelley is a media buyer for an advertising agency. "I was happy to be in this country but disappointed to be in a camp. . . . It was a beginning for us . . . and it's history."[85]

Vladimir Zabotin, who found himself in disfavor with the Nazis in Germany on two counts—he was Russian and had a Jewish wife— returned to Germany, the land where he felt culturally rooted, in 1954. A noted abstractionist popular in Oswego for his portraits and for his children's classes, he found some of his work still hanging in German museums and, at the age of seventy, had yet to paint much of his best work. His wife, **Adelheid** (Heidi), a medical laboratory technician and sculptress who refused to sculpt in the shelter but worked a bit as a landscape artist, had died a few years earlier in New York of cancer. He died in Germany in 1968.

Soon after arriving in Oswego, sixteen-year-old **Konstantin Zabotin** (Kostia) discovered that by leaving through the fence he and his friends could enjoy a few beers at a friendly bar near the camp. Much to his shock, he soon learned, however, that it "was not the place to be." Winner of an American Legion essay contest in Oswego High School with a paper entitled "The United States Constitution as Seen by a European," he could not understand why there were separate bars for blacks and for whites.

Kostia earned a B.A. from Brooklyn College and is today customer service manager for Air France at Kennedy Airport. He, his wife Anita, a travel agent, and Mischa, their twenty-year-old multilingual son, share an apartment in Manhattan lined with paintings by his parents, including several Oswego portraits by Vladimir and a watercolor by Adelheid of a barracks with seagulls in the background. Happy in this country, he has not forgotten the humiliation it imposed. "I've always resented being restricted in the United States. I could never understand why, at the same time, German POWs had more freedom to move about." Yet, "the horrible part . . . happened in Europe." Able to draw clear distinctions between victims and perpetrators as well as to articulate important differences in culpability, he has felt no need to repress or suppress Oswego memories. "The paintings are beautiful and so were the people."[86]

Dozens of former Oswego refugees cannot be located and have not made themselves known despite publicity surrounding publication of Ruth Gruber's *Haven* and the August 1984 fortieth reunion in New York. Some undoubtedly remain unaware of this new interest in Oswego. Others prefer to disassociate themselves from the past. The latter includes people who refused to talk to or correspond with either Gruber or myself or people who did so only off the record.

Those who communicated only off the record expressed angry or hurt feelings readily recognized and understood by others who eagerly cooperated but censored their own contributions in order to avoid anything that smacked of criticism of a country to which they personally owe much. Because omitting such feelings seriously skews the overall picture, I am including two such communications anonymously. The first consisted of a brief written response to my initial inquiry by a former Yugoslav who was nineteen when the camp closed. The brother of a woman who has been very helpful, he wrote, "My feelings of the Oswego era and past is that I wish to leave it just that way—past."

In the second case, a fashionable mother and daughter from Danzig graciously permitted me to visit them in their apartment but did not want to be associated with my work. In a recent telephone conversation, the daughter said with sadness, "I see Cubans and others coming to this country and that is good, but I know that if we Jews needed help again the response would be the same."

APPENDIX 1

Work: The Parent Generation in Europe,
the Shelter Experience, and the Younger Generation Today

European Occupational Backgrounds

Professional and Managerial	263
Skilled and Semi-Skilled	117
Clerical and Sales	68
Service	5
Agricultural	4
	457

Specific Vocations in Europe

Merchant, Tradesman, Salesman	192	Farmer	4
Bookkeeper, Clerk	45	Pharmacist	4
Manufacturer	27	Musician	3
Tailor, Dressmaker	25	Mechanic	2
Artisan	25	Technician	2
Executive	13	Jeweler	2
Lawyer	9	Dentist	2
Writer, Journalist	9	Engineer	2
Banker	6	Rabbi	2
Butcher	6	Masseuse	2
Artist	5	Driver	2
Physician	5	Photographer	2
Secretary, Stenographer	4	Architect	2
Teacher	4	Actor, Actress	2

The Shelter Labor Pool (Males)

Male residents between the ages of 16 and 65	336
Certified unable for any work	129
Certified for light work only	63
Excused from work for welfare reasons	5

American Occupations of Former Refugees Who Were Twenty-Eight
Years Old and Younger when the Shelter Closed

Accountant	1	Military	1
Architect	1	Occupational Therapist	1
Art Director	1	Osteopath	1
Attorney	5	Pharmacist	1
Bookkeeper	2	Photographer	1
Braillist	1	Producer TV/Film	3
Building Contractor	1	Professor	8
Civil Servant	4	Proprietor	5
Clerk/Secretary/Stenographer	7	Psychologist	2
Composer	1	Real Estate Broker/Investor	4
Computer Analyst/Programmer	4	Salesman	1
Corporate Executive	4	School Counselor	2
Dentist	2	Skilled Worker	2
Engineer	9	Social Worker	3
Fur Designer	1	Stockbroker	1
Housewife	18	Talmudist	1
Insurance Agent/Broker	3	Teacher	9
Manager	4	U.N. Organizational Representative	1
Manufacturer	2	Veternarian	1
Medical Researcher	1	Welfare Worker	1

121

The group includes eleven Ph.D.'s and one Ph.D. candidate.

SOURCE (for parent generation): IMS Study, April 19, 1945, p. 30.

APPENDIX 2

Oswego Volunteers for the American Armed Forces

Name	Age	Citizenship
MALES		
Aladjem, Avram	57	Yugoslav
Albrecht, Herbert	40	Stateless, formerly Aus.
Antic, Josip	57	Yugoslav
Auerbach, Jakob	44	Yugoslav
Aufricht, Paul	46	Stateless, formerly Aus.
Beer, Osias	45	Polish
Bogdanic, Leo	52	Yugoslav
Charasch, Jakob	56	Polish
Cohen, Richard (DDS)	46	Spanish
Drahline, Abraham	42	Stateless, formerly Rus.
Finger, Oskar	46	Czechslovak
Finzi, Moso	38	Yugoslav
Fischer, Oskar	53	Yugoslav
Flatau, Ernst	59	Stateless, formerly Ger.
Joachim, Fritz	47	Stateless, formerly Aus.
Kraus, Alfred	57	Stateless, formerly Aus.
Krauthamer, Naftali	42	Stateless, formerly Rus.
Maurer, Leon	17	Stateless, formerly Aus.
Merksamer, Max	43	Stateless, formerly Aus.
Merzer, Jakob	40	Polish
Munz, Pesach	46	Polish
Ouroussoff, Peter	45	Stateless, formerly Rus.
Pillersdorf, Josef	67	Stateless, formerly Aus.
Ruchvarger, Abraham (M.D.)	32	Yugoslav
Schwarzenberg, Ziga	39	Yugoslav
Singer, Robert	68	Stateless, formerly Aus.
Strichewsky, Vladimir	52	Stateless, formerly Rus.
Weiss, Otto	48	Yugoslav
Zalc, Srul	48	Polish
FEMALES		
Altaras, Renee	24	Yugoslav
Auerbach, Eva	41	Yugoslav
Aufricht, Margarete	36	Stateless, formerly Ger.
Baruch, Anita	22	Yugoslav
Baruch, Jenny	18	Yugoslav
Hanf, Lea	19	Yugoslav
Lederer, Mira	20	Yugoslav

Milinovic, Gordana	22	Yugoslav
Montiljo, Relly	31	Yugoslav
Ruchvarger, Zdenka	19	Yugoslav
Semjen, Edith	21	Yugoslav
Weiss, Edith	20	Yugoslav

SOURCE: "List of Volunteers for Military Service," Temporary Havens, VIII, RG 210, NA.

APPENDIX 3

The Shelter Population

Population on August 5, 1944	982
Population on September 14, 1945	918
Births	16
Deaths	11
Emigration	2

February 28, 1945: Elsa Neumann left the United States to join her children in South Africa.

July 28, 1945: Ludwig Reis, 63, left the United States to join his children in Uruguay.

Repatriation to Czechoslovakia	1

October 9, 1945: Cecilia Melcer, 44, left the United States to rejoin her husband, a member of the Czech Legion.

Repatriation to Yugoslavia	66

Yugoslavs Repatriated May 31, 1945

The group included Jakob and Katarina Kabiljo, who had a brother with the partisans; Herman Freudenfeld, who had a son and daughter with the partisans; Elvira Alfandari, Freudenfeld's fiancée; Alexander Grin, whose wife and seven-year-old son remained in Oswego while he returned to assess conditions; Zora Jakovljevic, who had a son with the partisans; and four men who had non-Jewish wives in Yugoslavia looking after their property.

Yugoslavs Repatriated August 23, 1945

The group included Alexander Grin's wife and son; Dr. Rafailo Margulis, who had terminal cancer and wished to spend his last days in Yugoslavia, with his wife and two sons; and Stevan Koen, a former president of the Belgrade Chamber of Commerce, and his wife.

Returnees in this group who had husbands still with the partisans included: Flora Atias and her nine-year-old daughter; Sofija Adanja and her two young children; Estera Altaras and her two children; and Vilma Market, her son, and her sister. Sarika Pesah, returning with her young son, had a husband formerly with the partisans and now a POW in a German camp. The two Montiljo families and the Papo family had children still with the partisans. Brothers Moric and Josef Montiljo, whom the partisans had evacuated to Bari so that they could recover their health, returned with crates of machinery needed to reestablish their shoe business. Brothers Abraham and David Kabiljo, who returned with David's wife and daughter, had also been discharged by the partisans because of ill health; they had a third brother still with the partisans. Hugh Ebenspanger had both a brother and sister with the partisans. And Zlata Levi, who returned with her husband and daughter, had parents with the partisans.

198

Arrangements for Oswego Refugees Who Left the United States

The WRA, NRS, and HIAS helped returnees obtain necessary documentation and visas. HIAS and the National Council of Jewish Women arranged emigration. UNRRA did the same for repatriation. All who left had first to obtain tax clearance from the New York office of the Alien Unit of the Treasury Department's Division of Income Tax. Each individual having less than $25.00 received that amount from the Coordinating Committee. The WRA donated two towels to each refugee who left in May. Those who left in August received an NRS-sponsored three-day trip to New York, as well as WRA sheets, blankets, and towels.

APPENDIX 4

Shelter Deaths

This information was compiled from the case files of RG210 in the National Archives, the only instance in which I used those records.

Hermine Ackermann, 69, died January 15, 1946.
Widowed in 1932, she had one son in a German prison camp and another still fighting with the partisans. Nervous and depressed but otherwise apparently healthy, she arrived at Oswego with her daughter, son-in-law, and three grandchildren, the Arnstein family. When rectal cancer was discovered the following year she underwent, on January 8, 1946, what was thought to be successful surgery at the State Institute for the Study of Malignant Disease in Buffalo. However, she died nine days later, only three days before the family left for resettlement in Cleveland.

Dagobert Barnass, 60, died December 12, 1944.
A brandy manufacturer from Germany, he arrived in poor health and was soon diagnosed at the Syracuse University Hospital as having terminal lung cancer. He returned to the shelter in early November to live out his last days with his fifty-eight-year-old wife, Herta.

Karolina Bleier, 34, died December 28, 1944.
Shortly before Karolina's suicide, shelter welfare worker Ruth Ehrlich quoted her as wanting to "sacrifice" herself. As news of Nazi brutalities increased, she had become preoccupied with the two children from her first marriage whom she had left in Europe and had become "acutely disturbed."

Efraim Blumenkranz, 43, October 24, 1945.
A Polish-born textile technician and Zionist who represented the firemen on the Labor Committee, he suffered from spinal meningitis. He died in the Syracuse University Hospital of pulmonary pneumonia and was buried in New York, where his parents and three siblings lived. His widow and two young daughters obtained a two-week convalescent leave to attend his funeral and visit his family.

Arpad Buchler, 42, died December 19, 1945; coal accident.

Emilia Buchler, 65, died June 15, 1945.
Mother of Arpad Buechler, she arrived ill with cardiovascular arteriosclerosis and suffered heart failure.

Salomon Gaon, 37, died June 25, 1945.
A tailor from Yugoslavia who left a widow and eight-year-old son, he was treated in two New York hospitals and at the Syracuse University Hospital for a fatal form of leukemia.

Baschie Gottlieb, 52, died May 24, 1945.
She was thought to be in good health until five weeks before her death. Treated at Syracuse University Hospital the last three weeks for Hodgkin's

disease, she died of bronchial pneumonia. Max, her fifty-nine-year-old inventor husband, was a refugee leader. A member of the Advisory Council, he also served as chairman of the Austrian group.

Feibish Koppelman, 63, died January 9, 1946.
Tortured for eleven months in Dachau before being interned for four years in Italy, he arrived at Oswego suffering from central nerve deafness, partial paralysis, heart disease, and persistent fever and nausea. A typhoid carrier who had lost most of his teeth and looked old beyond his years, he was sometimes a "little confused" and "childish." He died in Santa Monica, California, only a few weeks after being paroled to his wife and daughters.

Josef Schlamm, 76, died March 28, 1945.
A widowed ivory and timber merchant fluent in German, French, Italian, and English, he arrived in Oswego ill with a heart condition. His death from bronchial pneumonia denied him his dream of joining his only surviving daughter in Benares, India.

Philip Stajn, 46, died September 31, 1944.
A Yugoslav merchant who died of heart failure, he left a forty-year-old widow.

Alfred Thewett, 64, died June 24, 1945.
A theatrical set designer, portrait artist, and writer from Austria, he was fluent in German, French, Italian, and English. Separated from his wife for seven years because she obtained permission to enter England and he did not, he suffered a heart attack and died two months after she emigrated to the United States. While in the shelter he taught fashion design and wrote for the *Ontario Chronicle*.

Ida Zeitlin, 71, died March 16, 1945.
A Russian-born, widowed nurse hoping to join her daughter, son-in-law, and two grandchildren in England, she arrived alone and ill with diabetes and died of bronchial pneumonia.

Nathan Zindwer, 63, died September 1, 1945.
A medical school graduate turned businessman who was twice wounded while serving in the Austrian Army during World War I, he spent four months in Dachau and seven months in Buchenwald before being interned for four years in Italy. Alone in Oswego because his children had emigrated to the United States in 1938 and his wife had died in 1940, he devoted all his time in the shelter to the study of English. Welfare worker Gabriel Derenberg described him as "deeply grateful to be in this country" and "one of the most sincerely humble inhabitants of the shelter." Neither his daughter, a physician in Boston, nor his two sons, who lived in New York, were notified until three days after he developed abdominal pains, which were tentatively diagnosed as acute inflammation of the gall bladder. Within a week he was dead. They later complained bitterly about the condition of the shelter hospital, where he had gone into shock after getting out of bed and had not had an oxygen tent available.

APPENDIX 5

Closing Roster

United States citizens	23
(Babies born in the shelter were acknowledged to be American citizens when the attorney general ruled that residence in the shelter fulfilled the requirement for preexamination.)	
United States immigration	854
1. Permanent visas	766
2. Temporary visas for Yugoslavs awaiting permanent ones	88
Temporary visas for people awaiting repatriation	19
(This group included people returning to family or to search for family; most hoped to emigrate later. Five in this group learned their relatives were dead and chose to apply for permanent visas. One non-Jewish Austrian who had been a janitor at a stock exchange, a government job, returned to a pension he did not wish to lose.)	
Temporary visas for people awaiting emigration	8
(All joined relatives in third countries.)	
Deaths	14
Inadmissibles	19
(The inadmissibles obtained temporary visas, renewable annually for seven years, after which they became eligible for permanent residence but not immigration.)	
1. TB	11
(Most of these cases challenged their exclusion, which rested on old medical records, and obtained permanent visas.)	
2. Mental	5
3. Cancer	1
4. Epilepsy	1
5. General health	1
(This elderly woman, "too weak to go anywhere," remained in a convalescent center.)	
Total accounted for	983
(982 plus "International Harry" Maurer, born en route to Naples and not on the original roster.)	
Non-Jews listed on the final roster	73
1. Resettled by Catholic Committee for Refugees	38
2. Resettled by American Committee for Christian Refugees	35

NOTES

Chapter 1: Introduction

1. Martin Gilbert, *Auschwitz and the Allies: A Devastating Account of How the Allies Responded to the News of Hitler's Mass Murder* (New York, 1981), pp. 1–80.

2. Walter Laqueur, *The Terrible Secret: An Investigation Into the Suppression of Information About Hitler's 'Final Solution'* (London, 1980), p. 208.

3. Moses Rischin, ed., *Immigration and the American Tradition* (Indianapolis, 1976), p. xi.

4. The 1921 Act limited immigration from any single country to 3 percent of the U.S. population from that country as of the 1910 census. It permitted 360,000 visas and reserved nearly 60 percent of them for northern and central European people.

The 1924 Act allowed fewer than 300,000 immigrants for each of the next three years and stipulated that those from any single country not exceed 2 percent of the U.S. total population from that country. It pushed the reference point back to the 1890 census, which predated most arrivals from southern and eastern Europe. It also stipulated that, beginning in 1927, annual permanent-visa quotas would not exceed 150,000 and would be distributed in proportion to the total U.S. white population from each country of origin as of 1920. See Pastora San Juan Cafferty et al., *The Dilemma of American Immigration: Beyond the Golden Door* (New Brunswick, 1983), pp. 52–54.

5. Sheldon Neuringer, "American Jewry and United States Immigration, 1881–1953" (Ph.D. diss., University of Wisconsin, 1969), pp. 205–206.

6. Naomi W. Cohen, *Not Free to Desist: A History of the American Jewish Committee 1906–1966* (Philadelphia, 1972), pp. 128–29.

7. John G. Clark, et al., *Three Generations in Twentieth Century America: Family, Community, and Nation* (Homewood, Illinois, 1977), pp. 257–59.

8. Hadley Cantril, *Public Opinion 1935–1946* (Princeton, 1951), p. 383.

9. Ibid., pp. 381–83.

10. Theodore Achilles, Memorandum, November 1938, State Department Decimal File 194044, 840–48 Refs/900-1/2. The Nansen Office was established by the League of Nations in the early 1920s in order to make "passports" available to millions of Russian refugees who lacked papers. Those who decried its demise in late 1938 did not understand that secret agreements limited it in the 1930s to providing travel documents only for refugees from the Near East. It provided little more than documentation for refugees from Germany.

11. Gilbert, *Final Journey: The Fate of the Jews in Nazi Europe* (New York, 1979), p. 16.

12. Bernard Wasserstein, *Britain and the Jews of Europe 1939–1945* (London, 1979), pp. 218–19. The IGC's principal achievements consisted of obtaining agreement on a travel form to be used in lieu of passports, assisting five hundred refugees to travel to Sosua, the Dominican Republic, in 1940, and helping with a few refugee camps in southern Italy and in North Africa during 1944.

13. Maurice R. Davie, *Refugees in America: Report of the Committee for the*

Study of Recent Immigration From Europe (New York, 1947), p. 20; Lyman Cromwell White, *300,000 New Americans: The Epic of a Modern Immigrant-Aid Service* (New York, 1957), pp. 20–21.

14. Lucy S. Dawidowicz, *On Equal Terms: Jews in America 1881–1981* (New York, 1982), p. 107.

15. Henry L. Feingold, "Roosevelt and the Resettlment Question," in *Rescue Attempts During the Holocaust: Proceedings of the Second Yad Vashem International Historical Conference* (April 1974), pp. 150–51.

16. Henry L. Feingold, *The Politics of Rescue: The Roosevelt Administration and the Holocaust, 1938–1945* (New Brunswick, 1970), p. 153.

17. Ibid., p. 169.

18. Cohen, *Not Free to Desist*, p. 253.

19. *New York Times,* July 22, 1942.

20. Dawidowicz, *On Equal Terms*, p. 114.

21. Cohen, *Not Free to Desist*, p. 241.

22. Ibid.

23. Ibid., pp. 242–43.

24. Feingold, *The Politics of Rescue*, p. 177.

25. *Foreign Relations of the United States (FRUS)* 1943, I: 143.

26. Feingold, *The Politics of Rescue*, p. 194.

27. "Bermuda Conference," *Encyclopedia of Zionism and Israel*, 1971, vol I, p. 128.

28. Feingold, *The Politics of Rescue*, 199.

29. The *Irgun Zeva'i Le'umi* (National Military Organization) was founded in 1931 by commanders who split with the Haganah, the military organization controlled by the Jewish Agency (the quasi-official governing body of Palestinian Jewry). Both the Haganah and the Jewish Agency were dominated by Labor Zionists.

The Irgun split in 1937. Half of its members rejoined the Haganah while half aligned with Vladimir Jabotinsky and his Revisionist Zionists, militant idealogues who insisted on applying unrelenting pressure on the British rather than trying to cooperate with them.

30. Feingold, *The Politics of Rescue*, pp. 218–19.

31. Barbara Burstein, "Rescue in the Opening Rounds of the American Jewish Conference," in *Holocaust Studies Annual: America and the Holocaust* (1983), p. 159.

32. U. S. Congress, Senate, "Petition to Save the Jews in Nazi-Controlled Europe—Appeal by the Rabbis of America," *Congressional Record*, 78th Cong., 1st sess., October 6, 1943, vol. 89, 8107.

33. Monty Noam Penkower, "In Dramatic Dissent: The Bergson Boys," *American Jewish History* (March 1981): 192, and Sarah E. Peck, "The Campaign for an American Response to the Nazi Holocaust, 1943–1945," *Journal of Contemporary History* (April 1980): 372–73.

34. Feingold, *The Politics of Rescue*, pp. 221–22.

35. U.S. Congress, House, *Rescue of the Jewish and Other Peoples in Nazi-Occupied Territory,* hearings before Committee on Foreign Affairs on H. Res. 350 and H. Res. 352, 78th Cong., 1st sess., 1943.

36. Feingold, *The Politics of Rescue*, pp. 236–37.

37. Ibid., p. 241.

38. Ibid.

39. Memorandum, May 9, 1944, Temporary Havens, I, Records of the War Relocation Authority, RG 210, National Archives (NA), Washington, D.C.

40. Feingold, *The Politics of Rescue*, p. 241.

41. "Report to the Secretary on the Acquiescence of This Government in the Murder of European Jews," January 13, 1944, Vol. 693, pp. 212–36, Henry Morgenthau, Jr., Diaries (HMJr.), Franklin D. Roosevelt Library (FDRL), Hyde Park, New York.

Chapter 2: Rescue Proposal

1. "Report to the Secretary on the Acquiescence of This Government in the Murder of European Jews," January 13, 1944, Vol. 693, p. 214, HMJr., FDRL.

2. "Jewish Evacuation," March 8, 1944, Vol. 707, p. 221, HMJr., FDRL.

3. "Memorandum Submitted by the Washington Emergency Committee to Save the Jewish People of Europe," February 7, 1944, Box 7, War Refugee Board Papers (WRB), FDRL.

4. George Warren to the WRB, May 8, 1944, Part I, Series IV, Box 219, Edward Stettinius, Jr., Papers, University of Virginia, Charlottesville.

5. "Re: Peter Bergson," May 24, 1944, Vol. 735, p. 57; March 2, 1945, Vol. 825, pp. 81–106, HMJr., FDRL.

6. Memorandum to Secretary Morgenthau et al., May 20, 1944, Vol. 734, pp. 12–13, HMJr., FDRL.

7. John B. Friedman and Ted Mann, interview, Washington, D.C., May 20, 1981.

8. "Re: Peter Bergson," May 24, 1944, Vol. 735, pp. 24–36, 55–85, HMJr., FDRL.

9. "Views of the American Jewish Committee Regarding Palestine," January 10, 1944, State Department Decimal File, 867N.01/2222, RG 59, National Archives (NA), Washington, D.C.

10. "Attitude of Zionists Toward Peter Bergson," May 19, 1944, 867N.01/2347, RG 59, NA.

11. "Notes on Meeting with Mr. Pehle," February 25, 1944, Box 3, Joseph P. Chamberlain Papers, YIVO Institute for Jewish Research (YIVO), New York.

12. William Rosenwald to John W. Pehle, April 26, 1944, Box 17, WRB, FDRL.

13. "Jewish Evacuation," March 8, 1944, Vol. 707, p. 224, HMJr., FDRL.

14. Executive Order 9417, January 22, 1944, Official File 5477, FDRL.

15. Ibid.

16. "Jewish Evacuation," March 8, 1944, Vol. 707, pp. 212, 223, HMJr., FDRL.

17. Pehle, Memorandum, March 9, 1944, Temporary Havens, I, Records of the War Relocation Authority, RG 210, NA.

18. Henry L. Stimson Diaries, March 9, 1944, Library of Congress, Washington, D.C.

19. John W. Pehle, interview, Washington, D.C., May 19, 1981.

20. *FRUS* 1944, V: 563–77.

21. Henry A. Wallace Diaries, August 26, 1943, in possession of Theodore A. Wilson, University of Kansas.

22. Josiah E. DuBois, Jr., and John B. Friedman, "Report to the War Refugee Board," March 6, 1944, Temporary Havens, I, RG 210, NA.

23. Mathew Sargoy, "Memorandum in Support of Camp Project" (undated), Temporary Havens, I, RG 210, NA.

24. "Legal Basis for the Establishment by This Government of a Program Whereby Refugees Could Be Transported to the United States and Be

There Interned for the Duration of the War" (unsigned and undated), Temporary Havens, I, RG 210, NA.

25. Pehle, Memorandum, May 1, 1944, Vol. 726, pp 40–46, HMJr., FDRL.

26. Roland Young, *Congressional Politics in the Second World War* (New York, 1956), p. 103.

27. Ibid., p. 178.

28. *Kansas City Star,* February 28, 1944.

29. Ibid., February 29, 1944.

30. Ibid., March 2, 1944.

31. "Jewish Evacuation," May 2, 1944, Vol. 726, p. 149, HMJr., FDRL.

32. "Jewish Evacuation," April 8, 1944, Vol. 719, p. 4, HMJr., FDRL.

33. Pehle, Memorandum, April 15, 1944, Temporary Havens, I, RG 210, NA.

34. JED, Memorandum, March 25, 1944, Temporary Havens, I, RG 210, NA.

35. "Jewish Evacuation," May 2, 1944, Vol. 726, p. 146, HMJr., FDRL. A copy of the Gallup Poll taken April 14, 1944, is in Temporary Havens, I, RG 210, NA. Alfred Steinberg, "Mr. Truman's Mystery Man," *The Saturday Evening Post,* December 24, 1949, 24. This is the only Niles biography thus far discovered by Dr. Abram Sachar, who found several inaccuracies in it.

36. M. E. Ernst to Pehle, April 14, 1944, Vol. 721, p. 181, HMJr., FDRL.

37. Henry F. Pringle, "The History of the War," April 19, 1944, Temporary Havens, I, RG 210, NA.

38. "Re: Support For the "Idea of Temporary Havens of Refuge For Victims of Axis Oppression," May 9, 1944, Temporary Havens, I, RG 210, NA.

39. *New York Herald Tribune,* April 19, 1944.

40. Virginia Mannon to Pehle, April 19, 1944, Temporary Havens, I, RG 210, NA.

41. Pehle, Memorandum, May 11, 1944, Temporary Havens, I, RG 210, NA.

42. Ibid.

43. Ackermann to Pehle, May 5, 1944, Box I, WRB, FDRL.

44. "Conversation with Mr. McCloy," June 2, 1944, Vol. 738, p. 179, HMJr., FDRL.

45. "Re: Cabinet," May 26, 1944, Vol. 736, p. 70, HMJr., FDRL.

46. Alfred E. Smith to Charles G. Dawes et al., May 19, 1944; Smith to Pehle, with enc., May 26, 1944, Temporary Havens, I, RG 210, NA. The geographic spread of petition signers is evident from the identity of the governors: Chauncey Sparks (Ala.), Sidney P. Osborn (Ariz.), John C. Vivian (Colo.), Spessard L. Holland (Fla.), C. A. Bottolfsen (Idaho), Henry F. Schricker (Ind.), Simeon Willis (Ky.), Herbert R. O'Connor (Md.), Thomas L. Bailey (Miss.), Robert O. Blood (N.H.), Walter E.. Edge (N.J.), J. M. Broughton (N.C.), John W. Bricker (Ohio), J. Howard McGrath (R.I.), Olin D. Johnston (S.C.), M. Q. Shurpe (S.Dak.), Matthew M. Neely (W.Va.), L. C. Hunt (Wyo.).

47. U.S. Congress, Senate, S.R. 297, *Congressional Record,* 78th Cong. 2d sess., 1944, vol. 90, pt. 4.

48. Hadley Cantril to David K. Niles, April 14, 1944, Box 31, David K. Niles Papers, in possession of Abram S. Sachar, Brandeis University, Waltham, Mass. Pollster Cantril advised Niles that the objections raised by the 23 percent who disapproved of temporary havens needed to be met "head-on" if and when the administration announced such a plan. The objections boiled

down to a fear and dislike of foreigners, a concern that the refugees might not leave after the war, and questions about cost.

49. Pehle, Memorandum, June 1, 1944, Temporary Havens, I, RG 210. The House was in the midst of hearings on UNRRA appropriations, and it would have been inopportune to make known differences between the president and UNRRA Director Herbert Lehman.

50. *The Evening Star* (Washington), June 9, 1944.

51. Telephone Record, June 5, 1944, Vol. 739, p. 239; "War Refugee Board," June 7, 1944, Vol. 740, pp. 231–36, HMJr., FDRL. See also Henry L. Feingold, *The Politics of Rescue*, (New Brunswick, 1970), pp. 270–75, and Bernard Wasserstein, *Britain and the Jews of Europe, 1939–1945* (Oxford, 1979), pp. 209–10.

52. Pehle, Memorandum, June 1, 1944, Temporary Havens, I, RG 210, NA.

53. Memorandum, with enc., June 9, 1944, Official File (OF) 5477, FDRL. "Caring for Refugees in the United States," June 12, 1944, Temporary Havens, RG 210, FDRL.

Chapter 3: Diplomatic Gamesmanship

1. Handwritten Note on War Cabinet Memorandum, February 9, 1944, W 1953/16/48, Public Records Office (PRO), Kew, Richmond, England.

2. Anthony Eden, "Committee on the Reception and Accommodation of Refugees," February 7, 1944, W 1953/16/48, PRO.

3. War Cabinet Office Communication, March 10, 1944, W 3866/16/48, PRO.

4. Foreign Office to Washington Embassy, March 20, 1944, W 3867/16/48, PRO; for an explanation of British thinking, see Wasserstein, *Britain and the Jews of Europe*, 296–99.

5. "Jewish Evacuation," March 17, 1944, Vol. 711, p. 96, HMJr., FDRL.

6. Telephone Record, March 22, 1944, Vol. 713, p. 1, HMJr., FDRL.

7. Wasserstein, *Britain and the Jews of Europe*, pp. 327–28.

8. Pehle, Memorandum, February 10, 1944, Vol. 708, p. 272, HMJr., FDRL.

9. Sir F. Boverscher to Sir O. Sargent, February 24, 1944, W 1953/16/48, PRO.

10. Wasserstein, *Britain and the Jews of Europe*, pp. 209–10.

11. Ibid., pp. 206–11; *FRUS* 1944, I: 1013.

12. *FRUS* 1944, I: 1052–64.

13. "Proposed Refugee Camps in Tripolitania," March 8, 1944, W 2971/16/48, PRO.

14. Randall, Memorandum, March 2, 1944, W 2871/16/48, PRO.

15. Wasserstein, *Britain and the Jews of Europe*, p. 215.

16. "Proposal to Abandon the Establishment of a Refugee Camp at Zavia," November 15, 1944, WR 1824/6/48, PRO.

17. Minutes of HMJr./FDR Meeting, March 7, 1944, Vol. 5, p. 1339, Presidential Correspondence, HMJr. Papers, FDRL.

18. Wasserstein, *Britain and the Jews of Europe*, pp. 340–41; "History of the War Refugee Board and Selected Documents" (WRB History), I, 244, FDRL.

19. Ibid.

20. Bucknell to Randall, March 27, 1944, W 4787/16/48, PRO.

21. "War Refugee Board," May 20, 1944, Vol. 734, p. 7, HMJr., FDRL.

22. Ibid. For a brief summary of the main points discussed in London by

Stettinius and Dr. Chaim Weizmann; Stettinius, A. L. Easterman and Dr. Barou of the World Jewish Congress; and Wallace Murray and Foreign Office officials, see "Conversations in London on Palestine and Refugee Problems," undated, Vol. 730, pp. 110–11, HMJr., FDRL.

23. Pehle, Memorandum, February 10, 1944, Vol. 708, p. 272; "Jewish Evacuation," March 8, 1944, Vol. 707, p. 223; "Re: Peter Bergson," May 24, 1944, Vol. 735, p. 65, HMJr., FDRL.

24. Pehle, Memorandum, March 9, 1944, Temporary Havens, I, RG 210, NA.

25. *FRUS* 1944, I: 1123–24; C. Cheatham to Sir Herbert Emerson, September 15, 1944, WR 1078/12/48, PRO.

26. Foreign Office to Heathcote-Smith, Canceled Letter, August 1944, WR 1078/12/48, PRO.

27. Heathcote-Smith to IGC, with Appendixes "A" and "B," July 15, and Heathcote-Smith to IGC, July 18, 1944, WR 260/12/48, PRO; Edward A. Walker to Patrick Malin, August 11, 1944, WR 436/12/48, PRO; C. Cheatham, canceled.

28. Randall, Minutes, April 13, 1944, W 5497/16/48, PRO.

29. Michael Wright to Randall, May 30, 1944, W 9066/16/48, PRO.

30. State Department to Robert Murphy, May 27, 1944, Temporary Havens, II, RG 210, NA.

31. I. L. Henderson (consul in the Refugee Dept. of the Foreign Office) to Eastern Central Dept., June 6, with comments (June 10); Memorandum, June 7, 1944, W 9035/21/48, PRO.

32. Harry L. Coles and Albert K. Weinberg, *Civil Affairs: Soldiers Become Governors* (Washington, D.C., 1964), pp. 408–409, 332.

33. Ackermann, "Summary Report" (Ackermann Summary), November 4, 1944, Box I, WRB, FDRL.

34. Ibid.

35. Coles and Weinberg, *Civil Affairs*, p. 409; Ackermann to Pehle, May 3, 1944, Box I, WRB, FDRL.

36. Ackermann to Pehle, May 11, 1944, Box I, WRB, FDRL; *FRUS* 1944, I: 1078–79, 1092–94. Murphy insisted that the drop in refugee arrivals was due not to the restrictive order but to German advances against the partisans. He continued to defend the order as late as July 1944.

37. Ackermann to Pehle, June 17, 1944, Temporary Havens, III, RG 210, NA.

38. *FRUS* 1944, I: 1097–98.

39. Henriques to Henderson, July 25, 1944, WR 179/12/48, PRO.

40. War Office to IGC, June 20, 1944, WR 179/12/48, PRO.

41. *FRUS* 1944, I: 1125, 1097–98.

42. Ackermann to Pehle, May 11, 1944, Box I, WRB, FDRL.

43. Ackermann to Pehle, May 5, 1944, Box I, WRB, FDRL.

44. Ackermann Summary; WRB History, I, 239–40.

45. Major General Steel to Mr. Mason, October 20, 1944, WR 1457/6/48, PRO; *FRUS* 1944, I: 1063.

46. Pehle, Memorandum, June 1, 1944, Temporary Havens, III, RG 210, NA.

47. Memorandum, June 8, 1944, Vol. 741, p. 48, HMJr., FDRL.

48. Resident Minister Algiers to Foreign Office, May 24, 1944, W 8381/121/48, PRO.

49. Ibid.; RMA Hankey, Response, May 30, 1944.

50. Memorandum, September 27, Vol. 779, p. 161, HMJr., FDRL.

Feingold, *The Politics of Rescue,* p. 267. Wasserstein, *Britain and the Jews of Europe,* p. 264. *FRUS 1944,* I: 1125–26, 1142.

51. Lucy S. Dawidowicz, *The War Against the Jews 1933–1945* (New York, 1975), p. 382.

52. *New York Post,* October 26, 1944.

Chapter 4: Disparate Expectations

1. Ruth Gruber, "Eight Months Later," undated report to Secretary Ickes, pp. 13–14, Box XII, Records of the Fort Ontario Emergency Refugee Shelter (ERS), Columbia University (CU), New York.

2. Aulus Saunders, quoted in Lawrence Baron, "Haven From the Holocaust: Oswego, New York, 1944–1946," *New York History* (January 1983): 16.

3. Gruber, "Eight Months Later," p. 8.

4. Edward H. Spicer, "Story of Oswego," September 7, 1944, 2, Box XII, ERS, CU.

5. Eleanor Morehead, "Oswego, An Average U.S. Town, Chooses to Ignore its Refugees," *PM* (New York), February 27, 1945.

6. Gruber, "Eight Months Later," p. 8.

7. *PM,* February 27, 1945.

8. Robert A. Wilson and Bill Hosokawa, *East to America: A History of the Japanese in the United States* (New York, 1980), p. 215.

9. Henry A. Wallace Diaries, November 11, 1944, collection of Prof. Theodore A. Wilson, University of Kansas, Lawrence.

10. Dillon S. Myer, *Uprooted Americans: The Japanese-Americans and the War Relocation Authority During World War II* (Tuscon, 1971), p. 108.

11. Dorothy Swaine Thomas and Richard S. Nishimoto, *The Spoilage: Japanese-American Evacuation and Resettlement* (Berkeley, 1946), p. 26.

12. G. G. Beavers, "Final Report of the Internal Security System" (Beavers Report), February 28, 1946, I, RG 210, NA.

13. Pehle to Fortas, June 22, 1944, Temporary Havens, III, RG 210, NA.

14. Herbert Katzko to Ackermann, June 24, 1944, Temporary Havens, III, RG 210, NA.

15. Pehle to Ackermann, June 14, 1944, Box XII, ERS, CU.

16. Cable 1826 to Algiers, June 9, 1944, Temporary Havens, III, RG 210; Pehle to Ackermann, June 14, 1944, Box XII, ERS, CU.

17. Ackermann to Pehle, July 29, 1944, Temporary Havens, IV, RG 210, NA.

18. Miriam Sommerburg and Charles Abeles, "The Golden Cage," Scene 2, Box XII, ERS, CU. The play was staged in the shelter during September 1945.

19. "Departure for the United States of America" (unsigned and undated), Box 2331, Records of the Department of the Interior, Office of the Secretary, RG 48, NA.

20. Edward B. Marks, Jr., "Token Shipment: The Story of America's War Refugee Shelter" (Washington, D.C., 1946), pp. 109–10. This is the official history printed by the Department of the Interior: War Relocation Authority.

21. Ackermann to Pehle, June 22; Pehle to Ackermann, July 14, 1944; Box XVI, ERS, CU. Ackermann to Pehle, June 29, 1944, Temporary Havens IV, RG 210, NA.

22. "The Golden Cage," Scene 2.

23. David Levy and Zdenka Ruchwarger, taped interview, New York, October 28, 1979. Names of former Oswego refugees are first spelled in the

text in accordance with the spelling on the closing roster prepared by Unitarian Service Committee consultant Friedl Reifer on February 19, 1946. RG 210, NA. Name changes and corrections have been put in parentheses.

24. "The Golden Cage," Scene 4.

25. B. R. Stauber to Myer, with July 30 enc. (Stauber Memorandum), August 3, 1944, Box XII, ERS, CU.

26. Transport Commander to Commanding General Army Service Forces Washington, date unclear, Box II, ERS, CU. See also Myer, "Responsibilities on Mediterranean Mission," July 5, 1944, Box XII, ERS, CU.

27. Dr. David Hendell (formerly Hendel), taped interview, New York, October 31, 1979.

28. Fred Baum (formerly Fredi Baum), interview, New York, May 18, 1980.

29. Hendell interview.

30. *New York Post,* August 9, 1944.

31. *New York Times, New York Herald Tribune,* August 5, 1944. Case histories are not direct quotes.

32. Myer to Pehle, September 19, 1944, Temporary Havens, V, RG 210, NA; Allan Markley, "Final Study of Attitudes at the Fort Ontario Refugee Shelter" (Markley Reports), February 13, 1946, p. 5, RG 210, NA.

33. "The Golden Cage," Scene 5.

34. Letter, Olga Maurer to Sharon Lowenstein, May 30, 1980.

35. Ruth Karpf, "Displaced Persons: A USA Close-Up," *Survey Graphic* XXXIV (June 1945): 284.

36. International Migration Service, "A Study Made at Fort Ontario Shelter for Refugees" (IMS Study), Partial Report, April 9, 1945, pp. 6–7.

37. *New York Herald Tribune,* August 8, 1944; *Oswego Palladium Times,* January 19, 1946.

38. Society for Ethical Culture to Mrs. Roosevelt, March 5, 1945, Temporary Havens, X, RG 210, NA.

39. Edward B. Marks, Jr., to William O'Dwyer, with enc., March 20, 1944, Temporary Havens, XI, RG 210, NA.

40. *Ontario Chronicle,* April 5, 1945.

41. *Oswego Palladium Times,* January 24, 1946.

42. C. H. Powers to Dillon S. Myer, September 10, 1945, Box 408, RG 210, NA.

43. Joseph H. Smart to Joseph E. Beck, May 8, 1945, Box 408, RG 210, NA.

44. Kanus Goldberg and Paul R. Milton, "Voyage of the *Pentcho,*" *True* XVII (June 1945).

45. Brandt to Secretary of State, July 15, 1944; Kirk to Secretary of State, July 20, 1944, Temporary Havens, IV, RG 210, NA.

46. Ronald L. Loeb, "Final Report of the Health Section" (Loeb Report), February 5, 1946, p. 1, RG 210, NA.

47. IMS Study, June 8, 1945, p. 13. I matched the names to cases discussed in the IMS Study through the use of index cards that I compiled for every shelter resident.

48. *New York Herald Tribune,* August 5, 1944; Gruber, *Haven,* pp. 288–89.

49. *The News* (Greensboro, N.C.), September 22, 1944; *Oswego Palladium Times,* January 30, 1946.

50. Myer to O'Dwyer with enc., April 27, 1944, Temporary Havens, II, RG 210, NA.

51. *Ontario Chronicle,* July 26, 1946.

52. *Oswego Palladium Times,* January 26, 1946.

Chapter 5: Tenuous Beginnings

1. *Oswego Palladium Times*, August 6, 1944.
2. Ibid.
3. Fred Baum interview.
4. Stauber Memorandum. See also Spicer, "Story of Oswego," p. 4.
5. Ariel Tartakower, "Jewish Migrating Movements in Austria in Recent Generations," in Josef Fraenkel, ed., *The Jews of Austria* (London, 1967), p. 297.
6. Case Histories, Refugees, Box 2331, RG 48, NA.
7. Regina Gal, taped interview, New York, August 10, 1980.
8. IMS Study, June 8, 1945, p. 3.
9. Dawidowicz, *The War Against the Jews*, p. 191.
10. Smart (?), "Journal Memorandum," August 14, 1944, Box 408, RG 210, NA.
11. Michael G. Tress et al. to Israel Rothschild, August 6, 1944, Emergency Relief Center Papers, F-31-13-8, Agudat Israel of America Archives (AI), New York.
12. Fred O. Saunders, "Final Report of the Supply Section" (Saunders Report), undated, p. 2, RG 210, NA.
13. Bettie R. Schroeder, "Final Report of the Mess Operations Section" (Schroeder Report), February 20, 1946, p. 3, RG 210, NA.
14. Spicer, "Story of Oswego," p. 4.
15. Mendell Eller to Mr. Tress, undated, F-31-15-8, AI.
16. Cecilia Razovsky, "Some Suggestions on Camp Administration and Procedures," May 1, 1944, Box XIII, ERS, CU.
17. Director to WRB, Memorandum, undated, Box XII, ERS, CU.
18. Ruth Gruber, taped interview, New York, October 27, 1979.
19. Monthly Reports, December 5, 1945, 16, Box 411, RG 210, NA.
20. Jewish Labor Committee to Mr. Pehle, August 14, 1944, Temporary Havens, V, RG 210, NA.
21. Carl and Liesl Newman (formerly Karl and Elise Neumann), interview, Kansas City, March 16, 1982; Fred Baum interview.
22. Smart to Chief Inspector United States Customs Service, September 30, 1944; G. W. O'Keefe to Smart, October 6, 1944, Box 408, RG 210, NA.
23. Smart to Myer, September 29, 1944, Box 117, RG 210, NA.
24. Letter, Kitty Kaufman (formerly Kathe Kaufmann) to Sharon Lowenstein, October 12, 1979.

Chapter 6: Emotional Conflict

1. "The Golden Cage," Scene 5.
2. *New York Times*, August 10, 1944.
3. *Oswego Palladium Times*, January 28, 1946.
4. Gruber, *Haven*, p. 173.
5. *New York Post*, August 11, and September 7, 1944; *Oswego Palladium Times*, February 1, 1946.
6. *Ontario Chronicle*, February 8, 1945.
7. *New York Post*, September 6, 1944.
8. *Syracuse Herald Journal*, September 4 and 20, 1944; Gruber to Ickes, September 24, 1944, Box 416, RG 210, NA.
9. Carl Palmitesso, "The Refugees of Fort Ontario," paper given before the Oswego County Historical Society, November 17, 1953.
10. *Oswego Palladium Times*, December 27, 1945.

11. Jeanette A. Margolies, "Final Report of the Welfare Section" (Margolies Report), undated, p. 2, RG 210, NA.

12. *Oswego Palladium Times*, September 5, 1944. Examples of answers to rumors: (1) Oswego refugees did not get shoe stamps from the Oswego Ration Board but got them through the District Office and thus did not affect Oswego's allotment; (2) relatives of refugees did not waste gasoline by driving from California; the car with California license plates belonged to a WRA employee; (3) Oswego's new manufacturing plant would not rely on refugee workers—they could not accept outside employment or compete with local labor or private business in Oswego or elsewhere.

13. Myer, *Uprooted Americans*, p. 110; Memorandum, August 18, 1944, Box 411, RG 210, NA.

14. Memorandum, August 25, 1944, Box 1, ERS, CU.

15. Naomi Jolles, "Oswego Opens Its Heart to Refugees," *New York Post*, September 9, 1944. Lawrence Baron, "Haven from the Holocaust: Oswego, New York, 1944–1946," *New York History* LXIV (January 1983): 27.

16. Morehead, "Oswego, An Average U.S. Town, Chooses to Ignore Its Refugees," *PM*, February 27, 1945.

17. Markley Report, No. 7, January 28, 1946, p. 8.

18. Margolies Report, p. 2.

19. Memorandum, September 7, 1944; Mildred C. Whitaker to Smart, November 22, 1944, Box 411, RG 210, NA.

20. Judith M. Gansberg, *Stalag U.S.A.: The Remarkable Story of German POWs in America* (New York, 1977), p. 13.

21. Letter, Dr. Walter Arnstein to Sharon Lowenstein, January 21, 1980.

22. Ibid.

23. Hendell interview. Shelter records offer no hint of the POWs' presence. And the *Ontario Chronicle*, which did not appear until November 5, 1944, never mentioned them.

24. Newton L. Margulies, "Proper Treatment of War Prisoners: Reason for War Department's Management," May 15, 1945, *Vital Speeches* XI, no. 15: 479.

25. Ibid.

26. Ibid., p. 480.

27. Gansberg, *Stalag U.S.A.*, p. 22.

28. George T. Mazuzan and Nancy Walker, "Restricted Areas: German Prisoner-of-War Camps in Western New York, 1944–1946," *New York History* LX (January 1979): 70.

29. *Oswego Palladium Times*, September 20, 1944.

30. Weekly Report, January 3, 1945, Box 110, RG 210, NA; Smart to Myer, January 6, 1945, Papers of Jack Cohen, P-317, American Jewish Historical Society (AJHS), Waltham, Mass. Smart learned that in 1942 the Army rejected a plan to establish an anti-aircraft base at the fort because of the extreme winters, a decision reached after options had been taken on the land. See Smart to Myer, January 6, 1945, Box 2331, RG 48, NA.

31. Anne Dacie, "Yugoslav Refugees in Italy: The Story of a Transit Camp," pp. 8–9. This is a pamphlet, published in London in 1945 and available at the New York Public Library.

32. Gruber, "Eight Months Later," p. 22.

33. Margolies Report, pp. 1–4.

34. Loewenkron Hersch to Smart, November 4, 1944, Box 416, RG 210, NA.

35. Claudius K. Cirtautas, *The Refugee: A Psychological Study* (Boston, 1957), pp. 24–25.

36. Erving Goffman, *Asylums: Essays on the Social Situation of Mental Patients and Other Inmates* (Garden City, N.Y., 1961), 29.

37. Gruber, *Haven*, 321–23.

38. Curt Bondy, "The Emergency Refugee Shelter," January 1945, pp. 1–17, RG 210, NA. See also Bondy, "Problems of Internment Camps," *The Journal of Abnormal and Social Psychology* (October 1943).

39. Ickes to Myer, March 12, 1945, Box XII, ERS, CU.

40. Myer, "An Autobiography of Dillon S. Myer," (University of California at Berkeley Regional Oral History Office, 1970), p. 340.

41. Ickes to Myer, March 12, 1945, Box XII, ERS, CU.

42. Spicer to Bondy, January 26, 1945, Box XII, ERS, CU.

43. Gruber, "Eight Months Later," pp. 17, 19, 21.

44. Ibid., p. 19.

45. Telephone Record, Smart to Marks, March 14, 1945, Box 3, ERS, CU; "Mental Cases as of May 29, 1945," Box 419, RG 210, NA. Additional information added from my cumulative index file.

46. Dr. Rudolph Dreikurs, "Psychiatric Report," undated, pp. 3, 4–5, Gruber Papers. Dr. Dreikurs lectured, conducted group discussions, met with the staff, and interviewed fifty-nine refugees.

47. Ibid., pp. 10, 11.

48. Ibid., pp. 17–18.

49. Marks, "Token Shipment," p. 46; Memorandum, May 9, 1945, Box XIII, ERS, CU.

50. Margolies Report, pp. 18–19.

51. Dreikurs, "Psychiatric Report," pp. 6–7.

52. Minutes, March 31, 1945, p. 5, Gruber Papers.

Chapter 7: Persistent Problems

1. Cirtautas, *The Refugee: A Psychological Study*, p. 69.

2. Smart to Myer, with enc., September 29, 1944, Box 416, RG 210, NA.

3. Spicer, "Story of Oswego," p. 7.

4. Smart to Myer, September 4, 1944, Box 408, RG 210, NA.

5. Ibid.

6. Smart to Myer, August 29, 1944, Box 416, RG 210, NA.

7. Thomas and Nishimote, *The Spoilage*, p. 33.

8. Edward F. Quigley, "Final Report of the Fiscal and Personnel Section" (Quigley Report), March 2, 1945, p. 3, RG 210, NA.

9. Myer, *Uprooted Americans*, p. 61.

10. Resolution, September 22, 1944; Gruber to Ickes, September 24, 1944, Box 416, RG 210, NA. See also Myer to Pehle, September 8, 1944, Box IV, ERS, CU.

11. Marks, "Token Shipment," p. 60.

12. Gruber, *Haven*, p. 204.

13. David Levy and Zdenka Ruchwarger, taped interview, New York, October 28, 1979; Carl and Liesl Newman interview.

14. Paul Bokros interview, San Diego, January 4, 1980.

15. Letter, Zlatko Hirschler (present name not used by request) to Sharon Lowenstein, April 27, 1982.

16. Carl and Liesl Newman interview.

17. Smart to Colonel Enmet J. Bean, August 18, 1944; Joseph E. Beck to Pehle, September 29, 1944, Temporary Havens, I; "Observations Re: Procedures For Reimbursing the Refugees at Oswego in Dollars For the Lire and Dollars Deposited by Them With the Allied Control Commission in Italy," unsigned and undated, Temporary Havens, II; Pehle to Moses Leavitt, November 16, 1944, Temporary Havens, IV; Marks, "Recent Developments at Oswego," October 17, 1944; "Suggested Release at Fort Ontario on Conversion of Funds," unsigned and undated, Box 408, RG 210, NA.

18. Telephone Record, Marks and Smart, November 21, 1944, Box IV, ERS, CU.

19. Marks to Abrahamson, November 22, 1944, Temporary Havens, X; Smart, Memorandum, December 21, 1944, Box 409, RG 210, NA; Weekly Report, November 24, 1944, Box 110, RG 210, NA. See also *Ontario Chronicle*, March 8, 1945.

20. *Ontario Chronicle*, December 14 and November 23, 1944.

21. Telephone Record, Smart and Marks, December 5, 1944, Box III, ERS, CU.

22. Morris Burge to Dr. Bondy, January 15, 1945, Box 113, RG 210, NA.

23. Fred Baum interview.

24. Telephone Record, Smart, Marks, and Pitts, February 22, 1945, Box III, ERS, CU.

25. Telephone Record, Smart and Marks, February 21, 1945, Box III. ERS, CU.

26. Myer to Fortas, March 31, 1945, Box 2331, RG 48, NA.

27. Minutes of meeting held by Dr. Rudolph Driekurs in director's office, March 31, 1945, p. 4, Gruber Papers.

28. Margolies Report, p. 31.

29. Marks to Myer, October 17, 1944, Box 408, RG 210, NA.

30. Reuben Levine, "Final Report of the Administrative Management Division" (R. Levine Report), date unclear, p. 13, RG 210, NA.

31. Quigley Report, pp. 15, 17.

32. Letter, Smart to Lowenstein, April 19, 1982.

33. Ibid.

34. Pitts to Myer, June 18, 1945, Box 416, RG 210, NA.

35. R. Levine Report, 13.

36. Goffman, *Asylums*, pp. 6, 12, 7.

37. "Complaint Settlement Committee and Court of Arbitration," October 19, 1945, Box 415, RG 210, NA. Their records were not kept.

38. R. Levine Report, p. 14.

Chapter 8: Liberty's Struggle

1. "The Golden Cage," Scene 5.

2. Petition of the Residents of Fort Ontario to the Department of Interior–War Relocation Authority, December 1944, File 552, National Refugee Service Papers, YIVO.

3. Kent George Beam to Veterans of Foreign Wars, October 11, 1944, Box 113, RG 210, NA.

4. Morgenthau to Wolff, with enc., February 19, 1945, Temporary Havens, X, RG 210, NA.

5. Ibid.

6. Marie Syrkin, "At Fort Ontario," *Jewish Frontier* XI (September 1944): 9–10.

7. Bernard Dubin to Professor Chamberlain, January 26, 1945, with enc., Box I, Joseph P. Chamberlain Papers, YIVO.

8. Pvt. Frank D. Vranken to WRB, September 4, 1945, Box 409, RG 210, NA; Letter, Edith Semjen Starkman to Sharon Lowenstein, November 7, 1980.

9. Dillon S. Myer, "WRA: A Story of Human Conservation," p. 153, RG 48, NA. This is the final report of the director of the WRA.

10. *Congressional Record,* 78th Cong., 2d sess., Aug. 11, 1944, vol. 90, 6906–12.

11. *Washington Post,* October 24 and 25, 1944.

12. S. S. Wise to Ickes, August 14, 1944, File 552, YIVO.

13. Biddle to Ickes, September 16, 1944, Box XIV, ERS, CU.

14. Myer to Pehle, September 19, 1944, Temporary Havens, V, RG 210, NA.

15. Albert Abrahamson to Joseph Friedman, "Notes on a Possible Program Looking Toward the Removal of the Refugees From Fort Ontario," enc. in Memorandum, October 23, 1944, Temporary Havens, VII, RG 210, NA.

16. Marks, Memorandum, November 20, 1944, Box XVI, ERS, CU.

17. Gruber, *Haven,* pp. 241–42.

18. FDR to Biddle, January 17, 1945, OF 3186, FDRL.

19. Biddle to O'Dwyer, March 1, 1945, Temporary Havens, X, RG 210, NA.

20. Marks, Memorandum, September 7, 1944, Box 411; Myer to Ickes, "Status of the Refugees at the Fort Ontario Emergency Refugee Shelter," December 7, 1944, Temporary Havens, IX, RG 210, NA.

21. Ann Petluck to NRS Migration Department, September 5, 1945, Microfilm MKM 13, 27, National Refugee Service Papers, YIVO.

22. Marks to Myer, December 18, 1944, Box XVI, ERS, CU.

23. E. J. Shaughnessey to Mr. Carusi, December 28, 1944, Box I, Chamberlain Papers, YIVO.

24. Marks to Pitts, February 24; Marks to Myer, March 9, 1945, Box III, ERS, CU.

25. Biddle to Chamberlain, December 29, 1944, Box I, Chamberlain Papers, YIVO.

26. Ickes to O'Dwyer, April 12, 1945, Temporary Havens, II, RG 210, NA.

27. Marks to Myer, January 17, 1945; Telephone Record, Bernard Dubin and Marks, February 21, 1945, Box III, ERS, CU.

28. Ickes to Myer, March 12, 1945, Box III. ERS, CU.

29. Ibid.

30. Telephone Record, Smart and Marks, March 12, 1945, Box III, ERS, CU.

31. Fortas to Ickes, March 17, 1945, Box III, ERS, CU.

32. Ickes to O'Dwyer, April 12, 1945, Temporary Havens, XI, RG 210, NA. I have identified and summarized the cases: N.B. (psychiatric hospitalization in April 1945); N.B. (convalescent leave, September 9–Octover 9, 1945); E.L. (remained in the shelter); J.B. (foster home, September 14, 1945–January 11, 1946); O.B. (Long Island Convalescent Home, December 29, 1945–January 19, 1946), and B.G. (convalescent leave, October 12–November 17, 1945).

33. Myer to O'Dwyer, March 29; Ickes to O'Dwyer, April 10; Pitts to O'Dwyer, April 12, 1945; Temporary Havens, II, RG 210, NA.

34. Minutes, May 24, 1945, Box I, Chamberlain Papers, YIVO.

35. Meeting of Special Committee for Purposes of Considering Oswego

Situation, May 28, 1945, Refugee-Immigration 1945–50, American Jewish Committee Archives (AJC), New York; Harold L. Ickes Diary, June 9, 1945, Library of Congress.

36. Gruber, *Haven*, p. 242.

37. Marcus Cohn to George Hexter, June 5, 1945, Refugee-Immigration 1945–50, AJC. See also O'Dwyer, Memorandum, June 6, 1945, Temporary Havens, XII, RG 210, NA.

38. Harry S. Truman, *Memoirs I, Year of Decisions* (Garden City, N.Y., 1955), pp. 554–55.

39. Of the ten cabinet members Truman inherited, only Commerce Secretary Henry Wallace and Naval Secretary James Forrestal remained when the last refugees left the shelter February 26, 1946. Stettinius left in early July, Morgenthau in late September, and Ickes in mid-February 1946.

40. Francis Biddle to Harry Truman, June 28, 1945, Box XIV, ERS, CU.

Chapter 9: Freedom Achieved

1. *Washington Post*, April 8, 1945; *PM*, February 25, 1945; Dr. David Hendell interview.

2. Long to Hockworth, November 22, 1943, State Department Visa Division Decimal File 1945–46, 811.111 Refs/2138, RG 59, Federal Records Center, Suitland, Virginia.

3. "Message to Congress," June 12, 1944, "Temporary Havens, III, RG 210, NA.

4. Ann Petluck to Joseph Beck, August 22, 1944, File 556, National Refugee Service Papers, YIVO.

5. Ruth Ehrlich, "The Emotional Climate of Fort Ontario" (Ehrlich Report) (Appendix to Margolies Report), February 14, 1946, pp. 46–47.

6. Joseph H. Smart interview.

7. Memorandum, May 3, 1945; Smart to Myer, May 19, 1945; Five Page Fact Sheet, unsigned and undated; "Final Report of the Friends of Fort Ontario–Guest Refugees," January 4, 1946, Smart Papers.

8. "A Memorial to the President and the Congress of the United States Concerning the Freedom of Refugees Temporarily Living at Fort Ontario, Oswego, New York," May 1945, Temporary Havens, XIII, RG 210, NA.

9. Smart to Ernst Flatau, June 19, 1945, Box XV, ERS, CU; "Outline of Suggested Testimony at Fort Ontario Hearing, June 24, 1944, Smart Papers; *Washington Times Herald*, May 17, 1945.

10. Myer to Fortas, May 24, 1945, Box III, ERS, CU. The committee consisted of Dickstein, George P. Miller (D. Cal.), John Lesinski (D. Mich.), O. Clark Fisher (D. Tex.), Lowell Stockman (R. Ore.), James I. Dolliver (R. Iowa), and Justice Department counsel Thomas M. Cooley, II.

11. U.S. Congress, House, *Investigation of Problems Presented by Refugees at Fort Ontario Refugee Shelter*, Hearings before Subcommittee VI of the Committee on Immigration and Naturalization, on H. Res. 52, 79th Cong., 1st sess., 1945 (Dickstein Hearings), p. 13.

12. Ibid., pp. 59, 71.

13. *Oswego Palladium Times*, June 25, 1945.

14. Dickstein Hearings, p. 124; *Ontario Chronicle*, June 28 and July 5, 1945.

15. Albert G. D. Levy, "Acquisition of Nationality in the Emergency Refugee Shelter," *The American Journal of International Law* XXXIX (January 1945), Exhibit 6, Dickstein Hearings, p. 108.

16. Dickstein to O'Dwyer, with enc., July 6, 1945, Temporary Havens, XII, RG 210, NA; Memorandum, unsigned and undated, Box 5, National Refugee Service Papers, I-92, AJHS.

17. Harrison to Biddle, June 15, 1944, Box XIV, ERS, CU.

18. C. M. Pierce to Edward B. Marks, Jr., July 31, 1945, Box XIV, ERS, CU.

19. Marks to Myer, August 1, 1945, Box XIV, ERS, CU.

20. Marks to Myer, July 27, 1945, Box XIII,. ERS, CU.

21. Dr. David Hendell interview.

22. Powers to Myer, July 31, 1945, Box 414, RG 210, NA.

23. Powers, Memorandum, August 2, 1945, Box 414, RG 210, NA.

24. Weekly Report, September 13, 1945, Box 410, RG 210, NA. Five days earlier Powers reported that he would attempt to change the paper's staff if the editors did not agree to publish articles of a "morale-building" rather than "morale-destroying character." Monthly Report, September 8, 1945, Box 411, RG 210, NA.

25. Leonard Dinnerstein, *America and the Survivors of the Holocaust* (New York, 1983), pp. 34–38.

26. Tom Clark to Ickes, August 24, 1945, Box XIV, ERS, CU.

27. Myer to Beck, September 4, 1945, Box XII, ERS, CU.

28. Myer, "Further Notes on the Paneling of Fort Ontario Refugees" (Paneling Notes), October 1, 1945, Box IV, ERS, CU; Chamberlain to Clarence E. Pickett, September 29, 1945, Box I, Chamberlain Papers, YIVO.

29. "Classification for Use of Panel Members," Box XIV, ERS, CU.

30. Paneling Notes.

31. Weekly Report, September 13, 1945, Box 411, RG 210, NA.

32. Paneling Notes.

33. Phil M. Glick to Abe Fortas, December 6, 1945, Box IV, ERS, CU.

34. Ickes to Russell, December 10, 1945, Box IV, ERS, CU.

35. Ephraim, R. Gomberg to Emelie Levin, June 18; Levin to Gomberg, June 20; Bernard Dubin to Levin, November 1; Joseph E. Beck to Tom L. Evans, November 28; William Rosenwald to Clarence Decker, December 5; Beck to Sigmund Stern, December 5; Stern to Levin, December 5; Beck to Nathan E. Rieger, December 5, 1945; Eddie Jacobson to Emelie Levin, January 20, 1946; Levin to Beck, January 23, 1946; NRS Correspondence File, Jewish Family and Children Services (JFCS), Kansas City.

36. Z. Shister to Dr. John Slawson, October 24, 1945, Refugee-Immigration 1945–60, AJC.

37. Gruber, "Notes on Meeting with Mr. J. H. Smart, November 21, 1945" (Gruber/Smart Memorandum), Gruber Papers.

38. Minutes, December 12, 1945, Box I, Chamberlain Papers, YIVO.

39. Joseph P. Chamberlain et al. to Dean Acheson, December 14, 1945, Box V, Chamberlain Papers, YIVO; Gruber, *Haven*, pp. 268–69. The delegation also included Bruce Mohler, representing Cardinal Spellman and the National Catholic Welfare Conference; Clarence Pickett of the American Friends Service Committee; and Isaiah Minkoff of the National Jewish Community Relations Advisory Committee.

40. Glick to Powers, December 15, 1945, Box IV, ERS, CU.

41. Chamberlain to Harrison, December 19, 1945, Box V, Chamberlain Papers, YIVO.

42. *New York Times*, December 23, 1945.

43. Joseph E. Beck to Zlatko Hirschler, February 12, 1976 (copy of this letter to a former Oswego resident in the author's possession).

44. Feingold, *The Politics of Rescue*, p. 152.
45. Telephone Summary, Beck and Marks, January 5, 1946; Minutes, January 7, 1946, Box XV, ERS, CU.
46. Markley Report, No. 5, January 24, 1946, pp. 4–6.
47. Markley Report, No. 9, January 30, 1946, p. 7; Bernard Dubin, "Report on the Settlement by NRS of the Oswego Refugees" (Dubin Report), p. 4, File 447, NRS Papers, YIVO.
48. IMS Study, Statistics Memorandum, No. 5, September 15, 1944.

Chapter 10: Toward Renewal

1. *New York Post*, August 8, 1944.
2. Ibid.
3. R. L. Loeb to C. H. Powers, August 29; Sanford Sherman to John Provinse, September 4; Joseph Rubenstein to Powers, August 28, 1945, Box 419, RG 210, NA.
4. Loeb Report, pp. 22–23.
5. Marks, "Relations with Private Agencies in Connection with the Emergency Refugee Shelter," October 19, 1944, Box IV, ERS, CU.
6. Minutes, August 10, 1944, F 31-15-8, AI; Minutes, October 16, 1944, Box 411, RG 210, NA.
7. Smart to Max Stern, November 30, 1944, Box 415, RG 210, NA.
8. *New York Post*, September 9, 1944.
9. W. C. Schlosser, "General Summarization of the Vocational Training Situation as of December 25, 1944," Box 419, RG 210, NA.
10. *Oswego Palladium Times*, January 24, 26, 1946.
11. Manya Breuer to Sharon Lowenstein, New York, August 2, 1984.
12. Ehrlich Report, p. 50.
13. Markley Report, No. 4, January 22, 1946, p. 1; *Oswego Palladium Times*, January 19, 1946.
14. *Oswego Palladium Times*, August 30, 1945.
15. Ralph Manfred (formerly Ralph Manfred Kusnitzki), taped interview, San Francisco, January 13, 1980.
16. Ontario Chronicle, November 23, 1944.
17. Ibid., December 28, 1944.
18. Yosef Hayim Yerushalmi, *Zakhor: Jewish History and Jewish Memory* (Seattle, 1982), pp. 44–45.
19. Gruber, "Eight Months Later," pp. 13–14; *Haven*, pp. 227–29.
20. Pitts to Myer, June 5, 1945, Box 414, RG 210, NA.
21. Berta Choda, Medical Social Report (Appendix to Loeb Report), p. 9.

Chapter 11: Conclusion

1. Robert Dallek, *Franklin Roosevelt and American Foreign Policy, 1932–1945*, p. 336.
2. Amy Zahl Gottlieb, "Refugee Immigration: The Truman Directive," p. 7.

Epilogue

1. Boldface type is used for the names of former Oswego refugees as they appear in government records.
2. Adam Munz to Lowenstein, phone, taped, Nov. 9, 1984.

3. Walter Greenberg to Lowenstein, phone, taped, Nov. 12, 1984.

4. Manya Breuer, New York, Aug. 2, 1984; phone, taped, Nov. 10, 1984.

5. Gloria Bass Fredkove, New York, Aug. 2, 1984; phone, taped, Nov. 25, 1984.

6. Paul and Walter Arnstein, San Francisco, Jan 12, 1980; letter, Paul Arnstein to Lowenstein, Feb. 1, 1980 Walter Arnstein, signed questionnaire, Feb. 15, 1980.

7. Eva Auerbach, phone, taped, Nov. 25, 1984.

8. Magdelena Bader, phone, taped, Nov. 21, 1984.

9. Liesl Bader Friedman, letter, Dec. 1, 1979.

10. Jack Bass to Lowenstein, New York, Aug. 2, 1984.

11. Fred Baum interview.

12. Geza Bleier, phone, taped, Nov. 10, 1984.

13. Ibid.

14. Fred Bohm, phone, taped, Nov. 27, 1984.

15. Paul Bokros interview; phone, taped, Nov. 20, 1984.

16. Nelly Bokros Thalheimer, signed questionnaire, Aug. 2, 1984.

17. Sylvan Boni, phone, taped, Nov. 25, 1984.

18. Edith Bronner Klein, phone, taped, Nov. 23, 1984.

19. Paul Buechler, phone, taped, Nov. 12, 1984.

20. Sarah Danon Meller, phone, taped, Nov. 25, 1984.

21. Ruth Gruber, *Haven* (New York: Signet, 1984), p. 230.

22. Irene Danon, phone, taped, Nov. 22, 1984.

23. Gordana Milinovic Musafia to Lowenstein, phone, Dec. 3, 1984.

24. Salomon Dresdner, phone, taped, Nov. 24, 1984.

25. Herbert Druks to Lowenstein, New York, Aug 1, 1984.

26. Lily Ernst, phone, taped, Nov. 10, 1984.

27. Gruber, *Haven*, pp. 238–39. Mike Finci, phone, taped, April 28, 1985.

28. Lydia Finger, phone, taped, Nov. 22, 1984.

29. Fred Flateau, phone, taped, Dec. 5, 1984.

30. Sam Fraserman, phone, taped, Nov. 24, 1984.

31. Lidia Franco, phone, taped, Nov. 25, 1984.

32. Dr. Ernest Froelich, signed questionnaire, Aug. 2; phone, taped, Nov. 26, 1984.

33. Abe Forman to Lowenstein, New York, Aug. 10, 1980; signed questionnaire, Aug. 2, 1984.

34. Regina Gal interview; Gal to Lowenstein, New York, Aug. 10, 1980; signed questionnaire, Aug. 2, 1984; Charlotte Gal, signed questionnaire, Aug. 2, 1984; Albert Gal, signed questionnaire, Aug. 2, 1984.

35. Vera Gross, phone, taped, Nov. 25, 1984.

36. Hajim Hazan, phone, taped, Nov. 24, 1984.

37. Ruthe Hellner Zogut, phone, taped, Nov. 22, 1984.

38. Dr. David Hendell interview.

39. Zlatko Hirschler, letter, Jan. 29, 1980; phone, Nov. 22, 1984.

40. Gruber, *Haven*, pp. 227–28; John Hunter, phone, taped, Dec. 1, 1984.

41. Ray Harding to Lowenstein, New York, June 10, 1980.

42. Ibid.

43. Leon Kabiljo, phone, taped, Nov. 24, 1984.

44. Emica Kamhi Agrimi, signed questionnaire, April 5, 1980.

45. Kitty Kaufman, letter, Oct. 12, 1979; Eva Dye, interview, San Francisco, April 18, 1985.

46. Tina Korner Chernick, phone, taped, Nov. 27, 1984.
47. Liana Kramer, phone, taped, Nov. 24, 1984.
48. Suzanne Krauthamer Gurwitz, phone, taped, Nov. 22, 1984.
49. Ralph Manfred, letter, Dec. 2, 1979; taped interview, San Francisco, Dec. 13, 1980.
50. Gruber, *Haven,* pp. 251–52.
51. Mira Lederer Salomon, letter, Sept. 20, 1979. See also "Why Me?" in *Women: A Journal of Liberation* 6, no. 2: 24–26.
52. Gruber, *Haven,* pp. 244–45.
53. Eva Lepehne Rosenfeld, signed questionnaire, Feb. 5, 1980.
54. Levy/Ruchwarger interview.
55. Jack Wilson, signed questionnaire, Aug. 2, 1984; phone, taped, Nov. 25, 1984.
56. Irene Levy, phone, taped, Nov. 22, 1984.
57. Jack Liban, signed questionnaire, Aug. 2, 1984.
58. Gruber, *Haven,* pp. 221–222; Dr. Ralph Margulis, phone, taped, Nov. 27, 1984.
59. Sonja Mercer, phone, taped, Nov. 27, 1984.
60. Leo Mirkovic, phone, taped, Nov. 27, 1984.
61. Bella Moschev to Lowenstein, New York, August 10, 1980; Rosa Moschev Levy, phone, taped, Dec. 8, 1984.
62. George Newfeld, phone, taped, Nov. 22, 1984.
63. Gruber, *Haven,* p. 233.
64. Ibid., p. 233.
65. Dorrit Reisner Ostberg, phone, taped, Nov. 25, 1984.
66. Renata Romano; Clara Romano, phone, taped, Dec. 8, 1984.
67. Mark and Morris Rosenbaum to Lowenstein, New York, Aug. 2, 1984.
68. Ari Rothstein, phone, taped, Nov. 25, 1984.
69. Levy/Ruchwarger interview.
70. Irving Schild, phone, taped, Nov. 27, 1984.
71. Ilsa Schroeter, phone, taped, Nov. 27, 1984.
72. Gruber, *Haven,* pp. 247–48.
73. Ibid., p. 223.
74. Ibid., pp. 228–29; Sonja Sommerburg to Lowenstein, New York, Aug. 2, 1984.
75. Margaret Spitzer Fisse, letter, Sept. 26, 1979; taped interview, San Francisco, Jan. 13, 1980.
76. Steffi Steinberg Winters, letter, Sept. 25, 1979; interview, New York, Aug. 8, 1980.
77. Marion Strauber Siegel, signed questionnaire, Jan. 8, 1980.
78. Trudy Striks Ehrlich, signed questionnaire, Aug. 2, 1984; phone, taped, Dec. 8, 1984. Fanny Striks Saltz, signed questionnaire, Aug. 2, 1984.
79. Dr. Neva Svecenski Gould, phone, taped, Nov. 12, 1984.
80. Matilda Ternbach, signed questionnaire, Aug. 2, 1984; Lea Ternbach Ziering, signed questionnaire, Aug. 2, 1984.
81. Rudy Ternbach, signed questionnaire, Aug. 2, 1984; phone, taped, Nov. 12, 1984.
82. Gisela Tusak, signed questionnaire, Jan. 12, 1980.
83. *The Day,* April ?, 1960, P-317, AJHS.
84. Suzanna Waksman, phone, taped, Dec. 8, 1984.
85. Thea Weiss Sanders, phone, taped, Nov. 25, 1984.
86. Kostia Zabotin, phone, taped, Dec. 8, 1984.

BIBLIOGRAPHIC ESSAY

This study focuses on one unique development during the Holocaust years and is based primarily on original research.

Document Collections

Agudat Israel of America Archives, New York
  Papers of Emergency Relief Center, Oswego, New York
American Jewish Committee, New York
  Free Ports 1944
  Refugee Immigration
  Refugee Rescue
  United States Government War Refugee Board 1944
American Jewish Historical Society, Waltham, Massachusetts
  Papers of the American Jewish Congress
  Papers of Jack Cohen
  Papers of the Council of Jewish Federation and Welfare Funds
  Papers of the National Refugee Service
  Papers of Stephen S. Wise
American Jewish Joint Distribution Committee, New York
  Displaced Persons
  Italy
  Refugee Transit
Columbia University, New York
  Papers of the Fort Ontario Emergency Shelter
  Papers of Herbert H. Lehman
Federal Records Center, Suitland, Maryland
  State Department Box, "Refugees"
Ruth Gruber, New York
  Papers of Ruth Gruber
Institute for Mediterranean Affairs, New York
  Papers of the Emergency Committee to Save the Jews of Europe
Jabotinsky Institute, Tel Aviv, Israel
  Papers of Peter Bergson
  Papers of the Hebrew Committee of National Liberation
Library of Congress, Washington, D.C.
  Diaries of Harold L. Ickes
  Papers of Breckinridge Long
  Papers of Laurence A. Steinhardt
  Diaries of Henry L. Stimson
National Archives, Washington, D.C.
  Records of the Department of the Interior
  State Department Decimal File
  Records of the War Relocation Authority
Oswego County Historical Society
  Vertical File Fort Ontario Pamphlet Box 10

Public Records Office, Kew, Richmond, England
  Records of the Foreign Office
Franklin D. Roosevelt Library, Hyde Park, New York
  Papers of Francis Biddle
  Papers of Oscar Cox
  Papers of Stephen Early
  Papers of Harry L. Hopkins
  Diaries of Henry Morgenthau, Jr.
  Papers of Henry Morgenthau, Jr.
  Papers of Eleanor Roosevelt
  Papers of Franklin D. Roosevelt
  Papers of Samuel I. Rosenman
  Papers of Henry A. Wallace
  Records of the War Refugee Board
  Papers of John G. Winant
Abram Sachar, Waltham, Massachusetts
  Papers of David Niles, which in 1985 were given to the Harry S. Truman
    Library.
Joseph H. Smart, Salt Lake City
  Papers of the Friends of Fort Ontario Guest Refugees
Harry S. Truman Library, Independence, Missouri
  Eben Ayers Diary
  Papers of Matthew J. Connelly
  Papers of Clarence R. Decker
  Papers of Tom L. Evans
  Papers of Eddie Jacobson
  Diaries of Samuel I. Rosenman
  Papers of Samuel I. Rosenman
  Papers of Harry S. Truman
  Papers of George L. Warren
University of Virginia, Charlottesville, Virginia
  Papers of Edward Stettinius, Jr.
Theodore A. Wilson, Lawrence, Kansas
  Diaries of Henry A. Wallace
YIVO Institute for Jewish Research, New York
  Papers of Joseph P. Chamberlain
  Papers of the National Refugee Service

The documents used most extensively included the papers and diaries of Henry Morgenthau, Jr., and the records of the War Refugee Board, War Relocation Authority, and Department of the Interior, as well as those of the National Refugee Service and the British Foreign Office.

The documents of Henry Morgenthau, Jr., and of the War Refugee Board provided the core of the story behind the temporary havens proposal. The Morgenthau collection, housed in the Franklin D. Roosevelt Library, is divided into two parts, papers and diaries. Included in the diaries are summaries of cabinet meetings (official records were not kept), transcripts of telephone and office discussions, correspondence, and memoranda. The inserts in the diary entitled "Jewish Evacuation" and "Peter Bergson" offer crucial insights into the formation and functioning of the War Refugee Board. Morgenthau obviously had an eye on future historians, but he censored little.

The papers of the War Refugee Board are also in the Roosevelt Library. WRB Correspondence Papers Subject Files include documents concerning the proposal for temporary havens and the selection in Italy. Related material is also scattered among the hundreds of documents in the unbound, three-volume "War Refugee Board History." However, the principal WRB material relating to Oswego has been removed and filed instead with the records of the War Relocation Authority in the National Archives. Listed under "Temporary Havens," it consists of a chronological record of activities from March 1944, when the proposal officially went to the board, to mid-June 1945, when full responsibility for the shelter passed to the Department of the Interior.

Peter Bergson and his associates exercised considerable influence on the development of and campaign for the temporary havens proposal. The papers of the Emergency Committee to Save the Jews of Europe are housed at the Jabotinsky Institute in Tel Aviv, the Institute for Mediterranean Affairs in New York, and Yale University in New Haven. I found nothing useful in the first two collections, which are not indexed and consist largely of letters of appeal to world leaders, newspaper clippings, and other printed material. I did not examine the collection at Yale.

Whereas American archives file documents either topically or chronologically, the Public Records Office in Kew, Richmond, England, does both. Establishment of the War Refugee Board and its rescue campaign challenged previous State Department–Foreign Office understandings on refugee policy. The records of the Foreign Office provide a comprehensive account of the material related to each action or event. Rich in corrected drafts, penciled notations, and private memoranda, these records offer keen insights into the private meaning of public communications.

The War Relocation Authority administered the single shelter and campaigned throughout to have its occupants released into freedom. Its papers, in the National Archives, include comprehensive shelter administration records, a brief FBI summary on every adult, official camp photographs, press clippings, summary reports, and the International Migration Service studies.

WRA Records also include eleven feet of personal case histories, an alphabetical file that includes extensive medical and social data on every shelter resident. In October 1979 all case records were open to researchers as long as the material therein was not used with individual names. At that time, I merely glanced through one file for sampling purposes. In September 1982, when I wished to use the case records, the division had new personnel and a new policy. Researchers could examine only the records of deceased individuals. Having sampled the case records, I concluded that obtaining access through the Freedom of Information Act would prove more restrictive than helpful. Using administrative records, newspaper stories, and the camp newspaper, I compiled my own file for every shelter resident. Not bound by the rules of privacy covering case records, I strove for sensitivity without censorship. I used information freely that pertained to individuals presumably deceased but respected the wishes of people with whom I had contact and did not use full names in instances where medical and other sensitive material was used. If the case records become available, researchers can easily identify pertinent files.

Columbia University's Papers of the Fort Ontario Emergency Shelter, filed both chronologically and topically, are said to duplicate shelter administrative records in the National Archives. However, numerous reports and studies are not included in the Columbia collection, while items not found elsewhere, such as transcripts of telephone conversations between Marks and Smart, are here.

The records of the Department of the Interior, also in the National Archives, include five boxes under "Refugees" that pertain primarily to the WRA/Interior campaign for sponsored leave and regular immigration. These files also include the records (except the interviews of family heads) of the paneling conducted in September 1945 in the fort by Interior, State, and Justice representatives.

State Department records contain little that is not available elsewhere. They proved most interesting for their accounts, in the Decimal File on Palestine, of efforts by American Jewish leaders to have Peter Bergson drafted or deported.

Justice Department records pertaining to Oswego have been filed with closed Immigration and Naturalization records. I chose not to mount a challenge under the Freedom of Information Act because, except in the case of individual interviews, these records too will duplicate open Interior records.

Franklin Roosevelt insisted on maintaining shelter restrictions and Harry Truman finally released the group into freedom, but presidential papers proved to have limited usefulness. Roosevelt stood above the fray on refugee questions. His Official File and the Presidential Safe File include only a few items of note, most especially his December 17, 1945, letter to Biddle. A 1976 letter from NRS Director Joseph E. Beck to former shelter resident Zlatko Hirschler reveals that Beck drafted the Truman Directive with Samuel Rosenman and suggests that the NRS exercised considerable influence. However, the materials in the Truman Library offer no confirmation. A single entry in the diary of Assistant Press Secretary Eben Ayers indicates that Samuel I. Rosenman asked the president to consider several of the ideas later written into the document. The Rosenman papers include drafts of the statement but nothing regarding its history.

David Niles had no direct association with the shelter but he took an interest at critical times. Historians have long been intrigued by the role of this elusive special assistant to both Roosevelt and Truman, who died in 1952. The inaccessibility of his papers, willed to Abram Sachar, added to the mystery. In September 1983, having completed the manuscript for *The Redemption of the Unwanted,* Dr. Sachar, Chancellor Emeritus of Brandeis University in Waltham, Massachusetts, gave me free use of the collection, which was stored in his Brandeis office. The papers confirm but do not clarify Niles's interest in the temporary havens proposal, and they shed no new light on the story behind the Truman Directive. Niles's role remains an enigma.

Of the many private organizations involved with the shelter, the National Refugee Service played the dominant role throughout. Its papers were divided between YIVO and the American Jewish Historical Society. Reports, correspondence, and memoranda pertaining to social services, lobbying activities, and resettlement went to the American Jewish Historical Society. Papers related to immigration, including the disposition of inadmissible cases, went to YIVO. NRS Chairman Joseph P. Chamberlain, a non-Jew, was deeply involved throughout the thirties and forties in every question concerning refugees. His papers, also at YIVO, are essential for any study of the political climate surrounding refugee matters. They establish a strong link between the Oswego question and the larger Displaced Persons issue.

Rabbi Stephen S. Wise was the single most influential American Jewish leader of the time. He visited the shelter in August 1944 and was said to have prepared a lengthy report on his observations. However, the extent of Wise's interest must be inferred from occasional references in government and NRS records. The voluminous Wise papers in the American Jewish Historical Society in Waltham, Massachusettes, do not include Oswego documents.

A professional writer now living in Manhattan, former special assistant to Harold Ickes, Ruth Gruber collected copies of various shelter documents and kept an extensive record of her personal involvement in the project. She shared selected items with me. We exchanged addresses of former residents and officials. Most important, her book, *Haven: The Unknown Story of 1000 World War II Refugees* (New York, 1983), a warm and personal account of her own involvement, enabled many to speak of the experience for the very first time.

Joseph Smart, former shelter director, now retired and living in Salt Lake City, possesses the principal file on the Friends of Fort Ontario–Guest Refugees; see also the Jack Cohen Papers in the American Jewish Historical Society. A duplicate collection of the Jack Cohen Papers is in the B'nai B'rith Archives in Washington, D.C. Those papers in Mr. Smart's possession link his public campaign for immigration to Dickstein's efforts toward the same end. Mr. Smart also continues to treasure a large scrapbook that movingly confirms the rapport he established with many shelter residents.

Unpublished Materials

University of California, Berkeley
  Myer, Dillon S. "Autobiography."
Columbia University, New York
  Dickstein, Samuel. "Oral History."
Gruber Papers
  Dreikurs, Rudolph. "Psychiatric Report." Undated.
  "Haven." Unpublished draft.
War Refugee Board Records, Franklin D. Roosevelt Library
  Ackermann, Leonard. "Summary Report." November 4, 1944.
War Relocation Authority Records, National Archives
  Allen, George W. "Final Report of the Operations Division." February 26, 1946.
  Beavers, G. G. "Final Report of the Internal Security System." February 28, 1946.
  Bondy, Curt. "The Emergency Refugee Shelter." Undated.
  Brown, William E. "Final Report of the Buildings, Roads and Grounds Section." February 21, 1946.
  Gruber, Ruth. "Eight Months Later" (a report to Secretary Ickes). Undated.
  Huberman, Edward. "Final Report of the Community Activities Section." February 9, 1946.
  International Migration Service. "A Study Made at Fort Ontario Shelter for Refugees." June 8, 1945.
  Kray, Anna. "Final Report Refugee Employment." February 28, 1946.
  LaFave, James H. "Final Report of the Garage Section." February 20, 1946.
  Levine, Reuben. "Final Report of the Administrative Management Division." March 19, 1946.
  Loeb, Lotta. "Report of the Coordinating Committee for Fort Ontario." February 21, 1946.
  Loeb, Ronald. "Final Report of the Health Section." February 5, 1946.

Mackin, Robert H. "Final Report of the Electrical Section." February 21, 1946.

Margolies, Jeanette A. "Final Report of the Welfare Section." February 12, 1946. Appendix by Ruth Ehrlich. "The Emotional Climate of Fort Ontario." Undated.

Markley, Allan. "Attitudes at the Fort Ontario Refugee Shelter." 9 reports plus the final. January 18–February 13, 1946.

Miller, William L. "Final Report of the Carpentry Section." February 25, 1946.

Myer, Dillon. "WRA: A Story of Human Conservation." 1946.

Paino, George F. "Final Report of the Fire Department." February 27, 1946.

Quigley, Edward F. "Final Report of the Fiscal and Personnel Section." March 2, 1946.

Reifer, Friedl. "Closing Roster." February 19, 1946.

Saunders, Fred O. "Final Report of the Supply Section." March 1946.

Schroeder, Bettie R. "Final Report of the Mess Operations Section." February 20, 1946.

Sommerburg, Miriam, and Abeles, Charles. "The Golden Cage." Undated.

Spicer, Edward. "Story of Oswego." September 7, 1944.

United States Army Headquarters Second Service Command Security and Intelligence Division. "Paneled Fort Ontario, Oswego, New York, 8th August to 14th August, 1944."

Wolff, Ernst. "Storm in the Shelter." Undated.

It is unlikely that any group of people displaced by Hitler became the subject of more study than the Oswego refugees. Community Analyst Edward Spicer's eight-page "Story of Oswego" astutely noted national group differences and early relations with the community of Oswego.

Three reports provided a broad picture of the camp's emotional climate during its first eight months. Curt Bondy's January 1945 psychological assessment, "The Emergency Refugee Shelter," identified mounting problems in work and interpersonal relations. Dr. Rudolph Dreikurs's "Psychiatric Report" affirmed Bondy's observations and addressed the phenomenon of personality deterioration. Ruth Gruber's "Eight Months Later" described conflicting social and psychological trends. All three attributed problems more to current environmental conditions than to past traumas, conclusions supported by WRA Community Analyst Allan Markley's series of reports on "Attitudes at the Fort Ontario Refugee Shelter."

The study by the International Migration Service is based on work by several interviewers with varied training and needs to be used with considerable caution. The Army's Paneling report, completed during the first few days after the group arrived, and the WRA's Closing Roster offer more specific and a bit more reliable information than does the IMS Study. The former provides occupational backgrounds and is more accurate on places of birth. The latter includes immigration and resettlement information.

Miriam Sommerburg wrote the lyrics and Charles Abeles composed the music for "The Golden Cage," a musical revue in two parts and six scenes, presented in September 1945 to an audience that included State, Justice, and Interior representatives conducting panels within the fort. The script, deposited with shelter records at Columbia University, movingly suggests the pain and bewilderment of continued confinement. So does the essay "Storm in the

Shelter," written by Ernst Wolff and forwarded to Henry Morgenthau, Jr., by Eleanor Roosevelt.

Congressional Material

U.S. Congress. House. *Investigation of Problems Presented by Refugees at Fort Ontario Refugee Shelter.* Hearings before Subcommittee VI of the Committee on Immigration and Naturalization on H. Res. 52. 79th Cong., 1st Sess., 1945.

U.S. Congress. House. *Rescue of the Jewish and Other Peoples in Nazi-Occupied Territory.* Hearings before Committee on Foreign Affairs on H. Res. 350 and H. Res. 352. 78th Cong., 1st sess., 1943.

U.S. Congress. Senate. "Petition to Save the Jews in Nazi-Controlled Europe—Appeal by the Rabbis of America." *Congressional Record.* 78th Cong., 1st sess., October 6, 1943. Vol. 89, 8107.

U.S. Congress. Senate. Senator Reynolds speaking for the Amendment of Social Security Act–Unemployment Compensation, S. 2051. *Congressional Record.* 78th Cong., 2d Sess., August 11, 1944. Vol. 90, 6906–12.

With the Dickstein Hearings, held June 25 and 26, 1945, in the fort, the struggle to obtain the group's release from the shelter moved into the public arena. Dickstein Committee minutes, correspondence, and memoranda are closed for fifty years, thirty years longer than comparable Senate material. However, individual researchers occasionally gain access to closed materials through the chairman of the committee in question. I sought assistance from a congressman on the House Immigration and Naturalization Committee, but a secretary of the chairman screened material before it reached me so that I received only documents already available.

Interviews

Paul Arnstein, San Francisco, January 12, 1980.
Walter Arnstein, San Francisco, January 12, 1980.
Eva Auerbach, telephone, taped, November 25, 1984.
Magdalena Bader, telephone, taped, November 21, 1984.
Jack Bass, New York, August 3, 1984.
Fred Baum, New York, May 18, 1980.
Geza Bleier, telephone, taped, November 10, 1984.
Fred Bohm, telephone, taped, November 27, 1984.
Paul Bokros, San Diego, January 4, 1980; telephone, taped, November 20, 1984.
Bellina Boni and Raymond Boni, New York, August 10, 1980.
Sylvan Boni, telephone, taped, November 25, 1984.
Manya Hartmayer Breuer, New York, August 2, 1984; telephone, taped, November 10, 1984.
Paul Buchler, telephone, taped, November 12, 1984.
Tina Korner Chernick, telephone, taped, November 27, 1984.
Irene Danon, telephone, taped, November 22, 1984.
Salomon Dresdner, telephone, taped, November 24, 1984.
Herbert Druks, New York, August 1, 1984.
Bernard Dubin, telephone, August 4, 1981.

Eva Kaufman Dye, San Francisco, April 19, 1985.
Lily Ernst, telephone, taped, November 10, 1984.
Lydia Finger, telephone, taped, November 22, 1984.
Dr. Fred Flateau, telephone, taped, December 5, 1984.
Abe Forman, New York, August 10, 1980.
Lidia Franco, telephone, taped, November 25, 1984.
Sam Fraserman, telephone, taped, November 24, 1984.
Neti Levy Fredericks, San Francisco, January 13, 1980.
Gloria Bass Fredkove, telephone, taped, November 25, 1984.
John Friedman and Ted Mann, Washington, D.C., May 18, 1980.
Dr. Ernest Froelich, telephone, taped, November 26, 1984.
Regina Gal, New York, taped, August 10, 1980.
Dr. Neva Svecenski Gould, telephone, taped, November 12, 1984.
Walter Greenberg, telephone, taped, November 12, 1984.
Vera Gross, telephone, taped, November 25, 1984.
Ruth Gruber, New York, taped, October 27, 1979.
Suzanne Krauthamer Gurwitz, telephone, taped, November 22, 1984.
Raymond B. Harding, New York, October 31, 1979.
Hajim Hazan, telephone, taped, November 24, 1984.
Dr. David Hendell, New York, taped, October 31, 1979.
Elfi Strauber Hendell, New York, August 8, 1980.
Zlatko Hirschler, San Francisco, January 12, 1980; telephone, November 22, 1984.
Leon Kabiljo, telephone, taped, November 24, 1984.
Edith Bronner Klein, telephone, taped, November 23, 1984.
Liana Kramer, telephone, taped, November 12, 1984.
Edward Levitch, San Francisco, January 12, 1980, and New York, April 19, 1985.
Leon Levitch, New York, August 3, 1984.
David Levy and Zdenka Ruchwarger, New York (taped), October 28, 1979; San Francisco, April 19, 1985.
Irene Levy, telephone, taped, November 22, 1984.
Rosa Moschev Levy, telephone, taped, December 8, 1984.
Ralph Manfred and Margaret Fisse Spitzer, San Francisco, January 13, 1980.
Leon and Olga Maurer, New York, August 10, 1980.
Sarah Danon Meller, telephone, taped, November 25, 1984.
Sonja Mercer, telephone, taped, November 27, 1984.
Gordana Milinovic Musafia, telephone, taped, December 3, 1984.
Leo Mirkovic, telephone, taped, November 27, 1984.
Bella and Albert Moschev, New York, August 10, 1980.
Adam Munz, telephone, taped, November 9, 1984.
George Newfeld, telephone, taped, November 22, 1984.
Carl and Liesl Newman, Kansas City, March 16, 1982.
Dorrit Reisner Ostberg, telephone, taped, November 25, 1984.
John W. Pehle, Washington, D.C., May 19, 1980.
Sonia Sommerburg Rabin, New York, August 3, 1984.
Clara Romano, telephone, taped, December 8, 1984.
Renata Romano, telephone, taped, December 8, 1984.
Mark Rosenbaum, New York, August 3, 1984.
Morris Rosenbaum, New York, August 3, 1984.
Ari Rothstein, telephone, taped, November 25, 1984.
Thea Weiss Sanders, telephone, taped, November 25, 1984.
Irving Schild, telephone, taped, November 27, 1984.

Ilse Schroeter, telephone, taped, November 27, 1984.
Edith and O. Barnard Starkman, New York, August 10, 1980.
Rudy Ternbach, telephone, taped, November 12, 1984.
Suzanna Waksman, telephone, taped, December 8, 1984.
Jack Wilson, telephone, taped, November 25, 1984.
Steffi Steinberg Winters, New York, August 8, 1980.
Kostia Zabotin, telephone, taped, December 8, 1984.
Ruthe Hellner Zogut, telephone, taped, November 22, 1984.

Correspondents and/or Questionnaire Respondents

Emica Kamhi Agrimi
Paul Arnstein
Walter Arnstein
Denise Battat
Geza Bleier
Trudy Striks Ehrlich
Ralph Faust
Liesl Bader Friedman
Dr. Ernest Froelich
Abe Forman Furmanski
Albert Gal
Charlotte Gal
Zlatko Hirschler
Kitty Kaufman
Liana Kramer
Leon Levitch
Irene Levy
Jack Liban
Ralph K. Manfred

Harry Maurer
Adam Munz
Gordana Deutsch Milinovic Musafia
Eva Lepehne Rosenfeld
Fanny Striks Saltz
Thea Weiss Sanders
Fanny Schild
Irving Schild
Marion Strauber Siegel
Joseph H. Smart
Mira Lederer Solomon
Margaret Fisse Spitzer
Anna Stassen
Dora Langnas Stock
Matilda Ternbach
Nelly Bokros Thalheimer
Steffi Steinberg Winters
Kostia S. Zabotin
Lea Ternbach Ziering

The sampling of former shelter residents is not representative of the group as it was in Oswego. It is skewed in three ways. (1) It includes a disproportionate number of Yugoslavs. They were younger, they had more children, and, alone among the national groups, they retain a strong national identity and have, in many cases, maintained contact with each other. (2) It includes a disproportionate number of those interned with intact families, which were larger and easier to locate. (3) It includes a disproportionate number who were interned as youngsters. It thus favors those who have positive feelings. Those who remain bitter are less likely to come forth, less likely to permit an interview, and less likely to share their deepest responses. Nevertheless, although not in a proportion representative of the entire original group, this sampling includes people who convey the entire range of feelings and attitudes.

Cited Publications

JOURNALS AND MAGAZINES
American Jewish History
Foreign Relations of the United States
Jewish Frontier

Journal of Abnormal and Social Psychology
Journal of Contemporary History

Life
Mademoiselle
New York History
Oswego County Historical Society
Prologue

Saturday Evening Post
Survey Graphic
Time
True
Vital Speeches

NEWSPAPERS

Christian Science Monitor
The Day
Fort Ontario Chronicle
Kansas City Star
The News (Greensboro, North Carolina)
New York Herald Tribune
New York Post

New York Times
Oswego Palladium Times
PM
Syracuse Herald Journal
The Evening Star (Washington)
Washington Post
Washington Times Herald

Interest briefly soared when the group first arrived, rose slightly just before the November 1944 election, increased again during the Dickstein Hearings in June, as well as the paneling in September, and rose again during the camp's closing in January and February 1946. The shelter attracted far more press attention than its numbers warranted, particularly in the northeast.

BOOKS

Cafferty, Pastora San Juan, et al. *Immigration and the American Tradition.* New Brunswick: Transactions Inc., 1983.

Cantril, Hadley. *Public Opinion 1935–1946.* Princeton: Princeton University Press, 1951.

Clark John G., et al. *Three Generations in Twentieth-Century America: Family, Community, and Nation.* Homewood, Ill.: The Dorsey Press, 1982.

Cirtautas, Claudius K. *The Refugee: A Psychological Study.* Boston: Meader Publishing Company, 1957.

Cohen, Naomi. *Not Free to Desist: A History of the American Jewish Committee 1906–1966.* Philadelphia: Jewish Publication Society, 1972.

Coles, Harry L., and Weinberg, Albert K. *Civil Affairs: Soldiers Become Governors.* Washington, D.C.: Office of the Chief of Military History, Department of the Army, 1964.

Dallek, Robert. *Franklin D. Roosevelt and American Foreign Policy, 1932–1945.* New York: Oxford University Press, 1979.

Daniels, Roger. *Concentration Camps USA: Japanese Americans and World War II.* New York: Holt, Rinehart & Winston, Inc., 1972.

Davidowicz, Lucy S. *On Equal Terms: Jews in America 1881–1981.* New York: Holt, Rinehart and Winston, 1982.

———. *The War Against the Jews, 1933–1945.* New York: Bantam Books, 1976.

Davie, Maurice R. *Refugees in America: Report of the Committee for the Study of Recent Immigration from Europe.* New York: Harper & Brothers, 1947.

Dinnerstein, Leonard. *America and the Survivors of the Holocaust.* New York: Columbia University Press, 1982.

Encyclopedia of Zionism and Israel. New York: McGraw-Hill, 1971.

Feingold, Henry L. *The Politics of Rescue.* New Brunswick: Rutgers University Press, 1970.

———. *Zion in America: The Jewish Experience from Colonial Times to the Present.* New York: Hippocrene Books, Inc., 1974.

Gansberg, Judith M. *Stalag U.S.A.: The Remarkable Story of German POWs in America*. New York: Thomas Y. Crowell Company, 1977.

Gilbert, Martin. *Auschwitz and the Allies: A Devastating Account of How the Allies Responded to the News of Hitler's Mass Murder*. New York: Holt, Rinehart and Winston, 1981.

———. *Final Journey: The Fate of the Jews in Nazi Europe*. New York: Mayflower Books, 1979.

Goffman, Erving. *Asylums: Essays on the Social Situation of Mental Patients and Other Inmates*. Garden City, N.Y.: Doubleday Anchor, 1961.

Gruber, Ruth. *Haven: The Unknown Story of 1000 World War II Refugees*. New York: Coward, McCann, Inc., 1983. The paperback edition (Signet, 1984) includes a much lengthier epilogue, which I cite in my own epilogue.

Higham, John. *Send These to Me: Jews and Other Immigrants in Urban America*. New York: Atheneum, 1975.

Laqueur, Walter. *The Terrible Secret: An Investigation Into the Suppression of Information About Hitler's 'Final Solution'*. London: Weidenfeld and Nicolson, 1980.

Marks, Edward B., Jr. "Token Shipment: The Story of America's War Refugee Shelter" (booklet). Washington, D.C.: U.S. Department of the Interior, 1946.

Myer, Dillon S. *Uprooted Americans: The Japanese Americans and the War Relocation Authority During World War II*. Tucson: University of Arizona Press, 1971.

Rischin, Moses, ed. *Immigration and the American Tradition*. Indianapolis: The Bobbs-Merrill Company, Inc. 1976.

Sachar, Abram. *The Redemption of the Unwanted: From the Liberation of the Death Camps to the Founding of Israel*. New York: St. Martin's/Marek, 1983.

Thomas, Dorothy Swaine, and Nishimoto, Richard S. *The Spoilage: Japanese American Evacuation and Resettlement*. Berkeley: University of California Press, 1946.

Truman, Harry S. *Memoirs: Year of Decisions*. Garden City, N.Y.: Doubleday & Company, Inc., 1955.

Wasserstein, Bernard. *Britain and the Jews of Europe, 1939–1945*. London: Oxford University Press, 1979.

White, Lyman Cromwell. *300,000 New Americans: The Epic of a Modern Immigrant-Aid Service*. New York: Harper, 1957.

Wilson, Robert A., and Hosokawa, Bill. *East to America: A History of the Japanese in the U.S.* New York: William Morrow & Company, Inc., 1980.

Yerushalmi, Yosef Hayim. *Zakhor: Jewish History and Jewish Memory*. Seattle: University of Washington Press, 1982.

Young, Roland. *Congressional Politics in the Second World War*. New York: Columbia University Press, 1956.

ARTICLES

Baron, Lawrence. "Haven from the Holocaust: Oswego, N.Y., 1944–1946." *New York History* LXIV/1 (January 1983): 5–35.

Bondy, Curt. "Problems of Internment Camps." *Journal of Abnormal and Social Psychology* 38 (October 1943): 453–75.

Dacie, Anne. "Yugoslav Refugees in Italy: The Story of a Transit Camp." (Pamphlet.) London: Victor Gollancz Ltd., 1945.

Dawidowicz, Lucy S. "American Jews and the Holocaust." *New York Times Magazine*, April 18, 1983.

Feingold, Henry L. "Roosevelt and the Resettlement Question." In *Rescue*

Attempts During the Holocaust: Proceedings of the Second Yad Vashem International Historical Conference (April 1977), 123–81.

Goldberg, Kanus, and Milton, Paul R. "Voyage of the *Pentcho.*" *True* XVII (June 1945).

Gottlieb, Amy Zahl. "Refugee Immigration: The Truman Directive." *Prologue: Journal of the National Archives* 13 (Spring 1981): 5–19.

Jolles, Naomi. "Oswego Opens Its Heart to Refugees." *New York Post,* September 9, 1944.

Karpf, Ruth. "Displaced Persons: A USA Close-Up." *Survey Graphic* XXXIV (June 1945).

Margulies, Newton L. "Proper Treatment of War Prisoners: Reason for War Department's Management." *Vital Speeches* XI (May 15, 1945): 477–80.

Mazuzan, George T., and Walker, Nancy. "Restricted Areas: German Prisoner-of-War Camps in Western New York, 1944–1946." *New York History* LVIX (January 1978): 55–72.

Morehead, Eleanor. "Oswego, An Average U.S. Town, Chooses to Ignore its Refugees." *PM,* February 27, 1945, 5.

———. "Oswego Refugees Hurt Over Strict Internment." *PM,* February 26, 1945, 10.

———. "Refugees At Oswego Want to Go to the U.S.A." *PM,* February 25, 1945, 1.

Palmitesso, Carl. "The Refugees at Fort Ontario." *Oswego County Historical Society Yearbook* (1953): 65–71.

Peck, Sarah. "The Campaign for an American Response to the Nazi Holocaust 1943–1945." *Journal of Contemporary History* 15 (April 1980): 367–400.

Penkower, Monty Noam. "In Dramatic Dissent: The Bergson Boys." *American Jewish History* LXX (March 1981): 281–310.

Steinberg, Alfred. "Mr. Truman's Mystery Man." *The Saturday Evening Post,* December 24, 1949, 24–27.

Syrkin, Marie. "At Fort Ontario." *Jewish Frontier* 11 (September 1944): 9–12.

Tartakower, Ariel. "Jewish Migrating Movements in Austria in Recent Generations." In *The Jews of Austria,* edited by Josef Fraenkel. London: Valentine, Mitchell and Co., Ltd., 1967.

Works Not Cited but Relevant

BOOKS

Abella, Irving, and Troper, Harold. *None Is Too Many: Canada and the Jews of Europe 1933–1948,* New York: Random House, 1983.

Adamic, Louis. *America and the Refugees.* New York: Public Affairs Committee, 1939.

Adler, Cyrus, and Margalith, Aaron M. *With Firmness in the Right: American Diplomatic Action Affecting Jews, 1840–1945.* New York: The American Jewish Committee, 1946.

Agar, Herbert. *The Saving Remnant.* London: Rupert Hart-Davis, 1960.

Bailey, Thomas A. *The Man in the Street: The Impact of American Public Opinion on Foreign Policy.* New York: Macmillan Co., 1948.

Baram, Philip J. *The Department of State in the Middle East, 1919–1945.* Philadelphia: University of Pennsylvania Press, 1978.

Bauer, Yehuda. *American Jewry and the Holocaust.* Detroit: Wayne State University Press, 1981.

———. *The Holocaust in Historical Perspective.* University of Washington Press, 1978.

Bentwich, Norman. *The Rescue and Achievement of Refugee Scholars.* The Hague: Martinus Nijhoff, 1953.

Bernard, William S., ed. American Immigration Policy: A Reappraisal. New York: Harper, 1950.

Bowman, Isaiah. *Limits of Land Settlement: A Report on Present-Day Possibilities.* New York: Council on Foreign Relations, 1937.

Divine, Robert A. *American Immigration Policy, 1924–1952.* New Haven: Yale University Press, 1957.

Freidman, Philip. *Their Brothers' Keepers.* New York: Crown Publishers, 1957.

Friedman, Saul S. *No Haven for the Oppressed: United States Policy Toward Jewish Refugees, 1938–1945.* Detroit: Wayne State University, 1973.

Fuchs, Lawrence H. *The Political Behavior of American Jews.* New York: Free Press, 1956.

Gallup, George H. *The Gallup Poll.* 3 vols. New York: Random House, 1972.

Ganin, Zvi. *Truman, American Jewry, and Israel, 1945–1948.* New York: Holmes and Meier, 1979.

Grodzins, Martin. Americans Betrayed: Politics and the Japanese. Chicago: University of Chicago Press, 1949.

Halperin, Samuel. *The Political World of American Zionism.* Detroit: Wayne State University Press, 1961.

Higham, John. *Strangers in the Land: Patterns of American Nativism, 1860–1925.* New Brunswick: Rutgers University Press, 1955.

Hilberg, Raul. *The Destruction of the European Jews.* Chicago: University of Chicago Press, 1967.

Hirschmann, Ira. *Life Line to a Promised Land.* New York: The Vanguard Press, Inc., 1946.

Holborn, Louise W. *The International Refugee Organization.* London: Oxford University Press, 1956.

Isaacs, Stephen D. *Jews and American Politics.* Garden City, N.Y.: Doubleday & Co., Inc., 1974.

Israel, Fred L., ed. *The War Diaries of Breckinridge Long.* Lincoln: University of Nebraska Press, 1965.

Kanawada, Leo, Jr. *Franklin D. Roosevelt's Diplomacy and American Catholics, Italians, and Jews.* Ann Arbor: UMI Research Press, 1982.

Karpf, Maurice. *Jewish Community Organization in the United States.* New York: Bloch Publishing Company, 1938.

Klemme, Marvin. *The Inside Story of UNRRA.* New York: Lifetime Editions, 1949.

Leighton, Alexander H. *The Governing of Man: General Principles and Recommendations Based on Experience at a Japanese Relocation Camp.* New York: Octagon Books, Inc., 1964.

Michaelis, Meir. *Mussolini and the Jews: German-Italian Relations and the Jewish Question in Italy 1922–1945.* Oxford: The Clarendon Press, 1978.

Morse, Arthur D. *While Six Million Died: A Chronicle of American Apathy.* New York: Random House, 1967.

Murphy, Robert. *Diplomat Among Warriors.* Garden City, N.Y.: Doubleday & Company, 1964.

Proudfoot, Malcolm J. *European Refugees: 1939–1952: A Study in Forced Population Movement.* Evanston, Ill.: Northwestern University Press, 1956.

Rabinowitz, Dorothy. *New Lives.* New York: Avon, 1977.

Schechtman, Joseph B. *European Population Transfers, 1939–1945.* New York: Oxford University Press, 1946.

———. *The United States and the Jewish State Movement: The Crucial Decade,*

1939–1949. New York: Herzl Press, Thomas Yoseloff, 1966.

Shachner, Nathan. *The Price of Liberty: A History of the American Jewish Committee*. New York: American Jewish Committee, 1948.

Stember, Charles, et al. *Jews in the Mind of America*. New York: Basic Books, 1966.

Stevens, Richard P. *American Zionism and U.S. Foreign Policy, 1942–1947*. New York: Pageant, 1962.

Strong, Donald. *Organized Anti-Semitism in America: The Rise of Group Prejudice During the Decade 1930–1940*. Washington, D.C.: American Council on Public Affairs, 1941.

Vernant, Jacques. *The Refugee in the Post-War World*. London: Allen and Unwin, 1953.

Waldman, Morris D. *Nor By Power*. New York: International Universities Press, 1953.

Warren, Roland L. *The Community in America*. Chicago: Rand McNally & Company, 1966.

Wax, Rosalie. *Doing Fieldwork: Warnings and Advice*. Chicago: University of Chicago Press, 1971.

Wischnitzer, Mark. *Visas to Freedom: The History of HIAS*. New York: World Publishing Co., 1956.

Woodbridge, George. *UNRRA*. 3 vols. New York: Columbia University Press, 1950.

Wyman, David S. *The Abandonment of the Jews: America and the Holocaust 1941–1945*. New York: Pantheon Books, 1984.

———. *Papers Walls: America and the Refugee Crisis 1939–1941*. Amherst: University of Massachusetts Press, 1968.

ARTICLES

"Asylum in Britain and America." *New Republic* (August 30, 1943), 109: 311–13.

Auerbach, Jerold S. "Joseph M. Proskauer: American Court Jew." *American Jewish History* (September 1979) 69: 103–16.

Bauer, Yehuda. "Genocide: Was it the Nazis' Original Plan?" *The Annals of the American Academy of Political and Social Science* (July 1980) 450: 35–45.

Bentwich, Norman. "Wartime Britain's Alien Policy," *Contemporary Jewish Record* V (February 1942): 41–50.

Berman, Aaron. "American Zionism and the Rescue of European Jewry: An Ideological Perspective." *American Jewish History* LXXX (March 1981): 310–31.

Brody, David. "American Jewry, The Refugees and Immigration Restriction (1932–1942)." *Publications of the American Jewish Historical Society* XLV (June 1956): 219–47.

Capri, Daniel. "The Rescue of Jews in One Occupied Part of Yugoslavia." In *Rescue Attempts During the Holocaust: Proceedings of the Second Yad Vashem International Historical Conference* (Jerusalem, 1977), 465–507.

Davie, Maurice R. "Immigrant and Refugee Aid." *American Jewish Year Book* (1947–1948) 49: 223–36.

Dawidowicz, Lucy. "Indicting American Jews." *Commentary* 76 (June 1983): 36–44. Also see "Letters." *Commentary* 76 (September 1983): 4–28.

Feingold, Henry A. "Failure to Rescue European Jewry: Wartime Britain and America." *Annals of the AAPSS* 450 (July 1980): 113–21.

———. "The Government Response." In *The San Jose Papers*, edited by Henry

Friedlander and Sybil Milton, 245–59. Millwood, N.Y.: Kraus International Publications, 1980.

Higham, John. "American Immigration Policy in Perspective." *Law and Contemporary Problems* 21 (Spring 1956): 213–35.

Lipstadt, Deborah. "The *New York Times* and the News About the Holocaust: A Quantified Study." *Proceedings of the Seventh World Congress of Jewish Studies Holocaust Research* I (1980): 45–73.

———. "Witness to the Persecution." *Modern Judaism* 3 (October 1983): 319–38.

Maass, Ernest. "Integration and Name Changing Among Jewish Refugees From Central Europe in the United States." *Names* 6 (September 1958): 129–71.

Neff, Carol. "A Page in B'nai B'rith's History of Service: The Fort Ontario Refugee Project." *National Jewish Monthly* (May 1980): 22–23.

Rubin, Barry. "Ambassador Laurence A. Steinhardt: The Perils of a Jewish Diplomat, 1940–1945." *American Jewish History* LXXX (March 1981): 331–47.

Schneider, Catheren M. "The Displaced Person as a Patient." *American Journal of Nursing* (September 1945) 45: 690–92.

Segalman, Ralph. "The Psychology of Jewish Displaced Persons." *Jewish Social Service Quarterly* (June 1947) 23: 362–69.

Shalett, Sidney. "Prisoner Coddling is Denied by Army." *New York Times* (May 7, 1944), 14.

Strum, Harvey. "Fort Ontario Refugee Shelter, 1944–1946." *American Jewish History* LXXIII (June 1984): 398–422.

Syrkin, Marie. "What American Jews Did During the Holocaust." *Midstream* 28 (October 1982): 6–12.

"Truman Opens Gates to Refugees." *Christian Century* (January 2, 1946) 63: 2.

Tyhurst, Libuse. "Displacement and Migration: Study in Social Psychiatry." *American Journal of Psychiatry* 107 (February 1951): 561–69.

Wasserstein, Bernard. "The Myth of 'Jewish Silence.'" *Midstream* 26 (August/September 1980): 10–19.

Index

Names of former refugees are indexed according to spellings in government records. Parentheses indicate name changes or alternate spellings; brackets indicate married names.